Routledge Revivals

The Decline of Neutrality 1914–41

The Decline of Neutrality (1971) examines the impartial, disinterested neutrality as it was codified in the Hague Convention in 1907 and the changes the concept underwent from the beginning of World War I in 1914 up to Pearl Habor, December 1941. It deals with the different stages of neutrality during that period and looks at the reasons why the policy no longer worked. Some consideration has also been given to the attempts of uniting weak and strong neutrals in a common defence of neutral rights.

The Decline of Neutrality 1914–41

With Special Reference to the United States and the Northern Neutrals

Nils Ørvik

First published in 1971
by Frank Cass and Company Limited

This edition first published in 2025 by Routledge
4 Park Square, Milton Park, Abingdon, Oxon, OX14 4RN

and by Routledge
605 Third Avenue, New York, NY 10017

Routledge is an imprint of the Taylor & Francis Group, an informa business

© 1971 Frank Cass and Company Limited

All rights reserved. No part of this book may be reprinted or reproduced or utilised in any form or by any electronic, mechanical, or other means, now known or hereafter invented, including photocopying and recording, or in any information storage or retrieval system, without permission in writing from the publishers.

Publisher's Note
The publisher has gone to great lengths to ensure the quality of this reprint but points out that some imperfections in the original copies may be apparent.

Disclaimer
The publisher has made every effort to trace copyright holders and welcomes correspondence from those they have been unable to contact.

A Library of Congress record exists under LCCN: 75031804

ISBN: 978-1-032-95579-7 (hbk)
ISBN: 978-1-003-58558-9 (ebk)
ISBN: 978-1-032-95581-0 (pbk)

Book DOI 10.4324/9781003585589

THE DECLINE OF NEUTRALITY
1914–1941

The Decline of Neutrality 1914–1941

With special reference to the United States and the Northern Neutrals

BY

NILS ØRVIK

of the University of Oslo

SECOND EDITION

With a new foreword and supplementary chapter,
'NON-ALIGNMENT AND NEUTRALITY SINCE 1952'

FRANK CASS & CO. LTD.
1971

Published by
FRANK CASS AND COMPANY LIMITED
67 Great Russell Street, London WC1B 3BT
First published by Johan Grundt Tanum Forlag, Oslo, Norway

First published   1953
Second edition   1971

ISBN 0 7146 2696 1

All rights reserved. No part of this publication may be reproduced in any form or by any means, electronic, mechanical, photocopying, recording or otherwise without the prior permission of Frank Cass and Company Limited in writing.

Printed in Great Britain by Clarke, Doble & Brendon Ltd. Plymouth and London

Contents

FOREWORD TO THE SECOND EDITION............................ 7

PREFACE 9

I. THE EVOLUTION OF THE IDEA OF NEUTRALITY .. 11
    First American Neutrality 18
    The Traditional Neutrals 25
    Permanent Neutrality 28
    Neutrality in the «British Century» 29

II. NEUTRALITY DURING WORLD WAR I
    1. *The Failure of Impartial Neutrality* 38
    2. *Weak Power Neutrality* 50
        The Fish Agreement and the Submarine Warfare in the Arctic 53
        Copper and Coal 56
        Norway's War Losses 58
    3. *The Position of America as the Worlds Greatest Neutral* 62
    4. *The Aims of the Wilson Administration* 73
        Great and Small 73
        The State Department 76
        The President 82
    5. *Cooperative Neutrality and why it Failed* 89
        Neutral Proposals 91
        Scandinavia Asks for Defense of Neutral Rights 92
        Cooperation for Mediating a Peace 103
        Cooperation for War 106
        Latin-American Attempts to Cooperation 108
        The Unnatural Neutral 112

III. THE INTER WAR PERIOD 1919—1939.
    1. *Neutrality under the League Covenant* 119
        Article 16 and the Extent of Sanctions 122
        Neutrality Lives On 132
    2. *The Pact of Paris* 136

3. *Revision of the Concept of Neutrality* 145
   Swiss Neutrality 146
   The «New» Neutrality 148
   Neutral Cooperation Once More 153
4. *Neutrality without Rights* 157
   Towards Non-belligerency 167
5. *Small States Search for Security* 172
   Security through Alliances 173
   The Repudiation of Article 16 177
   Sweden 179
   Switzerland, Traditonal Neutral 180
   Belgium, «Realistic Neutrality» 183
   The Declaration of Copenhagen 185
   Sovereignty against Collective Security 187

IV. FROM NEUTRALITY TO NON-BELLIGERENCY

1. *American Neutrality in World War II* 195
   Cash-and-Carry 198
   All Help — Short of War 201
   Dynamic Non-belligerency 205
2. *The End of Norwegian Neutrality April 9, 1940* 216
   Military Preparedness 226
   The Iron Ore 229
   Watchful Waiting 332
   The Race 235
   «Lop-sided» Neutrality 238
   Necessity versus Legality 242
3. *Neutrality and the United Nations* 247
   Withdrawal and Expulsion 249
   Neutrality under the Charter 251
   Northern Neutrality in the Post War World 257

V. CONCLUSION 268

VI. APPENDIX: NON-ALIGNMENT AND
    NEUTRALITY SINCE 1952 279

BIBLIOGRAPHY 305

INDEX 315

Foreword
to the Second Edition

Since I wrote *The Decline of Neutrality* close to twenty years ago the world has changed, in many respects fundamentally. Due to some very special circumstances the neutrals had a renaissance in international politics. For a while they seemed to emerge as a third force.

In view of these changes, the publishers have asked me to revise the last chapters and bring the book up to date. Within the available time, this proved impossible. So we left the first edition unchanged, as it appeared then. We have, however, included an additional chapter in which I try to evaluate and summarize the development of neutral policies since 1952, when the first manuscript was completed.

I have found this a very frustrating experience. The two past decades have brought up new interpretations, concepts and connotations, all related to neutrality's basic theme—to be a third party in an international conflict. The narrow confines of a short chapter have precluded a representative account and analysis of the main trend in neutralism and non-alignment. What seemed feasible was to apply a wide perspective on the various forms of non-alignment and the phases they have gone through in the post-war period. In one way, it may have been appropriate to republish the book just at this stage. The non-aligned had their grandest hours in the fifties. Now the trend may once again be toward decline.

Without the brisk initiative and stimulating encouragement of Professor Ragnhild Hatton at the London School of Economics, I would probably never have thought of having the book republished. Further, I am particularly indebted to my long time friend Dr. Peter Lyon, whose advice and suggestions greatly improved the original manuscript. I am also grateful to Miss Carol Heller and Miss Mary Arnquist at the Berkeley Institute for International Studies, University of California, for editing and secretarial assistance.

Oslo, March 1970
Nils Ørvik
University of Oslo

Preface

The subject of this book is the impartial, disinterested neutrality as it was codified in the Hague Conventions in 1907. It has been my main purpose to find out what happened to the concept of neutrality from the beginning of World War I in 1914 up to Pearl Harbor, December 1941. I have dealt with the different stages of neutrality during that period and tried to point out the most important reasons why the policy no longer worked. Some consideration has also been given to the attempts of uniting weak and strong neutrals in a common defense of neutral rights. Though my actual research has been concentrated on the 1914—1941 period, the problems of the United Nations in its relations to neutrality are so similar to those of the League period that I have added a postscript with a few remarks on neutrality in the post war world up to 1950.

It soon became apparent that the basic principles of neutrality were practiced differently as each of the neutral states had to work out its problems in its own way. Swiss neutrality could not be identified with for instance Swedish or American neutrality. A full and general discussion of the whole problem of neutrality would therefore have necessitated a thorough treatment of the policies of each of the traditional neutrals. But that is not the scope of this study. I have limited my research to the United States as a great power with a strong tradition of neutrality, and as its counterpart chosen the northern neutrals, with particular reference to Norway as a typical representative of small states that have followed policies of neutrality. Both countries regarded themselves as traditional neutrals and attempted a policy based on the Hague definitions of neutrality; and they both failed. The United States because it was too big to abstain from influencing world affairs, while Norway lacked the economic and military force to make her neutrality policy valid.

This book is an abbreviated and somewhat popularized version of a doctorial dissertation written at the University of Wisconsin in 1950.[1] To reduce the cost of publication some chapters have been condensed or omitted completely. The one dealing with Norwegian neutrality policy in 1939—40 have been rewritten entirely on the basis of the considerable amount of material recently made available. However, the bulk of my source material has been obtained in the University of Wisconsin Library and in the library of the Wisconsin Historical Society. For the specifically Norwegian problems I have been given unrestricted access to the Norwegian state archives.

I am greatly indebted to my major professors at the University of Wisconsin, Chester V. Easum and Fred H. Harrington, whose encouragement and advice proved exceedingly valuable. I also like to express my deep gratitude to the *Norges Almenvitenskapelige Forskningsråd* for covering the expenses for the publication of this book.

Oslo, March 1953.

Nils Ørvik.

---

[1] Nils Ørvik. *The Changing Concept of Neutrality*, University of Wisconsin 1950, 443 pages.

I. The Evolution of the Idea of Neutrality

Neutrality signifies primarily a nation's status of non-participation in hostilities when other countries are at war. Yet in international law a neutral state also undertakes certain duties and claims certain rights. This conception is however of rather recent date. Until as late as two hundred years ago, the term had different meanings both in different times and places.

Most writers seem to agree that 1648 marks the beginning of neutrality as a formally recognized principle. But it was vaguely defined and could most properly be said to mean only «not full participation» in wars. It is illustrative of its small importance that Hugo Grotius, in his voluminous *De Jure Belli ac Pacis*, gave only a few pages to the discussion of neutrals, or the *medeii* as he called them, those who were «between peace and war». Grotius had not freed himself from the medieval conception of a struggle between good and evil forces, but apparently thought the neutrals themselves ought to decide which side was the more just and which unjust. He argued, however, that if the question of war guilt was debatable, «those who remain at peace should show themselves impartial to either side in permitting transit, in furnishing supplies to troops and in not assisting those under siege.»[1] These theories of his were later elaborated and supplemented by a great many writers building the foundations of international law.[2]

In the 17th and 18th centuries it was generally accepted that under certain conditions, a neutral could give direct and even

[1] Hugo Grotius, *De Jure Belli ac Pacis*, Liber III, 786. The principles laid down by Grotius make as interesting comparison to the famous Article 16 of the League of Nations Covenant.

[2] Christian de Wolff (1679—1754), Samuel Pufendorf (1632—1694), Christian Thomasius (1655—1728, Emmerich de Vattel, (1714—1767), Cornelius van Bijnkershoek (1643—1673).

important aid to one of the belligerents without being accused of unneutral action by the opposite party. Nor was is necessary for a state to justify its partial attitude by referring to one of the combatants as being more just in taking up arms. A neutral was looked upon basically as a friend that for various reasons chose not to take an active part in the war. For a while a neutral state seems to have been allowed to shift its favors much as it pleased, but in the eighteenth century the general conception grew that partiality was justified only when it could be shown to be in accordance with a treaty signed before hostilities began. Each belligerent thus knew in advance which of its friends would give maximum support and which would limit their assistance to troops, money and supplies.

There were two main types of these neutrality treaties. One provided for troops and extensive help from the neutral, while the other guaranteed that no assistance should be given to the enemy. There were also occasionally explicit promises to grant or deny certain privileges to troops of the other party and even pledges to remain strictly neutral. The last provision is particularly interesting for it shows that unless restrained by a treaty with one belligerent, a neutral might feel free to assist the other. It is evident that such provisions would not have been possible, had there not been a confirmed belief in treaties.

Since the late Middle Ages the European countries had become more and more dependent on trade. This was hardly noticed in times of peace, but it became painfully obvious whenever states were involved in war. It therefore soon became a natural claim that peoples not directly engaged in the armed conflict, should be allowed to carry on their trade as usual. As there were no adequate means of land transportation, the question of neutral trade became chiefly a *maritime* problem.

The great conflicts arising between neutrals and belligerents have nearly always been connected to the seaborne trade. The essence of the neutral problem can in fact be compressed into one gross simplification. In time of war each of the belligerents wanted to cut off all trade and, if possible, all relations between his opponents and the neutrals. The latter, on their part, wanted to keep up their trade and other relations with all belligerents, without interference from any of them. As none of those extreme claims was fully enforceable, it became necessary to find a compromise that might reduce the inconveniences for all concerned. The outcome of the struggle to establish such a modus vivendi has at all times been entirely dependent upon the economic and military strength, the strategic position and the perspicacity and persistence of the two sides. In short, the rules of neutrality are products of two forces pulling in opposite directions, the final result being determined by the relative bargaining power of the parties.

This is most clearly illustrated by viewing the practises concerning contraband and blockade, both expressions of the same basic principle. The belligerents, particularly the seapowers would have liked to see all articles destined for their opponents put on the contraband list and all ports declared in a state of blockade. On the other hand, since trade with belligerents usually was a very profitable business, the neutrals wanted all articles on the free list and no blockades at all.[3] The neutral freelists as well as the contraband lists were usually results of bipartite treaties. Apart from arms and ammunition there was no general agreement as to contraband and there was little consistency.

The destination of the cargo was naturally of major importance at an eventual seizure. From relating only to enemy ports, it was soon extended to include the principle of the «continuous voyage», when goods were transhipped in a neutral port and sent on to the enemy. The right to seize enemy property had never been disputed, but problems arose when an enemy ship was captured carrying a neutral cargo or when enemy goods were found on a neutral ship. The first attempt to settle this was made in 1494 in a collection of customary rules called *Consolato del Mare;* but the ship-cargo problem continued to be a source of endless quarrels between the belligerents and the neutrals. The result was a series of compromises in which the advantage rested with the most powerful party. Neutral ships were safe only when they carried exclusively neutral goods between neutral ports.

With ever-increasing colonial expansion and overseas trade it became more difficult for belligerents to control neutral shipping. The only way to find out about ships and cargoes was to patrol

---

[3] Generally speaking it has been the British who have primarily determined the rules of contraband, while the Swedes have laid the foundations for the practise of blockading enemy ports.

the seas, and «visit» the ships they encountered. If the ships papers gave reason for suspicion, a search was made. Disputes arising from such actions usually did not concern the principle of visit and search, but the manner in which it was applied. A detailed description of the legal procedure was often inserted in the treaties, and the ships papers therefore became of greatest importance. As such *lettres de mer* might give free passage or exemption from delay, neutral skippers were naturally tempted to falsify their papers or carry duplicate sets.

The eighteenth century saw a decline in the respect for such ships papers and an increased aggressiveness on the part of belligerents. As the neutrals' devices for protection were wrecked one by one, their only choice seemed to be to put actual force behind what they considered to be their rights. This situation provided the background for armed neutrality. It came about when one or several neutral countries joined forces and proceeded to dare belligerents by convoying their merchant ships with their own navies. Belligerents were then put in a difficult position. By violating neutral rights persistently, they ran the risk of provoking the neutrals into entering the war on the other side. It was force against force. Where the leagues of neutral states were sufficiently strong, they could succeed in protecting their trade, where they were not, the belligerents won.

With relation to recent applications of the same principle, it ought to be stressed that such armed neutralities were declared and applied to particular situations. They did not aim at a cooperation of neutrals on a broader basis and for a longer period. There could be no sense of permanence or solidarity because at that time belligerents and neutrals shifted roles incessantly. Neutral powers were driven together by the needs of an acute situation and their defensive cooperation ceased when there was no longer an urgent emergency calling for it. The conclusion evident from this experience was that if the neutral group was strong enough, the belligerents came to terms with it, but that if it was too weak, the neutrals themselves became involved in the conflict.

Without the force and influence which only a great power could provide, an armed neutrality league naturally failed. Russia's part in this period can be compared with the role later played by the United States during the First World War. Due to their military strength, their resources and great-power influence, those states became necessary trustees for the weaker neutrals. They were both unnatural neutrals as they were too big and influential to remain passive spectators of the struggle for world dominance. When they threw their influence to the side of one of the belligerents, the neutral cause was lost. Without the force behind its arguments, neutrality was not feasible. Lacking it, neutrals had to submit — or choose on which side to fight.

In this period neutrality was thus secured and guaranteed by the provisions of particular treaties. The neutral had to act in conformity with these agreements, whether they provided for a benevolent, partial or impartial neutrality; and neutrals in similar situations might have widely different rights and duties. In the sixteenth and seventeenth centuries there was a great respect for treaties in general. In the eighteenth century there was a greater tendency to disregard legalities, to adopt more fraudulent practices, — and there was less safety for neutral trade. The persistent demand of the neutrals was the recognition of the principle free ships, free goods and freedom of the seas. When they were in a strong position they came quite close to achieving their aim, but they fell far short when the belligerents had the advantage. Treaties concluded before the war, and bargaining power were the two factors which secured the neutrals their right to trade without interference. Up to the nineteenth century there was no general international agreement which codified neutral rights and guaranteed the same treatment to all neutral powers.[4]

Napoleon's gigantic attempt to gain world domination for one power alone, and Britain's firm determination to deny it to him, provides, in many respects, an interesting comparison to Kaiser Wilhelm and the First World War, and especially in relation to

---

[4] For more detailed information of the early stages of neutrality see, Nicolas Socrate Politis, *La Neutralité et la paix* (Paris 1935),

E. Thomas, «Theory of Neutrality», in *Annals of American Academy of Political Science.* 186.

Philip Jessup, «Historical Development of the Law of Neutrality» in *The Reference Shelf,* 10, No. 7.

Philip Jessup, and Francis Deak, *The Origins,* vol. I of *Neutrality, its History, Economics and Law,* (New York 1935).

T. Boye, *De væbnede neutralitetsforbund,* (Kristiania 1912).

Georg Cohn, *Neo-neutrality,* Translation from Danish, (New York 1939).

neutrality.⁵ The long and destructive wars of Napoleon actually killed the concept of neutrality in its previous sense. It proved that in a great general war, it can give no protection and has to be modified or abandoned. A hundred years later, the First World War proved the same thing. There was the same division into two great camps, which together included most of the civilized world. Measures were met with counter-measures and blockades with counterblockades; reprisals against violations were used to justify new violations. The struggle was not confined to actual battles between organized armies and navies; economic weapons were used as well. England's policy of starving out the Continent was not adopted as a means of extreme necessity, but as a well planned policy that would help her win. Already in 1709, when the food condition in France was desperate, she adopted the starvation policy as an efficient method of warfare.⁶ On the other hand, the continental plan for strangling England by closing her markets and destroying her trade, was outlined already in the National Convention, in 1793.⁷ The means were different from those used a century later when the submarines began their destructive operations, but the aims were the same.

The moral arguments also resemble the ones used in the First World War. Napoleon, especially during his early campaigns, declared that he was fighting for high ideals against the British tyranny, while the English, pointing to the revolutionary period of terror, justified their actions as being necessary in order to preserve civilization against the despotism and barbarism of the French emperor. Great Britain, the balance-keeper, strongly stressed the importance of the freedom and independence of all nations, which would be ruled out by a French domination. She then presumed that by fighting for civilization, she also fought in the interest of all nations. It was thus a privilege for the neutrals to be allowed to stand outside the armed conflict, and as she was fighting their war as well as her own, she felt justified in dealing with them somewhat high-handedly.

Moreover, on one side, there was a seapower that wanted to

---

⁵ Allison Phillips and Arthur Reede, *The Napoleonic Period*, Vol. II of the series, *Neutrality, Its History, Economics and Law*.
⁶ *Ibid.*, 13, 30.
⁷ Phillips and Reede, *The Napoleonic Period*, 29.

preserve the existing world order with the many sovereign states which facilitated her own domination. On the opposite side, there was a great landpower which could not impose its system without destroying the independence of the other states. While the struggle lasted, both sides openly disregarded the sovereignty of the small nations. Full sovereignty was found only in the two belligerent camps. As the war dragged on, it involved so many vital ideological principles that no compromise could be found. It developed into a deadly fight, not for a modus vivendi, but for complete domination by the victor and the destruction of the defeated enemy. Under such conditions, neutrality became a luxury that could no longer be afforded. Therefore, it had to disappear.

The Napoleonic Wars ended one stage of neutrality. The «gentlemens' neutrality,» the partial, treaty-bound neutrality policy of nonparticipation, which certain states occasionally chose to follow, had been a convenient and profitable measure when no particular interests or dangers made direct involvement advantageous or necessary. The policy of neutrality had not yet come to be identified with a certain group of states that consistently applied it. On the contrary, a state might be heading one of the belligerent sides in one war, and in the next be a peaceful neutral. Naturally, under such circumstances, no international agreement could be made to support neutrality. It was not until the last half of the eighteenth century that there was a basis for classifying some of the smaller states as being traditional neutrals. The partial or benevolent type of neutrality did not survive the wars following the French revolution. But the realization of complete failure did not prevent the principle of neutrality from a come-back which brought the concept up to its highest prestige and influence. In fact, even before the Napoleonic catastrophe, the foundations were laid for that strange and important political creation of the nineteenth century, impartial and passive neutrality or neutrality built on law.

The characteristic traits of this impartial neutrality were, in the first place, a policy carried out in accordance with rules laid down by municipal enactments, later also by international agreements. The weight now came to rest almost equally on the two main items of neutrality, *rights* and *duties*. By the new stress on duties, the neutral was obliged to take on certain obligations in return for the privilege of staying out of war and having its rights respected. The most important of these duties was the pledge to take an impartial and passive attitude and to prevent belligerent actions from being committed within its territory. This change in the conception of neutrality did not come overnight; it was a development covering a long period, and there seems to be a general agreement among the writers that it was founded and formulated by the United States in the 1790's.[8]

First American Neutrality.

The first official declaration of the new policy came with George Washington's famous «Proclamation of Neutrality» of April 22, 1793. For the first time impartiality was put up as one of the main duties of a neutral power. It read: «The duty and interest of the United States require that they should, with sincerity and good faith adopt and pursue a conduct friendly and impartial toward the belligerent powers.»[9] Equally important was the new distinction which separated the government and its citizens in their conduct of neutrality. Washington went on to proclaim that the state did not accept responsibility for the acts of those who rendered themselves «liable to punishment of forfeiture under the law of nations» by participating in hostilities against the belligerents, and those carring contraband would not receive the protection of the United States.

The proclamation must be seen against the background of the time when it was framed. In 1778, when the United States had fought most desparately for its independence, it had concluded a

[8] W. E. Hall, *A Treatise on International Law* (Oxford, 1924), 705; J. Whitton, «The Changed Attitude of Powers toward Neutrality Laws,» in *Current History*, 30 : 455 (July, 1929); Q. Wright, «Repeal of the Neutrality Act,» in *American Journal of International Law*, 36 : 15 (January, 1942); Fenwick, *The Neutrality Laws of the United States*, 6; Charles S. Hyneman, *The First American Neutrality* (Urbana, 1934), 7; «The first American neutrality perhaps more completely than any other marked the transition from the era of benevolent neutrality to the modern era of neutral conduct.» H. A. Smith, «Future of Neutrality,» in *Contemporary Review*, 33 : 317 (March, 1933); «The existing laws of neutrality is... really a child of American policy.»

[9] For the full text see *American State Papers, 1789—1794*, second edition, 44—45; Richardson, «*Messages and Papers of the President,*» 1 : 156; *International Conciliation Documents*, 1928, 384.

treaty of «Amity and Commerce» with France.[10] In this, the Americans obligated themselves to a definite pro-French attitude and gave the French extensive privileges which were to be denied to the enemy. As war broke out between France and England, Washington and his cabinet feared that if they should have to carry out the obligations they had taken on in the treaty with France, England might consider it to be a sufficient cause for war. At the same time they were afraid to abrogate the treaty outright because that might bring war with France. This could happen even if the treaties were only «temporarily and provisionally suspended» as Hamilton advised.[11]

But the United States did not want war with any country. Whether they were on the French or the English side was of secondary importance; it might be equally dangerous in both cases for their newly acquired independence. In order to avoid war and at the same time to maintain friendly relations with both belligerents, the Washington Administration therefore devised the policy of strict and impartial neutrality. This was the immediate problem, and both Hamilton and Jefferson, the two great political leaders, regarded the neutral policy as a way of dealing with an actual acute situation.

Emphasis on duty was a particularly interesting feature of the Jeffersonian principle of neutrality.[12] The world had often seen nations concerned about their neutral rights, but it had seldom seen them impartially emphasizing their own neutral duties.[13] It is not of major importance and it is hardly possible to point out a single man as being primarily responsible for this policy. However, most writers on the period seem to agree that «the work of Jefferson was indispensible in the formulation of a policy so truly impartial as that laid down for the United States in 1793».[14] There can be little doubt that he had very clear ideas on this point and saw the possibilities that such a policy offered to a small and weak

[10] Thomas Bailey, *A. Diplomatic History of the American People* (New York; 1946). 18, 71—89.
[11] Charles M. Thomas, *American Neutrality in 1793* (New York, 1931), 56.
[12] Hyneman thinks that Washington, while speaking of «duty» in his proclamation, thought more of duty to the citizens than of duty to international law. Hyneman, *The First American Neutrality*, 16.
[13] Thomas, *American Neutrality in 1793*, 92.
[14] *Ibid.*, 266.

country. In a letter to Morris, the United States minister to France, Jefferson said that

> they had produced proofs from the most enlightened and approved writers on the subject that a neutral nation must in all things relating to the war observe an exact impartiality towards the other parties; that favors to one, to the prejudice of the other, would produce a fraudulent neutrality of which no nation would be the dupe.[15]

Jefferson realized that the surest way to maintain neutrality was to convince the belligerents that the United States seriously intended to observe its duties impartially and was able to do so. The first requirement was that belligerents were not allowed to engage in hostilities within neutral territory.[16] Respect for neutral territory has ever since been the corner-stone of all neutral policy, since it involves the related question of *sovereignty*. This has always been a vital issue in the relations between states, but it was of particular importance in the system of balance of power which was based upon the thesis that all states were equally sovereign. A state might be restricted in all its outward activities, but as long as it could keep its territory inviolable, it could claim a full sovereign status. This was most important for the United States whose existence as an equal state still rested on a rather unstable foundation. It, therefore, became imperatively important for this new state that no justified doubt be raised as to the validity of its sovereignty.

Jefferson put strong stress on the distinction between the acts of a neutral government and those of its citizens. He stated that the United States would not prevent the sale of contraband, nor even of munitions to the belligerents. He justified it by the fact that «our citizens have always been free to make, sell and export arms;» and the prohibition was not required by the law of nations. The law «was satisfied with the external penalty of confiscation of

---

[15] Jefferson to Morris, August 16, 1793, *American State Papers*, I : 163.

[16] This involved the question of territorial waters. No international agreement existed as to the distance from the shore; it ranged from twenty miles to «the range of a cannon ball,» usually one league. Jefferson adhered to the «cannon shot» theory as the least margin the United States could claim (less territory to defend). Thomas, *Neutrality in 1793*, 106.

these munitions as should fall into the hands of any of the belligerent powers while on their way to the ports of their enemy.»[17] Neither did Jefferson think that provisions were contraband, but «the United States must either sell provisions to both warring powers or to neither. To do the latter would ruin our agriculture. Great Britain might feel the desire of starving an enemy nation but she had no right to do it at our expense.»[18]

This American innovation in international law of putting impartiality up as the main pillar of neutrality, was based more on sound reason than on legal precedents. Nevertheless, it was rapidly accepted by the powers. Hyneman says that

> within a few months after the issuance of the proclamation, it was regularly assented without contradiction that the law of nations imposed on all non-belligerent nations an obligation to be impartial in their relations with the parties at war.[19]

«Equal treatment of all nations, while preserving a decent regard for treaties,» was to be the policy of the United States. But the President and his advisers were from the very first aware that such a policy would involve compromises and skilful maneuvering if it was to prove successful. Hamilton stated what seemed to have been the universal opinion at that time, that certain stipulations of treaties made before the war, might not be influenced by the general policy of impartial neutrality. But this would not be effective for stipulations providing for military aid.[20] This seems to have been in accordance with the views maintained by writers on international law of this period. It was not until the twentieth century that it became generally recognized that a neutral was not permitted to give material assistance to one belligerent only, whether there existed a pre-war treaty or not.[21]

To effectuate and institutionalize this policy which was inaugurated by Washington's proclamation of neutrality, the United States entered upon a program of neutral legislation. By enacting municipal laws it aimed at two things: they would restrict their

[17] Thomas, *Neutrality in 1793*, 248—249.
[18] *Ibid.*, 253
[19] Hyneman, *The First American Neutrality*, 19.
[20] Hyneman, *The First American Neutrality*, 20—25.
[21] Hall, *International Law*, 709—710.

own citizens from committing acts which might cause conflicts with states at war, and the belligerents were forbidden to undertake warlike actions or to prepare such within the territory of the United States. In 1794, Congress adopted a neutrality law which defined some of the neutral duties.[22] This act forbade:

1. The commissioning of an American citizen to serve a foreign prince or state.
2. The enlistment or hiring to enlist in the service of another state.
3. The fitting out and arming of vessels to be used in a hostile manner against countries with which the United States was at peace.
4. The commissioning of such a vessel or the augmentation of its forces.
5. The setting on foot of military expeditions against foreign states within the territory of the jurisdiction of the United States.[23]

The underlying idea is again the distinction between the acts of individuals and those of the neutral state. The neutrals forbade the belligerents to carry the war into neutral territory, but laid themselves open for penalization by the powers at war when they ventured outside their pacified area. The neutral citizens could trade where, and in what articles they wanted; the only check upon them was the control exercised by the belligerent. And it was up to him to stop them.[24] Attempts made by neutrals to restrict their own citizens were not always successful. The failure of Jefferson's embargo of 1807 illustrates the difficulty which was involved when abstinence from trade meant sacrifice of profits.

The law of 1794 was supplemented in March, 1817, by «an act more effectually to preserve the neutral relations of the United States».[25] It provided that any armed vessel that left the jurisdiction of the United States was to give satisfactory assurance that

[22] *United States, Statutes at Large*, I : 381—384 (Boston, 1848).
[23] Fenwick, *Neutrality Laws*, 10—11.
[24] Syngman Rhee, *Neutrality as Influenced by the United States* (Princeton, 1912), 30—35.
[25] *Statutes at Large*, III : 370—371.

it was not to be employed in any warlike measures against any power with which the United States was at peace. This was a temporary enactment and in April, 1818, it was replaced by the Neutrality Act of 1818, designed to gather the previous enactments into a permanent legislation.[26] The provisions were more detailed and extensive than stated in the Act of 1794, but were essentially the same.

The legislative activity of the United States was followed with growing interest by all countries of the civilized world. The same can be said of the juridical decisions handed down, particularly by chief Justice Marshall, in the American courts. The legislation was municipal, with only national validity,[27] but before long the American pattern was followed by most European countries.[28] As early as 1819, Great Britain passed her foreign enlistment act, which, if not copied, was at least closely modelled on the American Act of 1794. In the following years, state after state enacted similar laws.[29]

One cannot help but wonder what the underlying reasons were for this new impartial neutrality of the nineteenth century. The Napoleonic Wars, which had effectively demonstrated the inadequacy of neutrality, were hardly over before most of the nations of the world started introducing municipal neutrality legislation. Thus, the reasons for this new attitude must go deeper than the particular American treaty with France of 1778. It was not accidental that the United States, then one of the weakest nations in the world, should be the one to formulate this policy and give the clue.

The efforts of the Washington Administration seemed to have concentrated on one basic point, to avoid being involved in wars. Randolph, one of Washington's prominent advisers explained this in a letter to Monroe, June, 1795. He said:

[26] *Ibid.*, 447—450.

[27] Fenwick, *Neutrality Laws*, 11.

[28] «It is this extreme regard for the duties of neutrality that Canning praised so highly a few years later and which has caused the conduct of the United States to be a model until the present day.» Thomas, *American Neutrality in 1793*, 92.

[29] J. Whitton, «The Changed Attitude of the Powers Towards Neutrality Laws,» in *Current History*, 30 : 456 (June, 1929); P. M. Brown, «Neutrality,» in *American Journal of International Law*, 33 : 727 (1939).

An infant country deep in debt; necessitated to borrow in Europe; without manufactures; without a land or naval force; without a competency of arms or ammunition; with a commerce closely connected beyond the Atlantic, with a certainty of enhancing the price of foreign productions, and diminishing that of our own; with a constitution little more than four years old; in a state of probation, and not exempt from foes, such a country can have no greater curse in store for her than war. That peace was our policy has been admitted by Congress, by the People, and by France herself.[30]

Hyneman stressed this point very strongly. He said that the men who had already fought for political autonomy, had to fight, in 1793, for commercial independence. Jefferson, in particular, had looked forward to the time when the distresses of Europe would enable the still poor and insignificant United States to get into the European markets and take advantage of the quarrels between the great powers.[31] The corner-stone of this policy was peace. To preserve this, all the states had to be given equal treatment. Thus, they would have no good reason for attacking them or provoking them into a war:

Such a program would recommend itself to the administration, and «once they decided upon a path of impartiality, what was more natural than to argue that the law, which was to be found primarily in sound reason, obligated the American Government to pursue the course it had chosen?»[32]

If this had been primarily an American problem, the principle would probably never have reached Europe at all. But the fact that it was adopted and recognized there, indicates that there was a need for such a policy. The reason seems to be that a great many of the European nations were confronted with the same basic problem

---

[30] Randolph to Monroe, June 1, 1795, *American State Papers*, I : 706.

[31] In 1790, he said that the «flames of war will be kindled between our two neighbors,» and that the United States should pray their soldiers would «eat a great meal». During the Russo-Turkish War, he wrote that «the life of the feeder is better than the life of the fighter. ... let us milk the cow while the Russians hold her by the horns and the Turks by the tail.» Jessup, *Origins*, 260.

[32] Hyneman, *The First American Neutrality*, 18—19. Washington said in his Farewell Address: «Europe has a set of primary interests which to us have none or a very remote relation,» Richardson, *Messages and Papers of the Presidents*, I, 222.

and could, therefore, make effective use of the same remedy. It involved the whole question of weak nations at the beginning of the nineteenth century.

The Traditional Neutrals.

It has been mentioned before that the pre-Napoleonic period did not know any traditional neutrals. Nations were sometimes neutrals in one war and belligerents in the next. When no treaties had been concluded, there was no way to predict which countries would be in or out of a future conflict. Neutrality was usually a profitable status, but if the state had sufficient strength and influence, it was likely to gain more by using its power to coerce, than it could get as a passive spectator. On the other hand, a weak nation would always profit from its neutral trade but run great risk if it was drawn into a war. By staying neutral such states would get compensation for their weakness without risking anything. Their aim was consequently to stay out, for if they got into a conflict, they would expose their actual inadequacy to all the world and thus endanger their existence as fully sovereign states.

Today, the weak states can easily be picked out, but looking backward, which of these considered themselves as such in the seventeenth and eighteenth century? Which ones thought of themselves as weak and timid states whose entire existence was dependent upon peace, international law, and the rivalries of the great powers? To make sure it will be necessary to make a short review of the then status of the hitherto more or less traditional neutrals of the twentieth century.

Belgium was at that time involved in the Spanish and French controversies and did not have any independent policy at all, but Holland did. She was the world's greatest carrier nation, and even if England claimed the seas as her sovereign domain, she had to share substantial parts of the supremacy with the Dutch, who were at least second in command at sea. By the end of the eigteenth century, Holland no longer challenged British supremacy in naval matters, but she was still a great colonial power and carried on an enormous trade all over the world. It was not likely that the Dutch with their glorious maritime tradition should pay more than casual attention to the principle of neutrality before the forty years of confusion which are clotted around the turn of that century.

The Scandinavian neutrals have more neutral tradition behind them than most others but what about their peaceful intentions in the eighteenth century? In the fourteenth century, Denmark had actually ruled the whole of Scandinavia. However, from about 1520, Sweden had broken loose from her grip and had since that time been in constant opposition to her former oppressor. By 1700, Sweden had gained the hegemony in Scandinavia, but she had not succeeded in beating the pride and ambition out of the Danes. They did not think much of a peaceful and neutral policy for the future, but were only waiting for a chance to pay Sweden back.

The Thirty Years War had brought Sweden to the status of a world power and for nearly a century her able and ambitious kings kept up her great-power reputation. Sweden conquered vast territories from Russia and could for a while speak of the Baltic Sea as «mare nostrum». It is true that she had considerable setbacks at the beginning of the century, and lost most of her conquests, but one would hardly expect Sweden to turn to the passive role of neutrality only a few decades after she had defeated the Imperial Russian army at Narva.

Thus, in the years preceding the French revolution, most of the states that later got the names of traditional neutrals were still living in an afterswell of their world-power position. That period was still too close to make them realize that the world had changed and that they would never again enjoy the same opportunities. The list of alliances in the eighteenth century shows lively participation by the small powers. They still seemed to live in the illusions of their potential might. They gave the impression that to them force was still the only means by which prosperity and greatness could be gained. Why then establish a system of law, which might only complicate things and make it harder for them to get what they wanted when «their time» came again? Apparently they felt no urgent need of security. They had done quite well in the past centuries. Their greatness had been won by force, and even if recently their armies had been defeated, they did not think it was going to be like that forever. They were still confident that their unrestricted state sovereignty could be preserved without exposing themselves to the humiliations and deprivations which the passive attitude of constant neutrality would imply. They looked at their tattered banners from the various battlefields of Europe and persuaded themselves that they were safe behind their glorious, but tiny armies.

The Wars of Napoleon were a formidable eye-opener to all Europe, but to the weaker states in particular. None of them managed to stay out. By different motives, by threat of force, insults, and by fear, they were all taken in. Neither their own wishes and intentions, nor their armed forces had been enough to save them. Their war profits might have compensated their actual monetary losses,[33] but they had seen with their own eyes how easily even more precious things could be lost. They realized that the state sovereignty and independence, which they up to that time had taken as a matter of course, were now at stake, and could be lost almost overnight. They could still enjoy their sovereign status, but it was painfully clear that this existed no longer as a result of their own strength. In times of crisis they were left at the mercy of the great powers and it was evident that their future would be determined by the decisions made by them. Treaties did not prove to be sufficient guarantees, nor did their arms. To establish leagues of weak neutral states, strong enough to withstand the belligerents for a longer period, was hardly practicable. The small weak states eventually came to the conviction that conquests and military adventures would play no great part in their future policy. From then on their aim and ideal was *security*.

Armed conflicts would expose their military and economic weakness and increase the danger of being swallowed up by the great powers, and secondly, the «dangerous» ideas of the French revolution had spread to all countries and caused unrest in great and small states as well. This growing unrest at home made the monarchs somewhat uneasy for the future of their thrones. If this movement was allowed to develop, it might mean the end of their governmental system, and they knew instinctively that war with its misery and distress would work to their disadvantage.[34] Thus,

---

[33] Phillips, *The Napoleonic Period*, Appendices.

[34] This does not have an equal bearing on all countries. The great nations did not fear war so much because they could still gain by it, whereas the small ones could only lose. The United States did not fear the ideas of the French revolution, but European imperialism which also was the main concern of the Swiss.

even if their full sovereignty was much of an illusion already, they were bent on keeping it up, but they also understood that the only way in which they could gain the security they now longed for was by staying out of wars and being neutral. But they had to find some new way of doing this. Treaties would not be too helpful, and a partial neutrality would obviously not be tolerated any longer. So the primary question was what to do to keep out of war without reducing their position as equals?

As we know, the answer was given by the Washington Administration in 1793, and by subsequent legislation. Thus, the American innovation of a neutrality built on law became the foundation of the imposing structure of the nineteenth century neutrality. It was the neutrality of a weak state, whose existence as a sovereign nation was entirely dependent upon being left alone to complete its internal development in peace. None of the weak states could any longer influence world affairs by forceful means. What gains they could still get had to be obtained in peace, even if some other states were at war. Wanting to be left alone, they adopted the principles of impartiality, absolute passivity and non-participation, so far as their governments were concerned. From that time on, Europe spoke of traditional neutrals.

Permanent Neutrality.

Some of the smaller states went even further. In 1815, Switzerland managed to get general recognition of its status of permanent neutrality. This was established by a treaty whereby that state was guaranteed the inviolability of its territory in return for obligating itself to a neutral attitude in any war that might break out.[35] This permanent neutrality is different from the ordinary, traditional neutrality, which is «une situation acute,» that arises when a war breaks out, and lasts only during the continuation of hostilities. Traditional neutrality can also be abandoned any time the neutral state wishes to join the war. Permanent neutrality is, however, guaranteed by an international treaty and is intended to last forever, in war and in peace as well.[36]

In 1839, Belgium obtained the same privileged status of permanent neutrality, and in 1867, Luxembourg was neutralized. These are the only three cases of neutralization. In 1898 and 1902, Norway put forward claims to be recognized as a permanent neutral and there seems to have been no general objection from the principal foreign countries. However, these attempts never amounted to anything as Norway at that time was united with Sweden and could not independently control her foreign policy. As Sweden refused to agree, Norway had to give up her plans for neutralization, and the proposal was not repeated.[37]

Neutrality in the «British Century».

In the nineteenth century, neutrality was regarded as the chief means to obtain security for those states that felt too weak and small to have their independence guaranteed by force. Permanent neutrality was the extreme consequence of this trend. The small states who would not or could not get recognition of such a status, went on fortifying the position of traditional neutrality to diminish the risks of involvement.

Since 1818 municipal legislation had been considered an effective means to this end and it had been adopted by most countries. The United States continued to develop domestic neutrality legislation along the same lines as it had been introduced in 1794. In 1838, Congress passed a bill which was intended to supplement the act of 1818,[38] and in 1841, President Tyler issued a proclamation against «secret lodges, clubs or associations on the northern frontier». In both cases the objective was to avoid conflicts which might endanger the peace and the good relations between the United States and Great Britain. In the fifties and sixties, Presidents repeatedly issued proclamations against filibustering and warned American citizens against giving armed assistance to the insurrections in the West Indies, Central America and Canada.[39]

---

[35] J. B. Whitton, «La Neutralité et la Societé des Nations,» Hague Academy of International Law, *Receul des Cours de l'Academie des Droits International*, 1927, 456 ff.

[36] Frede Castberg, *Folkerett* (Oslo, 1937), 58.

[37] For a more detailed discussion see, Trygve Mathisen, «Nøytralitetstanken i norsk politikk fra 1890-årene og til Norge gikk med i Folkeforbundet.» *Norsk Historisk Tidsskrift*, vol. 36, May 1952.

[38] The immediate occasion was the insurrection in Canada and the intention was to stop the transport of arms and ammunition over the Canadian border; Bailey, *Diplomatic History*, 204—209.

[39] Fenwick, *Neutrality Laws*, 43—48.

It was soon evident, however that neutrality legislation was not to be limited to municipal actions. Throughout the last half of the nineteenth century, the question of neutral rights and duties appeared to an ever increasing extent on the agendas of the international conferences until it finally culminated in the Hague Conventions at the turn of the century.

The first of these agreements was the Declaration of Paris, which was signed at the conference in Paris in 1856, following the conclusion of the Crimean War. This treaty came about partially as a result of the different practices of England and France in confiscating enemy goods in neutral ships and vice versa. Since France and England for the first time in centuries were on the same belligerent side, this issue caused some confusion in their relations to each other and to the neutrals. In March, 1854, the French and British Governments resolved to change their rules to the benefit of the neutrals. Neutral flag should cover enemy goods and neutral goods be free even on enemy ships.[40] Thus, England had eventually given way to the neutrals' century-old insistence on free ship — free goods. In April, 1854, the Russian Government issued a similar statement. In return, most neutral states declared that they would strictly fulfil their neutral duties. Some even announced that they would not permit privateers to enter their ports.[41]

At the Paris Conference in 1856, Count Walewski, the French Foreign Minister, made a proposal to close the conference with a declaration to end the recurrent conflicts between neutrals and belligerents at sea and aid the foundations for a uniform international maritime law. The proposal was supported by the British plenipotentiary, Lord Clarendon, and subsequently formulated and accepted. Recognizing that «the maritime law had long been the object of regretable contestation,» the plenipotentiaries declared that:

1. Privateering is and remains abolished.
2. The neutral flag covers enemy merchandise with the exception of contraband of war.
3. Neutral merchandise, with the exception of contraband, is not capturable under the enemy's flag.

[40] Boye, *Vaebnede neutralitetsforbund*, 322—323. Both states had already agreed not to make use of privateers.
[41] The Scandinavian countries, Belgium, Naples, Spain, Austria and Brazil. *Ibid.*, 324.

4. Blockades in order to be obligatory must be effective; that is to say, maintained by a force sufficient to really prevent access to the coast of the enemy.[42]

The Declaration was signed by all the powers at the conference except by Spain, Mexico and the United States. These three states refused to sign because they would not consent to the abolishment of privateering. The United States representative, Mr. Marcy, declared that he would have signed if the Declaration had provided that all private property on the seas should not be interfered with. If this could not be guaranteed, the United States with its small navy, had to reserve the right to make use of privateers.[43] This seems to indicate that the United States' insistance on a general respect for neutral rights and duties was primarily made on a regional basis and with a view to national interests. During the American Civil War and the Spanish-American War, it announced its adherence to the principles of the Declaration, but only for the duration of the war.[44] The question of universality as a requirement for a successful application of the Declaration of Paris has not been widely discussed, but the English writer and politician, T. Gibson Bowles, seemed to think that it was of some importance. He said that

> the refusal... of Spain, might, had it stood alone, have been treated with scorn; but the refusal of the United States and their continued maintenance of the old rules, are absolutely destructive of the Declaration itself, and reduce it at once from its proud pretentions as an exposition of maritime law in general, to a mere convention between the signatory states for special rules as between themselves alone.[45]

Even without the signature of the United States, however, the Declaration seems to have been important for the neutral cause in general. It meant a victory for the ideas of neutrality, which the neutrals could hardly have expected. The neutral rights of

---

[42] Thomas Gibson Bowles, *The Declaration of Paris* (London, 1900), 122—123.
[43] Bowles, *The Declaration of Paris*, 196—198; Boye, *Vaebnede neutralitetsforbund*, 326.
[44] For details see Bowles, *The Declaration of Paris*, 199—208.
[45] *Ibid.*, 195.

trade were now recognized in an international agreement. By having their rights acknowledged, they had greatly added to their security and strengthened their position in a future war. It meant, in fact, a recognition that a neutral status during a war was legally justifiable, as was belligerency.

The Declaration of Paris got its first test during the American Civil War, and even though it proved difficult to get a strict observance of its rules, the prestige of the Declaration does not seem to have been weakened. This is most likely due to the fact that Great Britain claimed a neutral status during this conflict. The subsequent Treaty of Washington, involving the *Alabama* question, also contained some statements relating to legal neutrality.[46] Article 6 of the treaty provided that a neutral government was obligated to use «due diligence» to prevent the fitting out, arming or equipping of any vessel that was meant to or suspected of being intended for warlike purposes against a power with whom the neutral was at peace. Secondly, not to make use of its ports and waters as a base of supply for belligerent operations, and to use due diligence in its own ports and waters, preventing any violation of the foregoing obligations and duties.

As this was a bilateral agreement, it had no direct importance, but it has indirectly contributed to the development of legal neutrality since the principles formulated in the treaty were later incorporated in an international agreement.

The conference in Brussels was, however, a direct step toward the codification of war and neutrality on an international basis. It was called by Czar Alexander II and met in 1873. As a result of the conference, the so-called Declaration of Brussels was issued. It was not ratified but was of importance nevertheless since some of its basic principles were adopted at the Hague Convention in 1899.[47]

On the whole, during the latter part of the nineteenth century, there seems to have been an increasing willingness on the part of the great powers to have war regulated and codified. It is difficult to understand, on the basis of power politics, why the great powers, who were bound to be belligerents in any future conflict, not only acquiesced in, but actively worked for, an international recognition of neutral principles. This attitude is hard to explain on strictly

---

[46] *Treaties and Conventions, 1776—1887* (Washington, 1889), 481.
[47] Boye, *Væbnede neutralitetsforbund*, 324.

political grounds. Was it due to concentration on internal domestic development, or was it the force and influence of the humanistic ideas of that century? Or did the great powers like England and Russia think they had gotten what they wanted and that future wars might only upset the balance and threaten their established positions? Was the codification meant to restrict wars so as to make them practicably impossible?

The development of legal neutrality is even more remarkable since at the turn of the century, the danger of a general European war was increasing year by year. Still, the legislative work apparently continued with absolute disregard for changing conditions and the realities of the situation. Was the coming catastrophe felt to such an extent that the statesmen of Europe turned to legislation in a last desperate effort to exhaust all means, to let nothing be unattempted, that might help to lessen the destructive effect of the coming war? Whatever the correct answer may be, the powers on the very eve of the First World War turned to the most gigantic legislative effort in the history of neutrality.

In response to an invitation sent out by the Russian Czar, Nicholas II, delegates from most countries met in the Hague to discuss means for preserving the peace. The first Hague Conference was held in 1899. Plans were laid for a world court of arbitration and governments were strongly urged to submit their quarrels and disputes to this institution but were put under no obligation to do so.[48] At the same time, an attempt was made to regulate «the rights and duties of neutral powers and persons in case of war,» and at the second conference in 1907, plans were laid for a constructive peace program.[49] For the first time, the whole system of neutral rights and duties, on sea and on land, was defined and officially incorporated in international law to its fullest extent. What had for centuries been the always shifting usages and interpretations of the «law of nations» were now put into an international code which had the official approval of all nations.

The Hague Conventions mark the top, the very climax of legalized neutrality. From *Consolato del Mare,* piece by piece had been added to the law of neutrality, until the 1907 Convention disposed

---

[48] Ferdinand Schevill, *History of Europe from the Reformation to the Present Day* (New York, 1946), 675.

[49] Fenwick, *American Neutrality,* 108.

of most of the controversial points in the relations between belligerents and neutrals.[50] Many of the provisions had already been known and respected for a long time, but new rules were also added, and now all were codified into one single body of international law. Of the many conventions the fifth Hague Convention was concerned with neutrality on land, while the eleventh, twelfth and thirteenth dealt with maritime neutrality.

These conventions are so well known that it will hardly be necessary to give a detailed discussion of the various articles. One of the first and most important asserted categorically that «the territory of neutral powers is inviolable»,[51] a key point in neutral theory. It was further stated that the neutral state could not be held responsible for the commercial transactions of its citizens. Most important of all, however, was the strong stress on impartiality. In two articles of the fifth and thirteenth conventions it was explicitly maintained that it was «for the neutral powers an admitted duty to apply these rules impartially to the several belligerents».

Finally there was the important stipulation that the Hague conventions had to be accepted by *all* powers to be binding. While all powers signed, ratification was not universally obtained, and thus, the Hague Conventions never became an international obligation in a strictly legal sense.

The results of the Hague Conferences in 1899 and 1907, mark a great step toward the complete legal recognition of neutral rights and duties on international grounds. There now existed an elaborate juridical system, approved if not ratified by all. It is, however, not accidental that the first article in both of the two conventions deals with the inviolability of the neutral territory. This was actually the basic point of neutrality and the other articles are more or less elaborations of the same idea. If the territory was not absolutely respected, the theory of full equality and the sovereign status could not be maintained, and the neutral's existence as an independent state was endangered. By the Hague Conventions, the belligerents

---

[50] Fenwick, *American Neutrality*, 110.

[51] For the full text of the Hague Conventions see *International Conciliation Documents*, 1928, 373—384. See also James Brown Scott, *The Hague Conventions and Declarations, 1899 and 1907* (Baltimore 1909), which gives a complete and detailed treatment. See also a Norwegian version, J. G. Ræder, *Utvalg av Norges Overenskomster med Fremmede Stater*, (Oslo 1936).

were told how far they could go, and the neutrals had a safe legal basis for their efforts to prevent them from going further. The advantage was definitely on the neutral side and, if the rules were followed, they appeared to give the weaker states a great amount of security.

It was felt, however, that the system could still be improved. This was clearly expressed in the invitation which the British Foreign Minister, Sir Edward Grey, sent to the governments of the great powers in February, 1908. He said that at the Hague Conferences there had been agreements on some important points, but on «various questions connected with maritime war, divergent views and practices prevailed among the nations of the world.» On some of these it had been impossible to reach an understanding. He therefore proposed that another conference should be called in the autumn of that same year. Its main purpose was to be the establishment of an international court of appeal in matters of prize, and the British Government was under the impression that «this would not meet with general acceptance so long as vagueness and uncertainty exist as to the principles which the court ... would apply to questions ... affecting naval policy and practice.»[52]

The invitation was accepted, and in December, 1908, the conference met in London. At the end of February, 1909, the delegates had agreed to a declaration concerning laws of naval warfare which has later been called the Declaration of London. They dealt rather thoroughly with objects so delicate and so closely connected with national interests, that the Hague Conferences had not even dared touch them.

The first chapter of the Declaration, comprising twenty-one articles, dealt with the law of blockade, while the second chapter, which was even more extensive, dealt with contraband, the most controversial of all the neutral issues. The remaining seven chapters dealt with unneutral service, destruction of neutral prizes, transfer of flag, convoy, resistance to search and compensation.[53] It was a courageous attempt to clarify and regulate international relations

---

[52] Sir Edward Grey to His Majesty's representatives in Berlin, Madrid, Paris, Rome, St. Petersburg, Tokyo, Vienna and Washington, February 27, 1908. James Brown Scott, *The Declaration of London, February 26, 1909*, a collection of official papers and documents (New York, 1919), 13.

[53] For the full text of the Declaration, see Scott, *Declaration of London*, 112—129.

in time of war, and meant an additional gain to the traditional neutrals. Many regarded the Declaration as a great step in the development toward an International Court.[54] The Declaration of London was meant as a code and a guide for the International Prize Court which later was to be developed into a general international court.

Reading the provisions of the Declaration it seems almost inconceivable that the powers could come to terms over the details and formulations of such a document, the more so since most of the articles were written in an unanbiguous and straightforward way which did not leave much room for doubt as to the interpretation. The main requirement concerning blockade was still that it must be effective in order to be recognized. But to the flat statement of the Declaration of Paris was now added a great number of special provisions which took care of most cases likely to cause disputes. Among them was the requirement that a blockade must be applied impartially to the ships of all nations.[55] Far more important, however, was the attempt to define contraband. The old Grotian conception was now revived, and a distinction made between absolute and conditional contraband.[56] In both cases, extensive lists were given, classifying the articles after their use and importance in war. Absolute contraband would always be liable to capture if it was destined to an enemy country or territory occupied by one of the belligerents. In the same article[57] it was stated that it was immaterial whether the carriage of the goods was direct or entailed trans-shipment or a subsequent transport by land. The question of destination was also important in the case of conditional contraband, but this could only be captured if it was shown «to be destined for the use of the armed forces or of a governmental department of the enemy state...».

There were also special articles taking care of neutrals who tried some kind of participation on either side. The principle of

[54] Elihu Root in an address delivered at the sixth annual meeting of the American Society of International Law, April 25, 1912, *Ibid.*, 10.

[55] Article 4.

[56] Fenwick considers it extremely optimistic to put up a new detailed classification of contraband at a time when science was developing so rapidly. Fenwick, *American Neutrality*, 87., Grotius, *De Jure Belli*, Vol. III. 602.

[57] Article 30.

armed neutrality was finally recognized and neutral vessels under national convoy were exempted from search,[58] while «forcible resistance to the legitimate exercise of the right of stoppage, search and capture involves in all cases the condemnation of the vessel.»[59] A final article provided that the Declaration must be treated as a whole and could not be applied in parts. The Declaration of London was not ratified, but was all the same used as a model for neutral conduct together with the Hague Conventions.

Thus, instead of declining after its complete failure in the Napoleonic Wars, the concept of neutrality was saved by the American introduction of disinterested, impartial and passive neutrality as being the cornerstone of this new concept. The special movements and events that came to dominate the nineteenth century happened to work in the same direction and permitted neutrality to develop into a sky-high artificial structure, which was crowned by the Hague Conventions and the Declaration of London. Neutrality, as it was formulated in those documents, is the neutrality of the twentieth century and the accepted conception of the term. According to present-day definitions, neutrality is «a legal status arising from the abstention of a state from all participation in a war between other states, and the recognition by the latter of its abstention and impartiality.»[60].

There is practical unanimity among writers on international law, that a status of neutrality is dependent upon strict *impartiality* and absolute non-participation and passivity.[61] A study of the decline or growth of the concept must, therefore, be based upon this definition.

[58] Article 61.

[59] Article 63.

[60] P. Jessup, «Neutrality,» in *Encyclopedia Britannica*, XI : 363. Whitton puts it this way, «The neutrals are under obligation not to give armed assistance to one or the other belligerent and to adopt toward them an attitude of strict impartiality. Whitton, «The Changed Attitude of the Powers Toward Neutrality Laws,» 457.

[61] W. E. Hall, «On the Nature of Neutrality,» documents illustrating the law of neutrality, in *International Conciliation*, Doc. 1928, 373; L. Oppenheim, *International Law*, 400; Q. Wright, «Neutrality and Neutral Rights Following the Pact of Paris,» in *American Society of International Law Proceedings*, 1930, 80—87; Fenwick, *American Neutrality*, 102; E. Borchard, «Dragging America Into War,» in *Current History*, 40 : 392—401 (July, 1935).

II. Neutrality during World War I

The Failure of Impartial Neutrality

The First World War brought the most severe test for neutrality since the wars of Napoleon. In fact, it was the first general conflict in a hundred years. The Crimean War had been a peripheral affair after all, though most European powers were in it. The great vital issues of European politics had not been involved; the war did not last very long and it was not fought with any deadly intensity. Bismarck's wars were short and concentrated and did not involve any of those maritime questions, which have always proved fatal to neutrality.[1] The American Civil War was also too far off to mean a serious danger to international relations in general. The Balkan controversies had so far not developed into more extensive wars. It had been a century of peace and a century of triumph for neutrality.

World War I was to be the touchstone. Neutrality, buttressed by an almost complete legal equipment, was therefore put to its first real trial and given a chance to prove itself as a sound and vital political principle. During the Napoleonic Wars, the neutral states had been in a period of transition and confusion. Many excuses could rightfully be made to explain why neutrality did not work then. But in 1914, it was fully formulated and established and still the failure was almost complete. This elaborate legal structure, the result of painstaking efforts through many years, proved to be built on sand.

The similarity between the war of 1914 and those a hundred years earlier has already been pointed out. The arguments on both sides were essentially the same. There was a sea-power against a land-power in a deadly fight for continental domination. England

---

[1] Quincy Wright, *The United States and Neutrality* (Chicago, 1935), 3.

and her allies were once again fighting for civilization, humanity, democracy, and freedom of all peoples for self-determination. These lofty ideals seemed to give them a moral justification for resorting to almost any action they believed necessary; for the neutrals were also interested in the preservation of civilization and humanity, but they were not prepared to fight for it.[2] The Allies considered themselves justified in asking for some collaboration in the non-military field and cared little for the legal arguments of neutrality. Both sides invoked the same retaliation policy.

Piece by piece the whole body of neutrality legislation crumbled, until at the end to the war, the bare backbone of the skeleton was left. This was the old compromise between belligerents and neutrals based on hard facts and naked realities.

By using all their economic and military bargaining power, the neutrals might have succeeded in staying out of war, but in so doing they had to submit to severe limitations of their sovereignty. On the other hand, the belligerents had to modify their demands to the minimum which was necessary to keep the neutral from joining the enemy. During the First World War, the important arguments were not based on international law; what counted was bargaining: if you will let us do this and have that, we will not press you quite as hard as we might like to. It will lead too far to go into details about the neutrals' struggle for existence during the First World War. But in order to understand the neutrals' dilemma, some controversial points will be dealt with here.

The most important of these was again the issue of contraband. The Declaration of London had three very extensive lists of articles that were clearly and unmistakably defined. One, for absolute contraband, the other for conditional contraband, and the third for commodities which were explicitly declared not contraband.[3] This was merely a formulation of a principle which had been known for some time. Grotius, writing in the seventeenth century had said, «We must make distinctions with reference to the things supplied. There are some things, such as weapons, which are useful only in war; other things which are of no use in war, as those which minister to pleasure, and others which are of use both in time of

[2] Edwin Borchard and W. P. Lage, *Neutrality for the United States*, Yale University Press (New Haven, 1937), 48.

[3] See Scott for the detailed lists, *Declaration of London*, 117—122.

war and at other times, as money, provisions, ships, and naval equipment.»

While he thought the first two classes were clear, he said regarding the third one, that the conditions of the war must be taken into consideration. «For if I am unable to protect myself without intercepting the goods which are being sent to the enemy, necessity, as we have elsewhere said, will give me the right to intercept such goods, but with the obligation to make restitution unless another cause arises.»[4] This gives us an illustration of the hopelessness of a strict definition at a time when the outcome of the war was determined not by the armies alone, but by the civilians as well.

Jefferson had a clear and realistic view of contraband, as well as neutrality at large.[5] He said in 1801, «What is contraband by the law of nature? Either everything which may aid or comfort an enemy, or nothing. Either all commerce which would accommodate him is unlawful, or none... Either all intercourse must cease between neutrals and belligerents, or all be permitted.»[6]

While Jefferson thus saw the point without illusions, the men who drew up the Declaration of London a hundred years later did not seem to make much use of his experience.

Of course, the Declaration was never ratified. In England it passed the House of Commons, but was defeated by the House of Lords in 1910 on the grounds that it would be too favorable to the neutrals.[7] The rejection by the British naturally wrecked the hopes of ratification by other countries. Nevertheless, it was constantly referred to and numerous attempts were made by the neutrals to have some of its provisions respected.[8] The course of the war very soon showed that such a distinction of contraband was impossible under present conditions.

August 4, 1914, the British issued a proclamation by which a great number of articles were declared contraband. This was

[4] Grotius, *Liber III*, 602.

[5] See page 30.

[6] Allen W. Dulles and Hamilton Fish Armstrong, *Can we be Neutral?* (New York, 1936), 16.

[7] Borchard and Lage, *Neutrality*, 9.

[8] The United States in August, 1914, tried to get the Declaration recognized as a basis for their neutrality, which was, of course, denied, since England had refused to ratify it even before the war.

generally in accord with the London Declaration, but in the list of September 21, 1914, a number of articles were moved from the free list to the one of conditional contraband. In the proclamation of October 29 and December 23, the list of absolute contraband was extended considerably. These lists were soon after adopted by the other allies.[9]

In the address which Germany sent to the neutrals on February 4, 1915, she pointed out that the British had violated international law by putting illegible war articles on the contraband list, and that this would invalidate the distinction between absolute and conditional contraband.[10] This did not check the Allies, and in March, 1915, the British transferred raw wool, hides and ammonia from the free list to the list of absolute contraband.[11] The Germans then in their proclamation of April 18, 1915, «in retaliation» to the measures adopted by the Allies, changed their own rules, which then became almost identical with the Allied contraband regulations.[12] By April, 1916, the British had abolished altogether the distinction between absolute and conditional contraband.[13]

The provisions regulating blockade did not fare better. The Declaration of London had twenty-one articles devoted exclusively to the purpose of regulating blockade, but from the outset of the war it was evident that these provisions, which might have been applicable in 1856, were completely out-of-date in the world of 1914. A blockade of that old type was used only in backward areas where there were no or inadequate means of land communication.[14]

The modern communications with a net of canals, railroads, and macadamized roads built for heavy traffic made an old-fashioned blockade meaningless.[15] This was clearly expressed in a note which the British Foreign Minister, Sir Edward Grey, sent to the

[9] Edgar Turlington, «The World War Period,» in *Neutrality, Its History, Economics, and Law*, III (1936), 9.
[10] «Foreign Relations of the U.S.,» for the year 1915, *Supplement*, 95. See also Torsten Gihl, *Den svenska utrikespolitikens historia*. Vol. IV. 1914—1919. (Stockholm 1951), p. 54.
[11] *Foreign Relations. 1915. Sup.*
[12] *Ibid.*, 165, 174.
[13] Fenwich, *American Neutrality*, 92.
[14] Turlington, *World War*, 35.
[15] J. L. Brierly, *The Outlook for International Law*, (Oxford 1945), 30.

Secretary of State, Lansing, July 23, 1915. He stated that the changed conditions necessitated a new type of blocade. This could not be limited to certain ports, because due to the exellent means of communication both within Germany and in her neighbor countries, commerce could pass conveniently through ports in such neutral countries as through those of Germany.[16] To be effective, a modern blockade must cover great areas and zones, and not just small and limited points of the enemy coastline.

The closing of such extensive territories would require new implements of war to be effective. Therefore, already in August of 1914, mines were laid in order to blockade certain points and routes of strategic importance to the enemy. The use of mines for blockading purposes is said to have been introduced by Germany.[17] As as consequence, the British in October, 1914, announced that since the Germans had started the mine-laying business, they found it necessary to adopt counter-measures. These measures consisted in the mining of an area from the English Channel into the North Sea.[18] This was, however, ony the beginnig, and a month later, on November 3, 1914, the British Government declared the whole of the North Sea to be a military area.[19] To make sailings to the Scandinavian countries, the Baltic, and Holland possible, the ships that wanted to sail on these routes were invited to make use of the English mine-pilots. If not, they had to go through the mine belts «at their own peril».

This closing of the North Sea was of course a heavy blow to the neutrals, but it meant a great advantage to the Allies. The sinking of neutral ships increased, and during the first six months of 1915, 68 % of all the vessels that entered the North Sea had been effectively controlled by the British authorities.[20] The neutral ships did not dare to risk being blown up while entering the mined areas on their own, and rather preferred the control and piloting by the British. The French, after a while, followed the same practice, and the visit and search for contraband became almost inevitable for the neutral traders.[21]

[16] *Foreign Relations Supplement*, 168—171.
[17] Turlington, *World War*, 36.
[18] *Foreign Relations Supplement*, 460.
[19] For the details of the notes, see *Ibid.*, 454—470.
[20] *Ibid.*, 459.
[21] Gihl, *Svenska utrikespolitikens historia*, IV, p. 70.

In retaliation against this practice of «establishing a blockade of neutral coasts and ports,» the Germans adopted countermeasures. One of these was the German Proclamation of February 4, 1915,[21] which was termed an answer to the Allied «hunger blockade» and warned that neutral ships would be sunk in the waters around Ireland and Britain. One of the justifications for this was that the British were misusing the flags of neutrals, making positive identification impossible for the Germans.

This German practice came to involve the United States particularly, and after the sinkings of the *Lusitania* and the *Sussex,* the Germans bowed to the American pressure and agreed May 4, 1916, not to sink vessels without warning and to make provisions for rescuing the crews.[23] This meant a temporary settlement of the submarine issue, and checked the Germans from answering the British blockade. In January, 1917, unrestricted submarine warfare was reintroduced, which caused the United States to enter the war in April of that year.

In retaliation to the German proclamation of February, 1915, the British in March announced that in order to stop all export and import from and to Germany they would take into port any ship suspected of carrying «goods of enemy destination, ownership, or origin.»[24] Most of the neutrals protested against this but they made no impression on the British. Their blockade proved very effective, and the number of ships detained and taken into port increased greatly.[25]

By this new blockade practice, Great Britain achieved effective control over neutral trade. The official excuse was that it only meant an extension of the principle of continuous voyage. The English maintained that great portions of what was imported to the neutral countries was re-exported to Germany, and that she thus had a right to stop such goods. This was no doubt true in many cases, for example, the case of Denmark importing great quantities of lard which could hardly be intended for home consumption.

There would probably not have been as many objections to this British argument if it had not been for the fact that Britain did

[22] *Foreign Relations Supplement,* 1915.
[23] *Foreign Relations Supplement, 1916,* (May 4, 1916), 257.
[24] *Foreign Relations Supplement, 1915,* 132.
[25] *Ibid.,* 54.

not apply the same principles to her own trade. In 1915, there was an increasing re-export from Great Britain to the neutral countries of goods which was stopped when being carried by the neutrals. Danish ships were thus condemned for shipping lard to Denmark, while in 1915, Great Britain herself exported, 1,155 tons of lard and fat to the same country, which could as well be converted into German nitro-glycerine as that which the Danes carried. This was also the case with cocoa.[26] This concept of the blockade «involved the attempt to supplant Germany in neutral markets and to maintain a mutually advantageous trade with the neutrals.»[27]

This practice caused the United States to send a note to the British Government on November 5, 1915, complaining against this blockade which in the first place was not effective, and in the second place was not being applied indiscriminately, since the British continued to trade with ports which they denied to the United States. Secretary Lansing pointed out that «the blockade is ineffective, illegal, and indefensible.»[28] The English, however, answered that the blockade was «in the spirit» of the old traditional rules and its effectiveness was best illustrated by the small number of vessels that escaped Allied control.

It was further stated in the American note that the blockade was a «retaliatory measure» and therefore illegal, but the British found themselves unable to admit this. Each belligerent was entitled «to meet his enemy on terms of equal liberty of action». If one makes an attack upon the other, disregarding neutral rights, his opponent must be permitted to act in similar fashion in prosecuting the struggle.[29] On February 16, 1917, an Order in Council was issued outlining still sharper measures to be taken. It provided that a vessel, encountered at sea on her way to or from a neutral port, having the same means of access to enemy territory, and which did not call at an Allied port, should be decreed to be carrying goods of enemy destination. In Article 2 it was stated that a ship carrying goods of enemy destination or origin was liable to condemnation.[30]

[26] Jessup, *Today and Tomorrow*, 37.
[27] *Ibid.*, 59.
[28] *Foreign Relations Supplement, 1915*, 578.
[29] *Foreign Relations Supplement, 1916*, 370.
[30] *Foreign Relations Supplement, 1917*, 494—504.

This Order in Council did not leave the neutrals much chance to determine for themselves, and very few tried to avoid calling at Allied ports. Visit and search in the old fashion on the high seas was no more of the same importance. The ships were taken into port and searched there. The justification for this was that modern ships were bigger and better equipped, so that they could continue even if the weather was too rough to permit regular visit and search. Also, should two ships stop together, this exposed them to a greater danger of submarine attacks.[31]

The development of the two old neutral principles, contraband and blockade, seemed to indicate that pre-war neutrality was no longer applicable. In order to exist, the neutrals had to submit to the belligerents; they were no more able to determine their own course. Their subservient position is perhaps even better illustrated by the numerous new restrictions which made the neutrals feel very painfully that the change in conditions to which the belligerents constantly referred, had certainly not been to their advantage.

It was only natural that the belligerents, from the very beginning of the war, established embargoes on export of certain articles which they themselves needed. Even those articles which remained on the export lists could not be released anywhere. The issuing of licenses was dependent upon their destination, and a declaration of ultimate destination was required. At the same time the British also claimed certificates of origin for goods imported into the United Kingdom, if the goods came from countries near to Germany. Both belligerents claimed guarantees against re-exportation as a condition for export of certain articles. More and more, as the war went on, export articles were put on the prohibition lists.[32] All the neutrals were more or less dependent on most of these embargoed commodities, and consequently the granting or refusal of export licenses became one of the most effective means of pressure which the belligerent had. In most cases the neutrals did not have much of a choice.

In 1915, Sweden secured permission to import certain goods from the Allies, only on the stipulation that she allowed articles, which she herself had prohibited from export, to pass through her

[31] Walter Millis, *Road to War, America 1914—1917* (N.Y., 1935), 118.
[32] Turlington, *World War*, 68—70.

territory in transit from the United Kingdom to Russia.[33]. Late in 1916, the Scandinavian countries and Holland were notified that they would be given no more export licenses on certain articles if these were considered to have been exported in greater quantities than their normal consumption seemed to justify.[34]

To make it difficult for Germany to pay the neutrals for the goods she bought, the transfer of money, securities, gold and silver to enemy nationals abroad was prohibited. This practice was adopted by all the Allies.[35]

The fact that most of the commodities in world trade were carried on steamships made it possible for the Allies to introduce a new pressure method in the «cold war» against the neutrals. As nearly all the bunker-depots in the world were under Allied control, the Allies would make neutral access to their fuel supplies dependent on certain concessions on their part.[36] All ships which were suspected of having the slightest connection with the enemy, were flatly refused coal at the Allied supply stations.[37] This practice was steadily developed, and in addition to the black-lists, there also appeared a white list. It stated which ships had accepted the numerous conditions imposed by the Allies and thus might bunker freely in all Allied ports.[38] However, if a ship «misbehaved», she was transferred from the white to the black-list.

One of the conditions provided that ships destined for the Scandinavian countries could not get coal supplies in Great Britain if they did not guarantee a return cargo to Allied territory. The official British excuse for these measures was the «shortage of coal supplies» which only permitted the sale of bunkers to «friends».[39] As long as the United States was non-belligerent, the neutrals could get along by taking in coal in such quantities in America

---

[33] Heckscher, «Sweden in the World War,» in *Sweden, Norway, Denmark, and Iceland in the World War*, (New York), 72.

[34] *Foreign Relations Supplement, 1916*, 443.

[35] *Foreign Relations Supplement, 1917*, Vol. II, 899.

[36] Turlington, World War, 73.

[37] The British declaration of the bunker control came April 25, 1916; ships lying in British ports should not be allowed to bunker unless return freights were guaranteed. Wilhelm Keilhau, «Norway in the World War,» in *Sweden, Norway, Denmark and Iceland in the World War*, 348.

[38] For the details of the conditions see *Foreign Relations Supplement, 1916*, 459.

[39] Jessup, Today and Tomorrow, 49.

that they did not have to refill at the Allied bunker stations; but when the United States entered the war, it became almost impossible for the neutral traders to avoid the Allied control.

As early as in 1914 the nationals of the Allied countries had been forbidden to trade with the enemy. This restriction was soon extended to include certain persons and firms in neutral countries that were suspected of carrying on a trade with the enemy. These black-lists were first distributed confidentially, and the first public blacklist did not appear until February, 1916.[40] It gave the names of suspect firms in most of the neutral countries of Europe. United States firms were first publicly blacklisted in July, 1916. The German Government then saw its chance to stand up for neutral rights and issued a memorandum to all neutral states branding the blacklisting practice as illegal; and warning the neutrals who yielded to it that they were violating the spirit of neutrality.[41]

The use of blacklists was strongly opposed by most neutrals, particularly the United States.[42] It meant a strong interference with their trade because one blacklisted firm on the cargo list was enough to arouse suspicion as to the destination. The blacklisted were given no chance to be heard in the prize courts. The British Government classified this measure as purely municipal legislation, because it was «inherent in sovereignty and national independence that a government could restrict the commercial activities of its own nationals.»[43] Consequently, additional blacklists were issued in the fall of 1916. The Germans also used blacklists, but on a smaller scale. When the United States, entered the war it used blacklists extensively, particularly in Latin America.[44] The blacklists were widely feared in all neutral countries and often used as a threat to obtain concessions.[45] The neutral duty of impartiality in dealing with the belligerents became in this connection increasingly difficult to fulfill.

The fact that the British controlled the trans-Atlantic telegraph cables also meant a great check on the communications between neutral countries. This was particularly annoying for the United

---

[40] *Foreign Relations Supplement, 1916*, 434.
[41] Turlington, *World War*, 81.
[42] *Foreign Relations Supplement, 1916*, 421.
[43] *Ibid.*, 353.
[44] Turlington, *World War*, 83—85.
[45] Vigness, *Neutrality of Norway*, 53.

States in all her relations with Europe. She was, therefore, among those who protested most vigorously.[46] Italy and Switzerland were also much aggrieved by the delay and inconveniences caused by the censorship.[47] Due to strong insistence by US. Secretary of State, Bryan, the British in 1915, conceded that they would give notifications of the cablegrams they stopped. But at the same time the British made it clear that they had the right to use their own cables as they wished.

This complete domination of the cables put the British in a strong position for bringing pressure upon the neutrals, and in 1917, they denied the Dutch the use of their cables for commercial messages in order to prevent the transportation of sand and gravel from Belgium to Germany. On this occasion they once again stated that they had an obvious right to use their own cables as they pleased.[48]

In 1915 the British began to remove letters and parcel mail from neutral ships being stopped on their way to or from Germany. As the United States protested and argued that this practice was against the international usage, the British instead brought the ships into port and searched them there for contraband in the mail. This did not alter the inconvenience, and the United States through most of 1916, objected very strongly to it.[49] The British explained their behaviour by pointing to the fact that the Hague Postal Convention, which stated that mail was inviolable on the high seas, was not signed by six of the belligerents, and thus was not applicable in this case.[50]

It may be added that the United States later as a belligerent, strongly supported the right to interfere with the mail.[51]

The requisition of neutral tonnage was perhaps the most painful

[46] *Foreign Relations Supplement, 1916,* 510—530.

[47] The British government picked up business information, and passed it on to their competitors in England. Jessup, *Today and Tomorrow,* 51.

[48] Turlington, *World War,* 96.

[49] But it was in this connection that Lansing stated that the United States had to be cautious not to be bound or tied to propositions that it would regret in the future. Fenwick, *American Neutrality,* 97.

[50] Fenwick, *American Neutrality,* 97—98.

[51] Wilson's complaints over the intercepting of the mail are interesting, seen in relation to his statement after the U.S. was in the war, namely that «interference with the mail was an obvious sovereign right». Charles Seymour, *American Neutrality, 1914—1917* (New Haven, 1925), 10.

of all the humiliations the neutrals had to endure.[52] The exercise
of *lex angaria* or the requisitioning of neutral ships that happened
to be in Allied or enemy ports, was applied in April, 1917, when
the British Government seized twenty-four Danish ships in British
ports. The consent was given by the owners' representatives while
the Danish Government made protests. In May of the same year,
eleven Dutch ships were requisitioned in British ports. These ships
were owned by companies controlled by British financial interests.
The British Government then claimed the right to protect British
interests by bringing these ships under the British flag and arming
them for self-defense. No serious protests came from the Dutch.[53]
Later, more than a half a million tons were requisitioned, of which
450,000 tons belonged to the Dutch.[54] Altogether, eighty-seven
Dutch ships were finally taken over by the United States. Six
were lost, and the rest turned over to the Dutch as soon as the
war was over; compensation was made for the lost ones.

This measure on the Allied side was necessitated by the shortage
of tonnage which followed the German re-introduction of the
unrestricted submarine warfare. It could not be expected that
Germany would consent to such a reduction in the effectiveness of
her submarine campaign, and in April, 1918, she announced that
ships of the neutral countries which had permitted their tonnage
to be requisitioned, would be regarded as being in enemy service.
Ships, considered innocent, could get German warrants of safe
conduct on certain conditions.[55] The Dutch, who felt the threat
aimed directly at them, protested vigorously against this measure
which lacked foundation in international law. The other neutrals
were not quite so concerned, and did not protest.

The United States became highly alarmed, however, at this new
German measure, and the statement was made that unless necessary steps were taken, neutral shipping might be «subject to enemy
control in a manner which will be as effective as the control we
exercise by virtue of our bunker control.»[56]

---

[52] Wilson also described the requisitioning of neutral tonnage as exercise
of «indisputable rights of a sovereign». *U.S. Official Bulletin*, Vol. II, No.
263, March 21, 1918.
[53] Turlington, *World War*, 96.
[54] *Ibid.*, 96.
[55] Turlington, *World War*, 97. Jessup, *Today and Tomorrow*, 71—73.
[56] Turlington, *World War*, 98.

2. Weak Power Neutrality

The small neutral countries were not given much of a choice as to the maintenance of their neutrality. Squeezed, battered, and beaten from both sides, they were compelled to do what was expedient, rather than what was desirable from their own point of view. But all neutrals did not submit to the same extent. Their actual bargaining power became the decisive factor in their gradual submission to belligerent pressure. The weaker they were, the greater were their humiliations.

To illustrate this fact it will be necessary to elaborate in some detail on what happened to the northern neutrals during this period. The Scandinavian countries were almost completely at the mercy of the Allies as far as trade was concerned. Previous reference has been made to the restriction on their import, but they were not much better off when it came to export. Before long the British had established control organizations in all these northern countries. By means of these half-camouflaged institutions they were able to control all neutral export and import, particularly observing that nothing was re-exported to places where it could reach the enemy.

Sweden, was better off than the rest, and, in fact, came very near to being economically self-sufficient.[1] Even so, she had to submit to measures that greatly reduced her sovereignty and her right of self-determination. An organization called Transito had been established in October of 1915 to control and regulate the transit over Swedish territory of goods to and from Russia. This institution was camouflaged as a joint stock company, but was actually controlled by the British Government and operated under orders from the British Legation at Stockholm.[2] It did not limit

[1] Turlington, *World War*, 101.
[2] Turlington, *World War*, 106—107.

its activities to the transit only, but had decisive influence on nearly all matters of import and export. The activities of this organization caused the Swedish Prime Minister, in December, 1915, to issue a declaration that the government would not permit the establishment, under foreign leadership, of a state within the state. The King made an announcement to the same effect in January, 1916, and in April a bill was passed that provided penalty for those who tried to place the economic life of Sweden under foreign supervision. Nevertheless, Transito continued to operate effectively until the end of the war.[3]

This indeed serves to illustrate the weakness of the neutral position. When such encroachments on an independent state's right to selfdetermination could go on in a relatively strong and well-to-do state such as Sweden, how then should the other northern neutrals be able to run their own affairs?

As long as the transit to Russia continued, Sweden had considerable bargaining power, of which she made efficient use. On one occasion she let the Allies inside her territorial waters and used the sheltered waterway, Kogrundsrennan in return for a certain amount of grain. The Schwartz-Lindemann and the Eden-Hellner governments, which followed the fall of Hammarskjöld, were in a less favorable bargaining position when they took over in 1917.[7] By that time, the Bolshevik revolution had greatly reduced the importance of the transit to Russia.

Sweden and to some extent also Denmark, due to their strategic positions and domestic production, were thus able to gain something from both belligerents by bargaining. Norway, however, was greatly dependent upon the import of all sorts of foodstuffs as well

---

[3] Jessup, *Today and Tomorrow*, 189.

The Swedes were asked to let through goods in transit to Russia, but at the same time they were not allowed to export more than a certain minimum of goods to Germany. «Aktiebolaget Transito» was administered by Mr. A. R. Bildt, who was responsible both to the British and the Russian legations.

Foreign Relations Supplement, 1915, 285. For more details on Transito see, Torstein Gihl, *Den svenske utrikespolitikens historia*, Vol. IV, *1914—1919*, 168 ff.

[7] Hekscher, *Sweden in the World War*, 92, 123.

He also makes this meditation: «If a great object is held to justify sacrifices, the deciding question will then be whether a strict adherence to a policy of neutrality really was such a great object.» (Page 4.)

as raw materials for industrial production. As shipping was her main source of income, she was from the very beginning in a difficult position, especially because her trade and commerce had for centuries been primarily tied up with Great Britain and the Western world. The situation did not appear serious at the beginning, since England stuck fairly close to the Declaration of London. But in October 1914, it became evident that this would not be the case in the future, and with the closing of the North Sea, November 5, 1914, Norway's foreign trade came to a great extent under British control.

The German submarine declaration of February 4, 1915, also caused great losses to the Norwegian Merchant Marine. In 1915, more than fifty Norwegian ships were sunk by German torpedoes, with heavy losses in lives, but this did not decrease the activity of Norwegian shipping.[8] During 1915, Allied control became effective even within the country itself, and by 1916, the businessmen in Norway were forced to take a stand for or against Germany so far as trade was concerned. By an indiscriminate use of blacklists, the merchants were pressed into the British-controlled system, and all sales to them were made on very strict conditions. In order to buy British goods, neutral merchants had to guarantee that the goods would only be used for specified purposes.[9] A strict neutral position was, therefore, unattainable for the Norwegian businessmen, even if they had wanted to preserve it. The Germans used the same methods, but could not enforce it to the same extent.

While Denmark effected a general trade agreement with Great Britain, Norway obtained only branch agreements which were much less favorable. Trade relations became more complicated and unstable, as each group of importers separately had to come to terms with the British government.[10] According to the provisions of the branch agreements, the British gained the privilege of inspecting the closest secrets and most confidential figures of the concerned industries. The first agreement of this kind was reached between Great Britain and the Norwegian cotton goods manufac-

---

[8] Wilhelm Keilhau, «Vaar egen tid,» in *Det Norske Folks Liv og Historie*, XL : 266 (Oslo, 1938).

[9] Vigness, *Neutrality of Norway*, 52.

[10] It is mainly due to the optimism of the Norwegian government that no general agreement was reached. They delayed it too long and let the right moment pass by. Vigness, *Neutrality of Norway*, 52.

turing union.[11] It made the union responsible for the conduct of its members; whose behaviour would consequently determine future trade. The conditions were made increasingly harder as time went on, and in some of the agreements made in 1916, British authorities actually got complete administrative domination even over Norwegian owned firms. In spite of the extremely humiliating provisions which the importers had to accept, the British made matters worse by claiming that the Norwegian Government should give its «unofficial approval» to the agreements.[12]

The Fish Agreement and the Submarine Warfare in the Arctic.

The most important of all these was the famous Fish Agreement of 1916. Fish is known to be Norway's most important export commodity, and before the war it was sent all over the world, particularly to South-European countries. Due to war costs and risks, the fish rose so high in price that those countries could no longer afford to buy it; but as the effect of the British blockade became felt in Germany in 1915, that country before long conquered the whole Norwegian fish market.[13]

This could not escape the attention of the British, and since they furnished Norway with 85 % of the means necessary for sustaining the fisheries, Great Britain had the power to stop the Norwegian fisheries completely if she should choose to apply full pressure.[14]

For different reasons she did not do so. Instead, ten million pounds were appropriated to buy the Germans out of the Norwegian market. This was done by making a Norwegian fish merchant an agent of the British Government.[15] At first the Germans did not know who was behind the merchant, but as prices rose and the Norwegian refused to sell to them, they would soon find out.

Later Great Britain questioned whether the same effect could

[11] Signed in London, August 31, 1915. Wilhelm Keilhau, *Norge og Verdenskrigen* (Oslo, 1927), 97.
[12] Keilhau, *Vaar Egen tid*, 269.
[13] Vigness, *Neutrality of Norway*, 82, Keilhau, *Norge og Verdenskrigen*, 70—85.
[14] Vigness, *Neutrality of Norway*, 71, 81, 82, Keilhau, *Norge og Verdenskrigen*, 70—85.
[15] Albert Martens, the owner of one of the greatest fishing concerns in Bergen.

be obtained in a cheaper way. As a result of this consideration, an agreement was made with the Norwegian Government on August 5, 1915, according to which the Norwegians were totally prohibited from exporting any kind of fish except canned goods.[16] As a special grace, however, fifteen percent of the total catch might be exported to «any other country». The remaining eighty-five percent the British would still buy, but at their own prices, and they might end their purchasing obligations after four weeks' warning.[17]

The Fish Agreement was definitely a violation of the principles of economic neutrality and as such inconsistant with Norway's duties as a neutral. This was an obvious fact to the Norwegian Government as well as to the British; and as a consequence, German reprisals had to be expected. It meant the risk of getting into the war, a risk Norway would never have taken if she had had a free choice. Additionally, the agreement also meant a financial loss to the national economy. The government, therefore, did not dare to announce the agreement publicly, but tried for a while to keep it secret. This was, of course, not possible because no plausible explanations could be given the Germans when they were denied further purchases of fish.

The Germans then on the twenty-first of September, 1916, told the Norwegian minister in Berlin, Thor von Ditten, that they did not consider these explanations satisfactory and that reprisals might be expected at any time.[18] A few days later a submarine campaign was started against Norwegian shipping in the Arctic waters off the coast of Northern Norway. By this campaign, the Germans wanted to strike a blow at Norwegian shipping and stop the traffic between Great Britain and Archangelsk. From September 26 to October 4, they sank eleven Norwegian ships in this area.[19] Due to the cold, many of the sailors froze to death and the rest suffered greatly before they were rescued.[20]

These sinkings caused great indignation in Norway, and public opinion demanded that the government should do something to

[16] Officially the agreement was made with the Fish Merchants Association, but the Prime Minister, Gunnar Knudsen, had the final responsibility. Keilhau, *Vaar egen tid*, 275.
[17] Keilhau, *Vaar egen tid*, 270—275.
[18] Keilhau, *Vaar egen tid*, 277.
[19] *Ibid.*, 277.
[20] Vigness, *Neutrality of Norway*, 87.

stop them. Since the submarines were likely to get up to the northern area through Norwegian territorial waters, the government issued a proclamation providing that war submarines were prohibited access to Norwegian territorial waters, except when it was necessary in order «to save human lives».[21]

This measure was more an expression of the indignation which was felt all over Norway than a move of wise diplomacy. The other neutral countries had prohibited submarines within their territorial waters except in the case of bad weather or shipwreck.[22] The Norwegian proclamation thus went much further, and the German Government sent an indignant answer and intensified their submarine warfare in the North. From the twentieth to the thirty-first of October, the Germans sank a total of thirty-three Norwegian ships at a value of twenty-five million crowns. What they wanted was a revision of the Fish Agreement and by the submarine activity force Norway to continue the fish export to Germany; but if Norway were to do so, the Allies would stop her imports and destroy her fisheries and industry.

The Allies also felt that the situation was critical. On the twenty-ninth of October, the French Prime Minister offered the Norwegian fleet ten submarines, and in November, the British put twelve airplanes at the disposal of the Norwegians.[23] Fortunately, these offers were declined by the Norwegian Minister of Defense.

More important was the support given by the Swedish and Danish Governments. The strong position which particularly Sweden took in this question may have had some weight with the Germans. They may have understood that the Norwegians were pressed to a point where they in desperation might enter the war on the other side, and as the Swedes and Danes had taken a unified attitude, these powers, might also be drawn in.[24]

---

[21] Keilhau, *Vaar egen tid*, 281. See also W. Keilhau, *Tidsrummet fra omkring 1875 til omkring 1920 in Det Norske Folks liv og Historie*, Vol. X, 510—511.

[22] (shipwreck — havari).

[23] Keilhau, *Vaar egen tid*, 283, 286. (The Russian Minister also declared that his government was willing to offer Norway every necessary assistance in case of a break with Germany. *Ibid.*, 286.)

[24] The Norwegian Government sent them a note which drew attention to the difficult position in which the country was put; but the Foreign Minister did not withdraw the submarine declaration nor did he promise a new fish agreement with Germany.

What motives the Imperial Government may have had, it altered its position by the end of November, 1916. The German Assistant Secretary of State told von Ditten that if the Norwegians would base the fifteen percent fish export to Germany on the average export for the last five years, maybe an agreement could be reached. This hint was enthusiastically grasped by Norway. Simultaneously, the Norwegians changed their stand on the submarine issue. The proclamation was not officially revoked, but it was put out of force by a secret instruction to the Norwegian Navy. On these conditions, an agreement could be reached, and on the ninth of February, the German Minister to Norway, Michahelles, communicated that the Imperial Government «betrachtet den Zwischenfall als erledigt».[25]

Copper and Coal.

About the same time, Norway had perhaps her most serious controversy with Great Britain; this time the issue was copper. Norway exported copper ore and imported electrolytic copper, primarily from the United States. Great quantities of the copper ore had for years been exported to Germany, but in the spring of 1916, the British Government informed the Norwegians that it disapproved of this traffic. As a consequence an agreement was made, whereby the Allies permitted eight thousand tons of copper to reach Norway. In return they were to get the copper ore. The British understood this to include all kinds of copper ore, while the Norwegian Foreign Minister held that ore with less than one-half percent copper might be exported elsewhere. He, therefore, permitted great quantities of this to be exported to Germany.

In the agreement of August 30, the British also had provided for a first claim to all supplies and production of copper in Norway until a certain amount was covered. To be sure of getting it all, they gave the Spanish-English company, Rio Tinto, the right of buying the rest. The provisions were not quite clear, and Ihlen, the Norwegian Foreign Minister, construed this to mean that the British had renounced their right to a first call for the contract

[25] Keilhau, *Norge og Verdenskrigen*, 138—152, Keilhau, *Vaar egen tid*, 289.

with Rio Tinto.[26] Thus he permitted increased sales of copper ore to Germany, with compensation in metallic copper, but on a much smaller scale. This had been made to bring about an understanding with Germany on the submarine issue, and was probably an absolutely necessary concession to make the Germans negotiate at all. Nevertheless, on the twenty-fourth of November, the British claimed that the export of copper to Germany should be stopped immediately. Yet, this Ihlen could not do, because it would undoubtedly have broken the negotiations with the Germans, which were evidently progressing satisfactorily. The export of copper ore to Germany was therefore continued.[27]

On December 1, 1916, Lloyd George took over the government in England, and shortly afterwards the Norwegian Government was warned that if the export of copper ore to Germany was allowed to continue, the coal export to Norway would be stopped.[28] Ihlen tried to delay this prohibition from taking effect, but immediately before Christmas the British allowed no more coal to reach Norway.

The agreement with Germany was, however, not yet concluded and Norway could, therefore, not yield to the Allied demand, but had to go on without coal. It had a very serious effect on the country's economic life and was painfully felt all over the country. Schools, churches, and theaters had to close. The gas was on only certain hours a day. The ships could not get into the ports, because the ice-breakers lacked coal to keep the passage open.[29]

By the beginning of January, 1917, the agreement with Germany was reached, and on January 24, Ihlen let the British know that he was willing to stop the export of copper ore to Germany if they would recall the ban on exports of coal to Norway. This was done on the seventeenth of February.[30] These episodes illustrate the dilemma that a small country had to face during the Great War.

---

[26] Keilhau, *Norge og Verdenskrigen*, 158—159.

[27] Keilhau, *Vaar egen tid*, 290.

[28] Keilhau, *Norge og Verdenskrigen*, 169.

[29] Vigness, *Neutrality of Norway*, 65—68.

[30] The official offer was made on February 14. Keilhau, *Norge og Verdenskrigen*, 177. (See this excellent book for details of Norway in the First World War.)

Norway's War Losses.

Norway's greatest asset was her merchant marine, but it could not always be used effectively for bargaining purposes because its services were imperative for paying for the export. In fact, Norway had to sail in order to live. The Allies got an effective control over her shipping through 1915 and 1916, and there was not much Norway could do about it. However, the Germans thought they could do something, and one of the aims of the unrestricted submarine warfare of January 31, 1917, was to scare the neutrals away from trade with Great Britain.

In the beginning it looked as if they should be successful. The Swedes and the Danes held back their ships, and during the first nineteen days of February, only five American ships set out for ports within the danger zone.[31] The Norwegian passenger liners suspended their sailings for a while, but the tramp steamer lines decided to go on regardless of the markedly increased risks.[32] The British were, however, still fearful that if the losses were too great Norway might withdraw her merchant marine, and February 3, 1917, the British Minister of Blockade, Lord Robert Cecil, suggested to the Norwegian Government that the British should buy a greater part of the Norwegian tonnage.[33]

This was rejected by the Norwegian Government on February 9, 1917. The official reason was that such a sale would be considered an unneutral act by Germany. The fact was that if Norway should sell her merchant fleet, she would lose what little bargaining power she had; and finally, the Norwegian shipping interests would be set aside with no chances for making large profits.[34] These were actually the major considerations.

The fact that Norway continued to sail when the others did not, made the British grant special privileges to Norwegian ships in

---

[31] Keilhau, *Vaar egen tid*, 295.

[32] The Norwegian-American line was willing to continue its sailings as before if they could lessen the risk by calling for control at Halifax instead of Kirkwall. This was refused by the British whereupon the line discontinued all sailings.

[33] Keilhau, *Norway and the World War*, 351. The sale of merchant ships was at that time conditioned by government approval, (laws of December 3, 1915 and July 21, 1916).

[34] *Ibid.*, 352.

regard to control and custom duties. But the losses were heavy; of the 590,545 tons which were the total world war losses in March, 1917, Norway alone lost 106,111 tons. There was a popular demand that the Norwegian ships should be armed, but the government refused to give its permission. Instead, British armed ships took over the most dangerous routes across the North Sea.[35]

While the Danish and Dutch ships were requisitioned, the Norwegians got a so-called tonnage agreement. This was made by the Norwegian Shipowners Association and a British shipping company which acted as an agent for the British Government. It provided for an exchange of tonnage and the lease of some Norwegian ships for the duration of the war. From April, 1917, all ships to or from Norway were protected by British convoys. This greatly reduced sinkings.[36]

All in all Norway lost 49.3 per cent of her merchant marine. No other merchant marine in the world lost that much, including the belligerents. Italy lost 46.9 %; France, 39.2 %, and Great Britain, 37.6 %. Due to the sinkings, more than two thousand Norwegian sailors lost their lives.[37]

It is obvious that the neutrality Norway claimed to maintain was not a real one. Although Norway must be recognized as a nonbelligerent, since no battles were fought within her territory and she did not participate in any acts of war, yet how much was left of her declared status? How many of those rules were enforced and respected? She was not impartial, nor was she passive; thus, what remained of her neutrality?

A few studies have been made of the attitude of the men that led the government in those days; but nothing has been brought forth so far to indicate that the administration tried to influence the Storting and the public opinion to favor one side in particular. In the case of Ihlen, the Foreign Minister, it is even today hard to determine where his own private sympathies lay.

It must be admitted that the Norwegian people were pro-British, as decidedly as the greater part of the Swedish people were pro-German. Both had been so for centuries, and this could not be changed by the war. Yet, even if they had their sympathies, there

[35] Keilhau, *Vaar egen tid*, 297—298.
[36] *Ibid.*, 299—301. In this connection the «Rautenfelsaffair» ought to be remembered. This indicated German sabotage against neutral shipping.
[37] Keilhau, *Norge og Verdenskrigen*, 204.

is every reason to believe that they did not want them to interfere with the policy of the country. They were not carried away by their sentiments to join any of the sides of the war. Common sense would forbid such actions by a small country. By getting in, she might lose all her independence, sovereignty, and domestic prosperity; by staying out and dealing impartially with both antagonists, she could press prices high and prosper — as Norway did when the British and the Germans competed for her fish market. There can be little doubt that the small countries which had the choice, preferred to stay neutral, because small and weak as they were, neutrality in its classic definition seemed to guarantee them just what they were afraid to lose: prosperity, sovereignty, political and economic independence. In spite of this, they were un-neutral, because they were too weak to resist the force of the belligerents, and consequently had to yield. What they lacked was not the will, but the force.

Great Britain could probably have destroyed the Norwegian fisheries completely any time she wanted to, but «as it would have aroused severe criticism in the other neutral countries, and the reaction of Norway could not be predicted, England first found it wiser to buy the fish in the open market.»[38] Vigness says, «Great Britain, as every Norwegian knew, possessed the power to bring about economic destruction of Norway any time she so willed.» Dr. O. Thommesen, famous editor and columnist, said that «a war with Germany would bring fearful misfortune upon us, but a war with England would be suicide.»[39]

Dr. Paul Vigness, who has made a special study of the Norwegian neutrality during the First World War states that Norway, even «if she was exposed to the worst provocations, never was carried away from her the determined will to keep the peace.»[40] That may be all right so far as will is concerned, but he also thinks that Norway had demonstrated to the world that it is possible even under such circumstances «to keep peace with honor». To this statement there can be raised some doubt. Of course Norway desired to preserve the peace, but she also wanted to carry on her

---

[38] Keilhau, *Norge og Verdenskrigen*, 73.
[39] Vigness, *Neutrality of Norway*, 94. (Thommesen.)
[40] *Ibid.*, 49. «The decline of the Norwegian sovereignty is clearly shown by the fact that she was not even allowed to export any of her imports to fellow-neutral Sweden, except on very special conditions.»

economic life as an independent sovereign nation and make decisions for herself. This she could not do. She was forced to accept such terms as she could get.

Because war as an instrument of practical politics was out of the question, Norway was left with one alternative: to keep peace at the sacrifice of her full sovereign status. She had to take what she was given, and what little bargaining power she had did not prove sufficient to preserve her the right of self-determination in her economic life.

3. The Position of America as the Greatest Neutral

While the Scandinavian countries chose to maintain their neutrality at the cost of depredations and hardships, the United States discarded neutrality in 1917. There is no unanimous agreement among American historians as to the causes for the war entry. Some have blamed big business and munition makers; others stress the influence of the British propaganda and the pro-British sentiment.[1] The most popularly accepted theory seems to be that the United States would not have become a belligerent if it had not been for the submarine issue.[2]

Charles C. Tansill who has made a very thorough study of the American war entry says that «America finally entered the war because of serious difficulties arising from the submarine warfare», and further, «if the President had taken any decisive action against the admission of armed British merchant men into American harbors and if he had been warned of the dangers that attended passage on belligerent vessels, America might well have been spared for the great sacrifices in 1917—1918.»[3] This indicates that the crucial points are the questions of armed merchant ships and the American losses due to the submarine activity of the Germans. These two issues, therefore, have to be dealt with in some detail.

The Germans started using submarines against neutral vessels February 19, 1915. But they had too few submarines then to effectively terrorize the seas, and most Americans took little interest in this campaign before the sinking of the British liner, *Lusitania*, in May, 1915. This event stirred up America, particularly, since more than a hundred United States citizens went down with the

---

[1] Walter Millis, *Road to War*.
[2] Charles Seymour, *American Neutrality, 1914—1917*, and *American Diplomacy During the World War* (Baltimore, 1934). Bailey, *Diplomatic History of the American People*, 645—646.

ship. The State Department sent a strong protest to Germany and the Germans actually changed the manner in which they conducted their submarine warfare.[4] They continued to be very cautious up to 1916, when conditions were changed because of the new use of the armed merchant men. Count Bernstorff, the German ambassador to the United States, wrote to Lansing on March 8, 1916, that England had made it impossible for submarines to act in accordance with the old rules of visit and search «by arming nearly all merchantmen and by ordering the use of guns in merchant vessels for attack».[5]

Edwin Borchard, who has made a special study of this problem, says that the British had prepared to arm their merchantmen since 1912.[6] A proposal was made March 27, 1913, by Winston Churchill[7] who said in effect that since Germany supported the right to convert merchantmen into auxilliary cruisers, Great Britain would take meassures to arm her merchant vessels. In March 1914, he stated that by the end of that year, seventy ships would be «armed solely for defensive purposes..., capable of self-defense against an enemy's armed merchantmen.»[8]

By the outbreak of the war, Great Britain already had forty armed merchant ships and within half a year later, about one thousand.[9] The *Lusitania* was listed as an armed ship but no satisfactory evidence has been brought to prove that she was armed at the time she was sunk.[10]

Thus, the arming of merchantmen was no new measure in 1915. What was new was the use of these ships. Up to that time, the armament had been considered to be exclusively for defensive purposes. However, on February 10 and 15, 1915, the British Admirality issued orders to their merchantmen to try to ram submarines if escape seemed impossible and to fire at them on

[3] Charles C. Tansill, *America Goes to War* (Boston, 1938), 288.
[4] *Foreign Relations Supplement, 1915*, 481.
[5] *Foreign Relations Supplement, 1916*, 190.
[6] Borchard and Lage, *Neutrality*, 83.
[7] Fenwick, *Neutrality Laws for the United States*, 154. Tansill, *America Goes to War*, 256.
[8] Charles Warren, «Safeguards to Neutrality,» in *Foreign Affairs*, 14 (1936), 210.
[9] Borchard and Lage, *Neutrality*, 94.
[10] *Ibid.*, 91, 93. See also T. Bailey, «The Sinking of the Lusitania,» in *The American Historical Review*, December, 1935, 54—73.

sight. These instructions reached the State Department via the American Embassy in Berlin.[11] This made the offensive character of the armed merchantmen rather obvious. There was a special provision in the instructions stating that «the ship pursued should open fire in self-defense, notwithstanding the submarine may not have committed a definite hostile act.»[12]

The Germans, on February 8, 1916, gave Lansing copies of confidential British instructions to attack submarines, and presented nineteen cases in which such attacks had been made by Allied merchantmen.[13] The British Government also offered prizes in reward to merchant ships which succeeded in destroying submarines.[14]

Those who saw the gun-crews of the British merchant marine in action have since testified that they were extremely efficient. «They handled their guns so skillfully that it was almost certain destruction for the submarine to emerge above the sea level in sight of the merchant ships.»[15] Naturally it was unreasonable to expect the submarines to conform to the old rules of visit and search under such circumstances; it would be suicide to give warning as the heavily armed cruisers could afford to do.[16] It was, therefore, possible to find some logic in the German complaints. In October, 1915, Lansing took the view that if the United States insisted that submarines must give warning «we should also insist that merchantmen be not armed.» If not, the advantage was all with the merchantmen and against the submarines.[17]

The Allies thought not, and Wilson was quite skeptical of views they presented. The same month he wrote that it was not «so simple as Balfour would make it. It is hardly fair to ask submarine commanders to give warning by summons if, when they approach as near as they must for that purpose, they are fired upon, as Balfour would evidently have them fired upon. It is a question of

[11] *Foreign Relations Supplement, 1915*, 653.
[12] Borchard and Lage, *Neutrality*, 95.
[13] *Foreign Relations Supplement, 1916*, 198.
[14] Warren, *Safeguards to Neutrality*, 211—212.
[15] Professor C. V. Easum in a seminar at the University of Wisconsin, August 1, 1949.
[16] Millis, *Road to War*, 263.
[17] Charles Seymour, *The Intimate Papers of Colonel House*, Vol. II (New York, 1926), 73.

many sides and is giving Lansing and me some perplexed moments.»[18]

On January 28, Lansing suggested a modus vivendi, which he presented to the Allied ambassadors in Washington. According to this the submarine should be bound by the rules for visit and search, while the Allies in return abandoned their practice of arming their merchant ships.[19] As a result of this note, the Allies were greatly disturbed and believed it to be disastrous if put into effect.

The Germans naturally were pleased at the suggestion, but apparently never took it seriously, because if it had been made effective, there would have been too few ships available to carry American goods to Europe. In this connection Bernstorff insisted that Lansing's note meant that «from that day the Americans would have had no more merchant ships at their disposal. For the fact is that there were no unarmed British ships.»[20] Millis says the proposal had not the slightest chance of success.[21] From what Lansing says in his *War Memoirs*, there is reason to believe that even he did not take it seriously.[22] Wilson let it be known that Lansing's proposal was purely tentative, and that according to custom, merchant vessels had the right to arm themselves defensively. Thus, if a submarine attacked an unresisting merchantman, with loss of American lives, it would be considered a breach of the formal assurances given by the German Government.[23]

This statement that merchantmen had a right to arm for defensive purposes was sent by Lansing to the diplomatic officers in European countries on February 16, 1916.[24] A week before, February 8, 1916, the German Government had announced that very soon it would regard armed merchant vessels as ships of war and treat them accordingly.[25] On this issue Morrissey says that «the United States asserted rights which never before had been claimed by a

---

[18] Wilson to House, October 4, 1915. Tansill, *America Goes to War*, 414—415, Seymour, *American Diplomacy*, 113.
[19] Morrissey, *Neutral Rights*, 106; Millis, *Road to War*, 263. Seymour, *American Diplomacy*, 113.
[20] Seymour, *American Diplomacy*, 115.
[21] Millis, *Road to War*, 264.
[22] *War Memoirs of Robert Lansing* (New York, 1935), 103.
[23] Seymour, *American Diplomacy*, 115.
[24] *Foreign Relations Supplement, 1916*, 70.
[25] *Ibid.*, 165.

neutral government,»[26] because it was impossible for a neutral to discriminate between defensive and offensive armaments. In her opinion the United States followed a policy of avowed discrimination between the belligerents.

Therefore, the submarine question cannot be dealt with separately, but must be seen in relation to the stand which the United States took on the issue of the armed merchantmen. In the period following the sinking of the *Lusitania,* where a great many American lives were lost, two more Americans were killed when the British liner *Arabic* was sunk. There were also other minor incidents, but sentiments were not brought to a high pitch until the attack on the unarmed French channel steamer, *Sussex.* This ship was torpedoed (not sunk) on March 24, 1916, by a German submarine which did not give warning. A great number of the passengers were killed or injured, but considering the events that followed, it is worth noting that *no* American lives were lost by the explosions on the *Sussex,* although quite a few were injured.[27]

Nevertheless, in spite of the fact that no American had lost his life on this occasion, in America the torpedoing of this steamer marked the decisive turn of the development towards war. Shortly afterwards Lansing sent a sharp note to Gerard for the communication to the German Minister for Foreign Affairs. He claimed that unless the Imperial Government would abandon its present methods of submarine warfare «the Government of the United States can have no choice but to sever diplomatic relations with the German Empire altogether.»[28] Mr. Gerard was instructed to

---

[26] Morrissey, *Neutral Rights,* 202—204.

In this connection it may be noted that the Dutch from the very beginning of the war firmly maintained that armed merchantmen should be treated as war ships. This in spite of continued indignant protests from the British.

Borchard and Lage, *Neutrality,* 100.

[27] Borchard quoting naval reports in his *Neutrality for the United States,* 217.; Tansill, *America Goes to War,* 493.; Seymour, *American Diplomacy,* 120.

The ambiguity of most writers on this point is rather remarkable in view of the enormous emphasis that was put on the loss of lives by German submarines. Turlington, *World War,* 43; Bailey *Diplomatic History,* 634; Millis, *Road to War,* 284, and many more, put it about this way: «Eighty persons, including a number of American citizens, were killed or wounded.» Millis even omits «or wounded» and says just «killed,» which gives a false impression of what happened.

[28] *Foreign Relations Supplement, 1916,* 234. Gerard was U.S. ambassador to Germany.

say that it had become painfully evident to the Government of the United States that this German practice was utterly «incompatible with the principles of humanity, the long established and incontrovertible rights of neutrals and the sacred immunities of non-combatants».[29]

These lofty statements were answered by Germany on May 4, 1916. The Germans said that the submarine question should not be allowed to interfere with the maintenance of peace between the two countries. They took the opportunity, however, of pointing to the inhumanity of the Allied starvation blockade of Germany.[30]

Thus, in order to keep the United States out of war, Germany yielded to the American claims. Consequently, no American ships were sunk without warning until the Germans reintroduced unrestricted warfare in 1917. This gave the United States an acceptable casus belli and she entered the war on the side of the Allies. In this connection Lansing says in *War Memoirs,* that the «submarine warfare may have been a blessing in disguise».[31]

When Wilson led the American people into war, he was conscious of the Allied violations of neutral rights, but he made an important distinction, which has become the classic one ever since. He maintained that the Allied violations caused only property damages, while the Germans destroyed human lives which was an indefensible violation of neutral rights for which there could be no compensation.[32]

It may seem that the natural reaction would have been to forbid the Americans to travel on belligerent ships. This would have eliminated the risk of bringing the country into difficulties because some American citizen might lose his life by traveling on the ships of a belligerent. Secretary of State, Bryan, was strongly in favor of such a prohibition. He regarded neutral rights of travel as no more sacred than neutral rights of trade, which had been infringed by the Allies.[33] This view was also held by most congressmen. After Lansing's modus vivendi note, the Gore-McLemore Resolu-

---

[29] *Ibid.*
[30] *Ibid.,* 257.
[31] Lansing, *War Memoirs,* 41.
[32] *Foreign Relations Supplement, 1915,* 99; Seymour, *American Neutrality,* 4.
[33] Seymour, *American Diplomacy,* 91.
[34] The Gore-McLemore Resolutions provided that American citizens should be warned against taking passage on armed merchantmen.

tions[34] were approved of by a majority in Congress, but they were still opposed by the administration. Wilson, February 21, 1915, summoned the congressional leaders and made the defeat of the resolutions a matter of personal prestige.[35] Consequently, they were duly defeated.

Secretary of State, Bryan, had wanted to give such warnings following the *Lusitania* incident. Wilson agreed then that «we ought to take steps as you (Bryan) suggest, to prevent our citizens from traveling on ships carrying munitions of war.»[36] But no such steps were taken. Neither were any warnings sent out, because the President thought that the people would travel anyway and because it should have been done long ago in order to have been of any help.[37]

Instead Wilson relied on a definition of sovereignty which clearly indicated the new status of the United States as a world power. It reminds us more of Canning's and Palmerston's proud declarations of British supremacy a hundred years earlier, than of the voice of a passive neutral power. At Topeka, February 2, 1916, Wilson said that it was necessary to protect and safeguard «the rights of Americans, no matter where they might be in the world.»[38] He vindicated the same view in his letter to Senator Stone during the discussions of the Gore-McLemore Resolutions.

> «For my own part, I cannot consent to any abridgement of the rights of American citizens in any respect. The honor and the selfrespect of the nation is involved. We covet peace, and shall preserve it at any price, but the loss of honor.» «... once accept a single abatement of right and many other limitations would certainly follow, and the whole fine fabric of international law would crumble under our hands piece by piece. What we are contending for in this matter is of the very essence of the things that have made America a sovereign nation, and she cannot yield them without conceding her own impotency as a nation, and make virtual surrender of her independent position amongst the nations of the world.»[39]

[35] Borchard and Lage, *Neutrality*, 114.
[36] Baker, *Neutrality*, 355.
[37] Morrissey, *Neutral Rights*, 65.
[38] R. S. Baker and W. E. Dodd, *The Public Papers of Woodrow Wilson*, Vol. II (New York, 1926), 89.
[39] Letter to Senator Stone, February 24, 1916, in *Foreign Relations Supplement, 1916*, 176. Baker and Dodd, *Public Papers*, 123.

The validity of this theory has been heavily attacked by Borchard. By referring to Chief Justice Marshall and other authorities, Borchard makes a good case for his stand that neutral individuals are not immune on belligerent ships.[40] If Wilson's view prevailed, all ships would have been effectively protected from attack by having American citizens on board as passengers. This would seem particularly unreasonable as they sailed through waters which were officially declared to be war zones. Ambassador Gerard compared it to having an American sitting on an ammunition wagon, which, however, could not prevent it from being fired upon on its way to the front.[41]

Borchard refuses to recognize any responsibility of the United States for the Americans who lost their lives when sailing on belligerent ships. They had no right of protection. He maintains that at the time the United States severed relations with Germany (February 3, 1917) only *three* American lives had been lost as a result of the submarine warfare.[42] These men were killed on board the *Gulflight* when that ship was torpedoed in May, 1915. (She did not sink.)[43] It is also significant that the *Gulflight* was not torpedoed on the high seas while alone. On the contrary, she was following a British patrol boat to a British port (Bishop) and was thus actually under convoy. Borchard emphasizes very strongly the point that the American ship was attacked when under belligerent naval convoy and thus not at all entitled to neutral protection.[44] It had in fact given up the protection of the neutral flag for that of a belligerent convoy.[45] According to this point of view, *no one* entitled to American legal protection, had lost his life by submarine activities until February 3, 1917.[46]

[40] Even Lansing in 1916 maintained that the flag of a ship covered alien passengers. *Foreign Relations Supplement, 1916*, 630—680.
[41] *Foreign Relations Supplement, 1915*, 461.
[42] Borchard and Lage, *Neutrality*, 212—235.
[43] The other American ship which was damaged in this period was the *Cushing*. It was hit by bombs, but no lives were lost. Borchard, *Neutrality*, 222.
[44] *Ibid.*, 229.
[45] Borchard maintains that the administration must have been aware of this fact. *Ibid.*, 229.
[46] This theory of Borchard does not seem to have been much discussed so far, either for or against. No references have been found to it in the literature of international law of the recent years.

This would, if it is true, make Wilson's standpoint on the loss of lives appear rather unsound, and would in fact invalidate his official reason for bringing America into the First World War. Without this issue, there seems to be little excuse for giving up neutrality and fighting the Germans. The issue of loss of lives formed, however, the central point in his Declaration of War, April 2, 1917.

> I am not now thinking of the loss of property involved, but of the wanton and wholesale destruction of the lives of noncombatants. ... Property can be paid for, the lives of peaceful and innocent people cannot be. The present German warfare against commerce is a warfare against mankind...[47]
> We will not choose the path of submission and suffer the most sacred rights of our nation and our people to be ignored and violated.[48]

Here we are right at the core of the *real* issue. The United States was no longer a conventional neutral. Its neutral rights were quite different from those of the other neutral states. The infringements on the American neutrality seemed like meager trivialities compared to the pressure and limitations to which the other neutrals were exposed. The United States suffered less than any other neutral country; still, it was the only one that found the situation so unbearable that it had to give up its neutrality and join the war. Even if we should condemn Borchard's theory as being false and incorrect, and instead accept the official figures, the American losses of lives and property are not impressive. In fact, they are negligible compared to those inflicted on many of the smaller neutrals. If the Americans traveling on belligerent ships be included, the total loss by April 6, 1917, was 194 American lives. Of these, 50 were enlisted as crew members, that is virtually in belligerent service, even if they still were American citizens. Apparently those 194 casualities convinced Wilson that neutrality had to be given up.

In comparison it may be of interest to note that Norway, a small country of a three million population, lost more than two thousand

---

[47] Address delivered at a joint session of both Houses of Congress, April 2, 1917. Baker and Dodd, *Public Papers*, Vol. III, 7.
[48] *Public Papers*, Baker and Dodd, Vol. III, 9.
[49] Borchard, *Neutrality*, 430, Appendix.

sailors, *doing their work on Norwegian ships*. Still, she did not find this a sufficient reason for giving up her neutrality.[50]

It is hard, and perhaps not fair, to compare two so widely different countries as the great United States and the small state of Norway. But even so, it seems as if these figures may throw some light upon neutrality in relation to sovereignty. The sovereign status of the United States would not admit that 194 Americans had lost their lives because they insisted on traveling on belligerent ships. Consequently, the administration thought itself justified in bringing the nation into the war.

On the other hand, the sovereignty of Norway seemed to permit more than two thousand Norwegians to be killed by belligerent actions. These men were not traveling about on passenger liners, but doing their jobs in carrying out the trade that was absolutely necessary for the existence of themselves and their country. Norway also lost the control of her foreign trade, was trodden upon, pressed and squeezed, and exposed to numerous humiliations from both belligerents. Still, she preferred to keep the peace and remained outside the war.

---

[50] During the whole war period, the *United States* lost on
American ships .... 469 lives
In the neutral period, on belligerent ships .... 194 «

Total loss for the whole war period 663 lives

(Borchard, *Neutrality*, 425—432, Appendices.)

During the whole war period, *Norway* lost on Norwegian ships
from belligerent activities .... 1,162 lives
Crews on ships that were «spurlos versenkt» .... 943 «

Total loss for the war period 2,105 lives

(Keilhau, *Norway and the World War*, 360.)

Loss of Ships and Cargoes During the War Period

Country	Ships lost by mines	Ships lost by submarines in war zones	Tons of cargo lost
Norway	97	701	75,000,000
Denmark	38	236	16,000,000
Sweden	76	155	14,000,000
United States	5	16	4,000,000

Turlington, *World War*, 64—65.

This disproportion between lives and property in two neutral countries indicates that concepts of neutrality and sovereignty exist on a national basis rather than on an international. It provides a very illustrative example of the wide difference between neutral rights when applied to a great and a small power. In spite of the recognized and accepted definition of neutrality, it is safe to say that the application of this principle during a general conflict is dependent upon the status of the country applying it. Each state will have its own definition of neutrality, as well as of its correlative, sovereignty.

4. The Aims of the Wilson Administration

Great and Small.

The neutrality of the nineteenth century with its stress upon impartiality and passivity, was formed by a weak power and enthusiastically adopted by other weak powers.[1] They had no surplus power, no yearning to extend beyond their own territories, and no more potential than was needed for their own development. Nineteenth century neutrality was a defensive and protective measure, the typical weak-country policy.

It has been pointed out before that the status of neutrality seems to be inseparably connected with and dependent upon the amount of sovereignty which a country enjoys. This sovereignty is determined by the freedom and independence with which the nation makes its decisions, without being influenced or forced by foreign pressure. A nation weak in an economic and military sense, will under the present world system be dependent upon its greater and more prosperous neighbors. It will necessarily not be able to enjoy a full and unrestricted sovereignty. Its degree of weakness will determine its limitations and consequently, the character of its neutrality. Neutrality will then be applied differently by great and small powers as, for example, the United States compared to one of the Scandinavian countries.

If we agree that the impartial and passive neutrality, introduced and formulated by the founding fathers a hundred and fifty years ago, was a typical weak-country policy, then it was an unnatural and abnormal status for the United States in 1914. For the Scandinavian states, however, it was the sole hope, the only means of avoiding economic destruction and possible loss of the independence and what sovereign status they still had left.

---

[1] Bradley, *Can We Stay Out of War?*, 111. «The doctrine of neutrality arose to make possible the refusal of weaker states to participate in the rivalries of their stronger neighbors.»

The period 1914—1917 marks a controversial point in the history of the United States. It has, therefore, been dealt with in detail by a great many of America's finest scholars in the field of history and international law. Hardly one of them goes to the extreme of defending every incident in this period as being in accordance with strict neutrality, but quite a few find that under the special circumstances, the United States was justified in taking the steps it took. When at last it was driven away from its path of neutrality, it was because one of the belligerents, by his inhuman warfare, became a menace to civilization.[2]

On the other hand, there are some writers who think that the United States was un-neutral from the very beginning of the conflict. They have found that it did not deal impartially with the two sides, but followed a policy of favoring one party.[3] As this became more apparent all the time, it could only lead to war, — sooner or later.

In such a case where so many complex problems are involved, it is impossible to say that one theory is completely false and the other is absolutely correct. It seems, however, as if recent writers tend to go along with the un-neutrality thesis. This may not be because the majority of the American people and government from the outset of the war did not want to be neutral; but because they tried to undertake a task that in its nature was impossible to perform.

The policy of neutrality was bound to fail, because it was inconsistent and out of harmony with the facts of the situation. It was inconsistent because it endeavored to deal with politics and economic development as if they were two separate and different things. It was the weak-power policy of Jefferson's America, applied to the twentieth century United States. No longer a tiny agrarian state, but a great power in every sense of the word, with an enormous productive capacity and with economic interests in most parts of the world. The United States was now a powerful nation, with all the earmarks of dominating greatness — except a

---

[2] Charles Seymour is one of the advocates of this theory. His book, *American Neutrality, 1914—1917*, puts the weight on the submarine question as the direct cause for American entrance in the war.

[3] Among those who stress this point are Charles G. Fenwick, *American Neutrality, Trial and Failure;* Edwin Borchard and H. P. Lage in *Neutrality for the United States.* See also Walter Millis, *Road to War.*

consistent foreign policy. As R. S. Baker puts it: «The foreign relations of the United States were based upon political isolation, but economically they were vitally entangled in every part of the world. The government could maintain neutrality, but could American industry and finance be kept neutral?»[4]

George Soule quotes W. H. Page, the American ambassador to Great Britain, to have said: «Once the war export business has grown to considerable dimensions, the fat is in the fire,» and adds for himself: «If the (Allied) purchases had not continued, our economy, warped to supply the war demands, would have collapsed.»[5] Allen W. Dulles said in speaking of the same period: «The world was being too interrelated economically to permit one great deal of it to stay outside.»[6] Baker sums it up by saying that: «It was all based upon the misconception that political isolation and economic infiltration were possible.»[7]

As we know, the Americans had once introduced the distinction between acts of government and acts of its citizens. A government could follow a course of strict impartiality and passivity, but it was not bound to restrict its citizens from supplying and giving assistance to one of the sides.[8] What would have happened if the United States had abolished this distinction and cut off its economic connections with the rest of the world, no one can tell. But the experience of the Jefferson Embargo of 1807 does not indicate that such a large-scale experiment would have been met with success.[9] If an embargo proved unsuccessful at a time when the United States was primarily an agrarian society, how could this principle then be expected to work when it was the greatest industrial producer in the world, with economic tie-ups in all countries.

It is safe to assume that strict neutrality would have been out of the question for the United States, whatever policy it had

---

[4] Ray S. Baker, *Neutrality, 1914—1915*, Vol. V of *Woodrow Wilson, Life and Letters* (New York, 1935), 164. See also Charles Seymour, *Saturday Review of Literature*, December 7, 1935, 6.

[5] George Soule, «Price of Neutrality,» in *The Reference Shelf*, 10 : 121, No. 7. «The economic price of neutrality amounts to the abandonment of trade.»

[6] Allen W. Dulles and Hamilton F. Armstrong, *Can We Stay Neutral?*, (New York, 1936), 88.

[7] R. S. Baker, *Neutrality*, 26.

[8] See page 43.

[9] Baker thinks it could not have been done. Baker, *Neutrality*, 181.

adopted, because her widespread interests made some kind of participation necessary. It seems, however, rather futile to discuss what might have happened if things had not been just the way they were. This can be nothing but speculation and provides no basis for a conclusion.

If, on the other hand, it were possible to find out something about the ideas and opinions of those men who ran the affairs of the country, some light might be thrown upon the neutrality problem of this period. The men in the administration must have known the facts and details of the actual situation better than anybody else, since only they had all the information available. If they arrived to the conclusion that strict neutrality would serve the interests of the country, they were likely to have done something to preserve it. If, however, we find that the men in the leading positions did not want to be neutral, it can be taken as an indication that neutrality no longer was the natural and adequate policy for the United States.

The State Department.

The position taken by the Wilson Administration has been widely discussed in later years. Some writers have defended it, while others have charged it with the responsibility of having committed the United States to unneutrality from the very beginning of the conflict. When considering this, it should be remembered that the Administration's position was extremely difficult. The inconsistency of the political and economic situation made their task almost impossible. To adapt a weak country policy to a world power is as difficult as trying to put a little boy's suit on a grown-up man.

Did the administration really want to be neutral even if it had been possible? E. Thomas says, «... we never were neutral ... our ambassador to Great Britain was unneutral, our Secretary of State was unneutral and the American people ... were not neutral.»[10] Borchard makes a flat statement, «we were unneutral and we paid the price. Our unneutrality began as early as August, 1914.»[11] He states further that «after the middle of 1915, the administration did

---

[10] E. Thomas, «Theory of Neutrality,» in *Ann. of Am. Acad.*, 186 : 166.
[11] Borchard and Lage, *Neutrality*, 34, 199.

not desire to stay neutral any longer.»[12] R. S. Baker says, «By October, 1914, perhaps earlier, our case was lost.»[13]

Besides President Wilson himself, three men had a great influence on the shaping of the nation's policy. These were the United States Ambassador to Great Britain, W. H. Page, Secretary of State, R. Lansing, and the President's Counsellor, Colonel House. Colonel House expressed the attitude of these men when he wrote to Page, October 29, 1914, «I cannot see how there can be any serious trouble between England and America, with all of us feeling as we do.»[14]

Page is generally said to be the most pro-Allied of them all, and there can be little doubt as to the stand which he took. He does not even seem to have taken pains to conceal his sympathies, and made a great many statements that indicate his unneutrality from the very beginning. He thought the best solution would be to get the President of the United States and the King of Great Britain to stand up side by side and let the rest of the world take a good look at them. In his correspondence there is plenty of evidence of his partial attitude. To quote a few lines from his numerous letters; September 15, 1914, he wrote to House, «...they (the Allies) are going to knock Germany out and nothing will be allowed to stand in the way. Pray God, don't let the Peace Old Women get the notion afloat that we can or ought stop it before the Kaiser is put out of business... civilization must be rescued.»[15] Still, he was allowed to keep a key position through all the years, and the question of replacing him with a man of a more impartial attitude was never an issue. Lansing has given a frank description of Page's personal and official unneutrality in London, and wondered why Wilson let Page remain ambassador to England through all this period.[16]

Colonel House said that «the trouble with Page is that he sees but one side of the question.»[17] There may, however, be raised serious doubts as to whether House himself had an unbiased

[12] *Ibid.*, 170.
[13] Baker, *Neutrality*, 181.
[14] C. Seymour, *The Intimate Papers, of Colonel House*, Vol. I, (New York, 1926), 309.
[15] *Ibid.*, 333—334.
[16] R. Lansing, «Difficulties of a Neutral,» in *Saturday Evening Post*, 203 : 102 (April, 18, 1931).
[17] Seymour, *Intimate Papers*, Vol. II, 73.

conception of both sides. August 22, 1914, he said to the President that «if Germany wins, it means the unspeakable tyranny for generations to come... Germany's success will ultimately mean trouble for us. We will have to abandon the path which you are blazing as a standard for future generations.»[18] Obviously a personal conviction like this would preclude an impartial attitude. Later statements show that he fully realized what the unneutrality of the United States meant for the Allies. On October 6, 1915, he wrote, «We have given the Allies our sympathy and we have given them the more substantial help that we couldn't offer Germany, even if we were so disposed — that is, an unrestricted amount of munitions of war and money. In addition to that, we have forced Germany to discontinue the submarine warfare.... We have done as much as any nation could do to help her (Great Britain) without actually entering the war. On the other hand, the British have gone as far as they possibly could in violating neutral rights, although they have done it in the most courteous way.»[19] Baker, writing about the same issue, states that, «the United States was furnishing supplies — supplies essential for the continuation of the war — to the belligerents on only one side.»[20]

In January, 1916, House was deeply engaged in discussions with the British King and the most prominent statesmen, and on January 4, Page and House had a conversation with Lloyd George and Austin Chamberlain. During this, «the amateur diplomat», as he later has been nicknamed, was asked what the United States wanted Great Britain to do. To Page's great admiration, House answered that «the United States would like Great Britain to do those things which would enable the United States to help Great Britain to win war.»[21] As to House's efforts for general peace, Baker writes that «House was envisaging his errand in England as a means of assuring the Allies that we considered their cause our cause, while Wilson wanted more pressure made upon the British for their infractions of neutral rights.»[22]

Secretary of State, Robert Lansing, had, next to the President, the greatest direct influence on foreign policy. He tells frankly in his

[18] Seymour, *Intimate Papers*, Vol. I, 285.
[19] *Ibid.*, Vol. II, 72—73.
[20] Baker, *Neutrality*, 180.
[21] Seymour, *Intimate Papers*, Vol. II, 124.
[22] Baker, *Neutrality*, Vol. VI, 139.

War Memoirs that from the first he knew that the United States would have to enter the war on the Allied side. But he, nevertheless, realized that the American people had to be educated and prepared for the war. As long as the people were nearly unanimous in their determination that the United States should stay out, Congress would not agree to take up arms against Germany. For the administration it was thus felt «hard to await the slow process of complete conversion to the cause of the Allies, and a right appreciation of the menace to human liberty in the case of a triumphant Germany.» But, as Lansing expressed it, there was in the autumn of 1914 no other cause for the administration to take.[23]

The *Lusitania* incident made him even more convinced that a war entry would be inevitable and on July 11, 1915, he wrote a memorandum «to his own guidance». He stressed there over and over again, that whatever happened «Germany must not be allowed to win this war or to break even, though to prevent it this country is forced to take an active part. This ultimate necessity must be constantly in our minds in all our controversies with the belligerents. American public opinion must be prepared for the time, which may come, when we will have to cast aside our neutrality and become one of the champions of democracy.»[24] This conviction was always in his mind and it explains much of the apparent inconsistency which marks the correspondence between the State Department and Great Britain. As they ultimately would become allies, «it would not do, therefore, to let our controversies reach a point where diplomatic correspondence gave place to action.»[25]

Consequently, no action could be taken to enforce respect for neutral rights. If the United States was likely to become a belligerent any day, and the administration really wanted war, it would be foolish to establish respect for rules which they in a short time would have to violate. Lansing saw clearly the danger which such a policy might involve. He held that «it was of the highest importance that we should not become a belligerent with our hands too tightly tied by what we had written.»[26] The United States would then have to adopt some of the policies which the British had adopted, if not all of them, because its aim would be

---

[23] Robert Lansing, *War Memoirs of Robert Lansing* (New York, 1935), 18.
[24] Lansing, *War Memoirs*, 21.
[25] *Ibid.*, 128.
[26] *Ibid.*, 128.

the same as theirs, «... and that was to break the power of Germany and destroy the morale of the German people by economic isolation, which would cause them to lack the very necessities of life.»[27]

There are not many of the essentials of neutrality left in this statement. There are no signs of the impartial and disinterested passivity which was supposed to be the earmark of a true neutral. With this noble aim in view, great care must obviously be taken to prevent the appearance of issues that might commit any of the two countries to definite actions and statements. Lansing gives a good description of the diplomatic correspondence of the State Department in its relations to the Allies:

> The notes that were sent were long and exhaustive treatises which opened up new subjects of discussion rather than closing those in controversy. Short and emphatic notes were dangerous. Everything was submerged in verbosity. It was done with deliberate purpose. It insured continuance of the controversies and left the questions unsettled, which was necessary in order to leave this country free to act and even to act illegally when it entered the war.[28]

Under such circumstances, it is easier to understand why Bryan had to leave the administration. As he was seriously concerned about maintaining a real and working neutrality, he would be pulling down what the others were building up, or vice versa. Colonel House makes the rather nebulous statement that «he (Lansing) concurs in my opinion that Mr. Bryan did more to endanger the peace of this country than any other man by his 'peace at any price policy'.»[29]

By the time of the *Lusitania* crisis, the slow «gradual process of education and enlightenment of the American people» had not gone far enough to make a declaration of war possible. Thus Lansing had to restrain his feelings. He would, however, have found it much more satisfying to have «denounced the whole wicked business, to have sent Bernstorff home, and declared war.»[30] This line of thought is quite consistently followed through the whole of his policy.

Of course, the statements made in Lansing's *War Memoirs*, are

[27] Lansing, *War Memoirs*, 128.
[28] *Ibid.*, 128.
[29] Seymour, *Intimate Papers*, Vol. II, 86.
[30] Lansing, *War Memoirs*, 23—26.

all made long after the war, except for such documents, as the memorandum of July, 1915. Things often look somewhat different when seen in retrospect and one has to be cautious in dealing with them. But, incidentally, these memoirs were published after Lansing's death, and it is not likely that they were written for any specific purpose, such as to strengthen his position in politics or society. For that reason Lansing's memoirs appear to be more reliable than most books written immediately after the events have taken place and when their effect still might mean something to the future position of the author.

The policy of Lansing was utterly realistic, and even if he at times seemed to wander in the high and hazy spheres of democracy and humanity, he did not go away from the firm conviction which became the basic principle in his policy, namely that the prosperity and safety of the United States depended upon an Anglo-American combination. This combination should be powerful enough to secure an effective domination of, and eliminate the dangers from, continental European powers and the rest of the world. His views on the foreign policy of this period fall well in line with the ones he presented in his *Notes On Sovereignty*. This book was published in 1921, but according to Lansing it was written long before the war.[31] From the theories and conclusions, which are found in this early work, it is quite clear that the fiction of legal neutrality had no weight with Lansing.

His major theme is sovereignty, both within the state itself and in relation to other nations. He states there that «the equality which they speak of (the publicists on international law) is not an equality of power and influence, but of legal rights ... rights unsupported by actual power are only moral precepts which may possess influence but never positive force. An equality of sovereigns to be real must be an equality of might, otherwise it is artificial.»[32] He evidently has a great suspicion of legal structures lacking the force behind them which make them real. He has no illusions as to mutual agreements which supposedly can take the place of the only thing that is real, namely, power. Lansing says that «political

---

[31] R. Lansing, *Notes on sovereignty*, from the standpoint of the state and the world. (Washington, 1921), 55, Lansing says the notes were prepared in 1906 and in part printed in the *American Journal of International Law* in 1907.

[32] *Ibid.*, 65.

mastery depends upon the physical power to coerce,»[33] and further, «stability of government rests entirely upon the physical strength to compel obedience and not upon a legal right to command. ... clearly *the question is of fact and not of law.*»[34]

This explains much of Lansing's apparent inconsistency in the neutrality question. He was an international lawyer, but he did not get stuck in the labyrinth of legal formalism. He had managed to keep his mind free from the web of theoretical legality and appreciate the essentials of twentieth century political philosphy. As a realist, Lansing's basic argument was that if the United States entered the war and won, they could gain influence with the Allies and be able to moderate the peace terms, thus regaining the good will of Germany which they had already lost.[35] He never intended to be neutral because he did not believe in the principle. Lansing seems to have seen clearer than any one else in the administration, the facts and the realities behind the lofty phrases and the legal spider-webbing. He had reached beyond nineteenth century idealism, and become a statesman of the twentieth century type.

The President.

While Lansing, House and Page safely can be said to have been unneutral and pro-Allied in their sentiments as well as in their policy, it is not so easy to place the Chief Executive, President Wilson, himself. Even those who have made a special study of his foreign policy do not seem to have arrived at any definite conclusion in this matter. Did he honestly and sincerely try to maintain a true and impartial neutrality, or did he not?

In his neutrality proclamation of August 4, 1914, he said that though the laws of the United States did not interfere with the free expression of opinion and sympathy, they nevertheless «impose upon all persons who may be within their territory the duty of an impartial neutrality during the contest.»[36] On the 18 of August, he

---

[33] *Ibid.,* 82.
[34] *Ibid.,* 92.
[35] Harley Notter, *The Origins of the Foreign Policy of Woodrow Wilson* (Baltimore, 1937), 437, 473.
[36] «Proclamation of Neutrality, August 4, 1914,» in *International Conciliation Documents* (Worchester, 1928), 392.

extended this to mean impartiality of thought as well, and he also appealed to the American citizens to «act and speak in the true spirit of neutrality which is the spirit of impartiality and fairness and friendliness to all concerned.» [37]

Wilson seems in this early period of the war to think of neutrality in terms of the traditional American pattern. Harley Notter has tried to show that Wilson's conception of neutrality had a striking resemblance to the views put forth by Washington and Jefferson.[38] His proclamation of August 4, has many traits in common with the first proclamation of American neutrality. There is the same strong stress on the duties of the citizens, the same tendency to go into details to make sure of a right interpretation. There was the same strong element of isolationism in the neutrality policy of this early war period. The fact that the United States was about the only neutral that did not protest against the German violation of the Belgian neutrality is an indication of this isolationism.

Wilson appears in the beginning to have thought of the war as being strictly European and as such it was as strange and peripheral as those wars were at the time when George Washington gave his Farewell Address.[39] Like many Americans, Wilson thought of America as the only sane country in a mad world. He said on August 3, 1914, «I want to have the pride of feeling that America, if nobody else, has her selfpossession and stands ready with calmness of thought and steadiness of purpose to help the rest of the world.» [40]

This statement, in fact, covered his basic attitude throughout the whole of the war period, even if he later changed his opinion as to how and by which means this help should be given. The most important thing was that he still thought this could be done by being impartial. Here his most burdensome problems arose. Due to the Allied blockade, Great Britain and her allies thus gained what approached a monopoly of the American market, and the United States assumed perforce the appearance of a supply base for the Allies. This constituted unneutrality to the Central Powers,

---

[37] *Foreign Relations Supplement, 1914,* 551—552.
[38] Harley Notter, *The Origins of the Foreign Policy of Woodrow Wilson,* 317—319.
[39] *Ibid.,* 316.
[40] Notter, *The Origins of the Foreign Policy of Woodrow Wilson,* 135.

but it does not seem to have been clearly realized in the early stage of the war.[41] Wilson believed firmly that America had a unique moral obligation to all mankind: «My thought is of America, a Nation, which keeps herself fit and free to do what is honest and disinterested and truly serviceable for the peace of the world.»[42]

These high ideals Wilson thought could be best reached by a neutral policy. The fact that he urged a verification of the Bryan peace treaties and supported his theory of money being the most nefarious kind of contraband, indicates that he sincerely believed in a strict neutrality during these first months.

It is hard to say how and when the change came about. Wilson was himself of British ancestry and he had always been a strong admirer of the English culture.[43] There can be no doubt that he made an honest and sincere effort to maintain genuine neutrality, but he had arrived at this conviction by reason and will-power. As he, emotionally and sentimentally, was inclined to be pro-Allied, it was harder to resist the many attempts that were made to pull him over to the Allied side and make him see their points only.

Wilson did not get much help from his cabinet as far as strict neutrality was concerned. As we have seen they all, except Bryan, tried to convince him that the Allies were fighting for the right cause and Germany was in the wrong.[44] The famous letter which the Harvard President, C. W. Eliot, wrote him on August 12, 1914, probably made a very deep impression on him.[45] After having read it he said, «I am afraid that something will happen on the high seas that will make it impossible for us to keep out of the war.»[46]

During the fall of 1914, there must have been a process of conversion going on, even if it is hard to say when it was completed. Wilson was very cautious not to make statements of unneutrality and there are few instances where he officially committed himself to a partial and decidedly unneutral attitude. He made some remarks, however, which definitely committed him to one side.

[41] Ibid., 323.
[42] Baker and Dodd, Vol. III, *Public Papers*, 158.
[43] Bailey, *Diplomatic History*, 615.
[44] Ibid., 614.
[45] Notter, *Origins of Foreign Policy*, 326—328.

Already on August 30, 1914, Colonel House wrote, «I was interested to hear him (Wilson) express as his opinion... that if Germany won, it would change the course of our civilization and make the United States into a military nation.»[47] He added that German philosophy was «essentially selfish and lacking in spirituality». On August 19, he wrote to Grey saying he felt that «we are bound together by common principle and purpose.»[48] In a cabinet meeting early in 1915, Wilson said he was «by inheritance, tradition and rearing at all times a friend of the Allies». Further, that «the Allies were standing with their backs to the wall fighting wild beasts, that he would permit nothing to be done by our country to hinder or embarrass them in the prosecution of the war unless admitted rights were grossly violated, and that this policy must be understood as settled.»[49]

It seems as if he had accepted Grey's statement (well known in principle from the Napoleonic Wars) that «America must remember that we are fighting her fight as well as our own to save the civilization of the world». Consequently, he said to Mr. Tumulty that «England is fighting our fight and you may well understand that I shall not in the present state of affairs, place obstacles in her way.»[50] In October, 1915, he said to Colonel House that «he had never been sure that we ought not to take part in the conflict ... and if she (Germany) did win, our turn would come next.»[51]

These statements indicate that during the fall of 1914 the conversion process had been completed and by early 1915, Wilson had taken his stand. He had not officially given up neutrality, but he had gone away from the Washington and Jefferson definition of it. In fact, he had returned to the partial neutrality advocated by Grotius, according to which the neutral should do nothing to hinder the belligerent that fought for the just cause.[52]

---

[46] Joseph R. Tumulty, *Woodrow Wilson As I Know Him* (New York, 1921), 186.
[47] Seymour, *Intimate Papers*, Vol. I, 293.
[48] Baker, *Neutrality*, 56.
[49] Told by Attorney General Gregory in *New York Times*, Jan. 29, 1925; quoted by Borchard, *Neutrality for United States*, 35—36. See also Seymour, *Intimate Papers*, Vol. II, 49—50.
[50] Tumulty, *Woodrow Wilson*, 230—231.
[51] House to Polk, Seymour, *Intimate Papers*, Vol. II, 84—85.
[52] See page 14.

Notter says that «both the President and the American people had become partisan before the war had lasted six months. And they had become partisan while the dominant dispute in their foreign affairs was over the British trade restrictions and *before* any controversy had developed over German naval policy.[53]

Wilson still believed that America was to play a major part, that she had «obligations to all mankind,» but no more by disinterested service, rather by helping what he thought to be the right side to win. Only then would a world peace be obtainable. From the early attempts to be neutral, his policy passed into a second stage, that of peace efforts and preparedness.[54] The peace program had been kept up all the time, but it was not until July, 1915, that the agitation for preparedness began.[55]

There is no reason to doubt the fact that Wilson sincerely wanted peace, but not peace at any price. The above statements show his attitude toward Germany and he was not likely to welcome a peace with Germany as a victor. He seems to have conceived peace as some form of reversal to the status quo of 1914, which meant discounting of the German military victories. This partial attitude greatly weakened his importance and influence as an acceptable mediator to both sides.

May 30, 1916, Stresemann spoke on this issue in the German *Reichstag*. He said that his party (the National Liberals) would reject Wilson as a mediator. If a vote were taken he thought that only a minority of the German people would be in favor of the «protector of American sale of arms and ammunitions, and of England's starvation warfare.» A mediation of a real neutral country, for instance Switzerland, would, however, be welcomed.

Incidentally, von Jagow, the German Foreign Minister, informed the American ambassador in Berlin, that he hoped the President knew the position of the German Government so he would not be affected by what Stresemann had said in the Reichstag.[56] This would indicate that the government did not object to Wilson as a mediator, which was the thing that counted. Stresemann's statement shows, however, that there were those who thought otherwise and would prefer mediation by some other neutral country.

From about the middle of 1915, German-American relations

---

[53] Notter, *Foreign Policy*, 382.
[54] Ibid., 444.
[55] Ibid., 431.

became steadily worse. This was mainly because of the submarine activity. At times it seemed as if any of these more serious incidents might be followed by war. In this period Wilson admitted that his thoughts «ran much along the same lines» as Lansing's had been doing all the time.[57] He must then seriously have considered whether a war entry on the Allied side would not be the best policy after all.

On January 12, 1916, Wilson had a conversation with Mr. Brand Whitlock, the American ambassador to Belgium. Whitlock was very outspoken in his anti-German statements and Wilson agreed that also in his heart there was no such thing as neutrality and that he was pro-Allied. «No decent man, knowing the situation in Germany, could be anything else.» He let it be known that this was his personal opinion, but admitted that in great parts of the country, people did not think that way.[58] However, this does not mean that he kept his personal opinions to himself. In an address made October 11, 1915, he said that: «Neutrality is a negative word. It does not express what America ought to feel.»[59] This was said in connection with the great stress he now put upon humanity which was more important than legal neutral rights and therefore, ought to concern all. But even if Wilson had chosen his «right» side by that time, there is no reason to believe that he would have America join the war before it was absolutely necessary to prevent the «wrong» side from winning.[60] However, the *Sussex* ultimatum took the final decision out of his own hands. This was a definite commitment that excluded the United States from enjoying her full freedom of action and prevented reconsideration and deliberation on the basis of the actual situation. It also changed Wilson's attitude to the conflict. Before the *Sussex* incident he had contemplated in his peace plans only the use of America's moral force; after that episode, he was ready to go the full distance to physical force.[61]

Thus by the end of 1916, neutrality was a past stage as far as Wilson was concerned. In a campaign speech October 26, 1916, he

[56] *Foreign Relations Supplement*, 1916, 33.
[57] Notter, *Foreign Policy*, 437.
[58] Wilson to House, Seymour, *Intimate Papers*, Vol. II, 50.
[59] Baker and Dodd, *Public Papers*, Vol. III, 375—381.
[60] Notter, *Foreign Policy*, 482.
[61] *Ibid.*, 515.

made this fact painfully clear. He first spoke of the present war as being the last one «that involves the world that the United States can keep out of. I say this because I believe that the business of neutrality is over; not because I want it to be over, but I mean this, that war has such a scale now that the position of neutrals sooner or later becomes intolerable.»[62] This statement could leave no illusions as to the future of American neutrality. At last Wilson had come down to the essentials of his foreign policy. Facts and necessity got the better of the lofty ideals; the luxury of a dead and unenforceable law could no more be afforded.

Baker says about this period: «One cannot avoid the impression that... the administration's defense of American policy was in reality a defense of the British blockade and furnished the British Government with a whole arsenal of arguments against our own criticism of that blockade.»[63] It must thus be admitted that with the exception of Bryan, the Wilson Administration was decidedly unneutral in its policy as well as in its personal attitude. There is nothing to show that they wanted to be neutral even if such a policy had been possible. It probably was not. There is a great deal of evidence[64] to prove that political isolation was absolutely incompatible with the high degree of economic expansion at which the United States had arrived by 1914. Most likely the administration had no choice at all. They might have perceived this fact and they probably did. What cool calculations Wilson may have kept behind the shining facade of high ideals of morality, humanity and democracy, no one will ever know. But Lansing knew for himself; he had no illusions as to the real issue. He knew that what counted at present were the facts, not the law. If there was no force behind the law, it was useless. If the neutrals were unable to put actual power behind their rights, the law was dead and might as well not have existed.[65] It is, therefore, a question of the greatest importance for the whole history of neutrality why an international collaboration for the defense of neutral rights had to fail.

---

[62] Baker and Dodd, *Public Papers*, Vol. II, 381.

[63] Baker, *Neutrality*, 237.

[64] See page

[65] Osten B. Undén, *Neutralität och folkrätt* (Stockholm, 1939), 8. When a statute of law is repeatedly violated «it loses its power and will bind nobody.»

5. Cooperative Neutrality and Why it Failed

Taken separately the small neutrals obviously did not have a chance against the great belligerents. Even if several small nations combined, their strength would have been proven inadequate. Of all the world's neutrals, just one had its neutrality balanced by a sufficient force to have the laws obeyed, the United States. This raises the question — could neutrality have been saved if all the neutrals had combined their forces with those of the United States? Would that have been sufficient to force the belligerents to respect their rights and reluctantly obey the laws of war and neutrality?

There was at least one statesman who realized the part which the United States played in the society of neutrals. Sir Edward Grey, England's master diplomat, once characterized the United States as being «in a sense a trustee of the rights of the weaker neutrals.»[1] He observed further that, «the Allies soon became dependent for an adequate supply on the United States. If we quarreled with the United States we could not get that supply. Blockade of Germany was essential to the victory of the Allies, but the ill will of the United States meant their certain defeat. It was better, therefore, to carry on the war without a blockade, if need be, than to incur a break with the United States about contraband and thereby deprive the Allies of the resources necessary to carry on the war at all, or with any chance of success.»[2]

Of course, the Wilson Administration could not help seeing the importance and responsibility of their strong position. In a letter of October 28, 1914, Wilson wrote a statement of the duties of the United States «as the only powerful neutral» to preserve neutral rights.[3] He has also made some statements that show his interest in

---

[1] Edward Grey, *Twenty-Five Years*, Vol. II (New York, 1935), 110.

[2] Grey, *Twenty-five Years*, 107.

[3] Notter, *Foreign Policy*, 350. Wilson to Page: «Not the least part of this war is going to be the satisfaction of opinion in America and the full performance of our utmost duty as the only powerful neutral.»

the principle of cooperation, describing it as «the vital principle of social life.»[4] Why then did they not put it into effect? Did the small neutrals refuse to collaborate, or did the fault rest with the United States?

Quite a few writers have suggested that the United States ought to have collaborated with the other neutral powers in order to establish an effective defense of their rights. Norman Angel, among others, made a statement as early as 1915, in which he stressed strongly the role of the United States in an interrelated world and its obligation to stand up for neutral rights.[5]

Borchard, who upon the whole is very skeptical of America's neutral position, says that the United States was definitely unwilling to make its protests effective against the Allied violations and did not want to collaborate with the other neutrals.[6]

Philip c. Jessup, who himself elaborated a theory of neutral cooperation, mentions that the Scandinavian countries, particularly Sweden, pressed hard in 1916 to bring about a conference for the planning of cooperation. Jessup has this information from diplomatic correspondence, but has used it for the purpose of making a case for a revision of neutrality. He thought that some kind of a new armed neutrality league could be established.[7] Several other writers on international law have made casual references to the cooperation question.

From the diplomatic correspondence of this period, it appears that the first step towards common action by the neutrals was taken by the Belgian group of the Interparliamentary Union. On August 3, 1914, its members sent out a request to all neutral countries to take energetic steps to safeguard peace and respect treaties. As Secretary of State Bryan pointed out, this was too late, since the war already had broken out.[8] But only two weeks after that Van Dyke, the United States Ambassador to the Netherlands, wrote the State Department a long comment on violations of Belgian neutrality.[9] He pointed out in strong terms that no

[4] Baker and Dodd, *Public Papers*, Vol. II, 430—438.
[5] Norman Angell, *The World's Highway* (New York, 1915), 36—40.
[6] Borchard, *Neutrality*, 12—25.
[7] Jessup, *Today and Tomorrow*, 165—170.
[8] *Foreign Relations Supplement, 1914*, 36.
[9] It should be kept in mind that the United States did not protest against the German violation of the Belgian neutrality.

national prerogatives would be secure and none could hope that an establishment of peace through justice could be attained. There would be no prospect of pacific cooperation of Europe «if the guaranteed neutralities of sovereign states are swept away like burnt paper on the plea that necessity knows no law.» He then went on to stress the position of the United States. Even if it stood outside the sphere of conflict, it had a real interest in it, not only for its own sake, but for the sake of humanity. The Dutch Government was at that time much shaken up by the events, but the fact that the United States had declared its neutrality greatly encoraged them. It was Van Dyke who first suggested that it would be a great advantage for the United States to act in cooperation with the other states that were still neutral.[10]

A Dutch paper, the «Gazette de Hollande», of November 17, 1914, had an article in which the same view was set forth. The paper contended that the governments of the United States and the Netherlands must collaborate to «save what was yet to be saved». What it proposed, was however, mediation and not collaboration for neutral rights.[11]

Neutral Proposals.

The question of mediation seemed to have been much discussed during this early period of the war, and it appears that Spain took a great interest in it. The Spanish Foreign Minister sent a note to the State Department in December of 1914, in which he brought up the mediation issue. It could not have been the first time this issue was introduced because he stressed that «even if earlier inquiries as to cooperation for mediation had been met with cold response», Spain still wanted to work together with the United States in cordial cooperation. Bryan answered that the President did not think the time had come for mediation, which incidentally did not stop Spain from again emphasizing her cooperative attitude.[12]

[10] *Foreign Relations Supplement, 1914*, 81.
[11] *Ibid.*, 146.
[12] *Foreign Relations Supplement, 1914*, 147. It is worth noting that Bryan, who is said to have been sincerely working to preserve neutrality did not show any interest in neutral cooperation. Probably more because he did not realize its importance, than from unneutral intentions.

In November, 1914, Great Britain began to hold up business telegrams between Switzerland and the United States. Due to this, financial and commercial relationships between the two countries were greatly impeded. Therefore, the Swiss President proposed to the Secretary of State, through the Swiss Legation in Washington, that the two countries should take joint action both in London and in Paris. In his memorandum of November 20, 1914, the Secretary of State informed the American Legation in Switzerland that he had instructed the American ambassadors in London and Paris to «cooperate in every possible way with the Swiss ministers in those capitals in the matter of censorship of commercial cable messages between the United States and Switzerland.»[13]

Page was thus instructed to cooperate with the Swiss Minister, but «the department prefers, however, to have presented a separate protest,» in order to arrive at an arrangement that can «lessen the hardships and inconveniences and loss of money which now entailed upon the commercial houses of the United States.» The same message was sent to the American ambassador in France.[14]

Scandinavia asks for Defense of Neutral Rights.

Although the kings and ministers of the Scandinavian countries did not meet until December, 1914,[15] they had started their own cooperation at an early stage of the war.

On the fifth of November, the Swedish and Norwegian Governments issued protests against the British closing of the North Sea.[17] The day afterward Schmedeman, the American minister to Norway cabled the Secretary of State and told him about the protest from Norway to Great Britain. He also mentioned that Sweden and Denmark would do the same. This information had

[13] *Ibid.*, 516.
[14] *Foreign Relations Supplement, 1914*, 517.
[15] The meeting took place on December 18—19, 1914, in Malmø and was called by the Swedish King.
[16] Gihl, *Svenska utrikespolitikens historia*, IV, 70—75.
[17] For a more detailed account of the early Scandinavian cooperation see Keilhau, *Tidsrummet fra omkring 1875 til omkring 1920*, in *Det norske folks liv og historie*, Vol. X, 501—503 and Keilhau, *Vaar egen tid*, 260. *Foreign Relations Supplement, 1914*, 465.

been given to him by the Norwegian Foreign Minister, who had expressed the hope that the United States would also protest.

A few days after, on November 10, 1914, the State Department cabled Schmedeman and directed him to inform the Norwegian Minister of Foreign Affairs that «this government does not see its way at the present time to joining other governments in protesting to the British Government against their announcement that ships entering the North Sea after November 5, do so at their own peril.»[18] Incidentally, this did not keep the Scandinavian states from trying again.

In January, 1915, Sweden sent a memorandum to the Secretary of State through the Swedish Legation in Washington. The Swedish Government took the opportunity to tell about the conference which the Scandinavian states had held in Stockholm. In that conference they had agreed on a protest drawn up in general terms and directed against «certain measures which are inconsistent with the principles of international law» which the belligerents had recently utilized. In this note, which was sent to the governments of the major belligerents, Sweden also complained about the arbitrary alterations in the laws of contraband and the seizure and search of vessels.

The Swedish minister, in presenting this message to the Secretary of State hoped to ascertain the position of the United States with regard to these questions. In his conclusion he very cautiously approached the central issue: whether these steps taken toward the «preservation of rules laid down by international law» received the support of the United States.[19] The State Department answered on January 22, 1915, but made no comments. The Department proposed that the matter be deferred until it had received the text of the note of protest.[20]

The proposal for active collaboration now seemed to have been given up, at least temporarily, since the Scandinavian countries went no further than to ask for sympathy for their actions. Such an official approval was not given, but this does not mean that the

---

[18] *Foreign Relations Supplement, 1914,* 465.
[19] *Ibid.,* 472.
[20] *Ibid.,* 473. Those notes were sent to the State Department on February 18, 1915, *(Foreign Relations Supplement, 1915,* 139) but no further answer to these can be found.

United States took no interest in what the other neutrals were doing.

The step toward collaboration taken by the Scandinavian countries when their kings and foreign ministers met in the Swedish town Malmö, seems to have gained the attention of the United States in particular. In the beginning of 1915, the United States minister to Denmark, Mr. Egan, had a conversation with Mr. Scavenius, the Danish Foreign Minister. The reason for this meeting was that Mr. Egan wanted to know whether the three Scandinavian countries had made a secret agreement in Malmö. Scavenius denied emphatically that such an agreement had been reached, but stated that the ministers of foreign affairs had signed a protocol by which the parties agreed not to make any serious decisions as to trade and economic relations without common consulation, and further, that the neutral position of the three countries should be maintained. «No more could be done,» he added resignedly. He did not on this occasion, express any request for collaboration with the United States, but the conversation gave an impression of his resignation and pessimism as long as the Scandinavian countries had not secured the aid of the greater neutrals.[21]

On October 29, 1914, the British issued a new Order in Council. In connection with the position of the United States on Article Two of this order,[22] the Danish minister in Washington, Mr. Brun, had a conversation with the solicitor of the State Department.[23] The latter had intimated that to insist too strongly in London on the rights of the United States and its trade with other countries would probably create difficulties for the smaller neutrals under the existing conditions. But he also mentioned that perhaps the time had come for a conference between the United States and the other neutral countries, with a view toward taking common action to protect their legitimate trade.

The Danish minister shortly afterwards wrote a memorandum to the State Department[24] stressing the collaboration of the three Scandinavian countries in relation to the recent Malmö Conference, and stating that «any step that the United States might decide to

---

[21] *Foreign Relations Supplement,* 1915, 7—8.
[22] *Foreign Relations Supplement, 1914,* 262. Article Two referred to contraband.
[23] December 23, 1914.
[24] December 28, 1914.

take for the support of the smaller neutrals in this matter» would be very satisfactory to the Danish Government.[25] A prompt reply was received on January 7, 1915, to the effect that the State Department «found itself unable to make a categorical answer to the question propounded,» particularly, as it «called for statement of the action which would be taken by the government in advance of the event.»[26] However, in cases where Article Two might be applied, its position would be taken by the facts and circumstances of the actual case. This was only a partial answer to the unmistakable point in the Danish request. The proposal for collaboration was by-passed in silence and no comment made on it.

It thus seems as if the State Department did not want to enter into collaboration with other neutrals. This is even more remarkable, since it would not involve commitments of any kind. The Scandinavian neutrals had asked the United States to join them in a protest against the British measures in the North Sea, and as no one could deny that this was a violation of American neutral rights as well as of any other country, it could not be regarded as a break with the traditional policy of isolation. On the other hand, though the United States did not protest the British closing of the North Sea, it protested very vigorously when the Germans declared their war zones on February 4, 1915. The note which the State Department sent the Germans on February 10, was written in a very straightforward manner and left no doubt as to its interpretation. The Imperial Government was bluntly held «to strict accountability for such acts of their naval authorities.»[27]

In style and choice of words there was a marked difference between this message and the ones which were sent to the British. In connection with reports regarding the misuse of the American flag by the British, a State Department note read: «The government of the United States desires very respectfully to point out to his Britannic Majesty's Government, the serious consequences which may result to American vessels and American citizens if this practice is continued.» This was the Secretary of State to Page on February 10, 1915, and Page was not likely to put more teeth into the protest. Simultaneously the three Scandinavian neutrals sent

---

[25] *Foreign Relations Supplement, 1915,* 296.
[26] *Ibid.,* 298.
[27] *Foreign Relations Supplement, 1915,* 99.

a joint protest against the misuse of neutral flags on English ships. This, however, was stated in more determined terms.[28]

The governments of neutral countries were not the only ones to remind the United States of its responsibilities as the world's greatest neutral. The United States representative to the Netherlands, Van Dyke, sent a telegram to the Secretary of State on February 16, 1915, saying that the Foreign Minister of the Netherlands had asked certain questions in relation to the German declaration of open submarine warfare. He wanted to determine whether, if a Dutch vessel should be sunk by mistake by a German war vessel under this naval declaration of February 4, the Netherlands could count on the moral support of the United States?[29]

Bryan answered on February 17, that if «such a situation should arise, the Netherlands may count on sympathetic attitude of the United States. Do not understand what moral support means!»[30]

On the same day, Van Dyke wrote a long letter to the Secretary of State strongly emphasizing the point that the interests of the Netherlands and the United States were so close in this case that they ought to pursue a common line of action. The same thing would also apply to certain of the other neutral countries such as Norway, Sweden, Denmark and Italy. He went on to say that «it would in my judgment be very desirable if a certain unity of attitude and action among all these neutral countries could be attained in regard to this particular subject of the protection of our commerce and the lives of our citizens at sea.»

The ambassador did not state what he meant by this unity of action, that is, whether it should be limited to protests and notes or develop into something more substantial, but he did suggest that it should at least insure «as far as possible, a consolidated moral support for such measures as may... safeguard common rights and interests.»[31]

On March 6 Van Dyke once more stressed the point which he had made in his letter of February 17. He first mentioned the public resentment in Holland against both belligerents and

[28] *Foreign Relations Supplement, 1915*, 100.
[29] *Ibid.*, 109.
[30] *Ibid.*, 110.
[31] *Foreign Relations Supplement, 1915*, 131.

maintained that the measures taken by both sides were unlawful attacks upon the economic life of neutral nations. It was not only a measure of reprisal between belligerents; it was an illegitimate action against the neutrals as well. It was intended as a means to make them take sides in the war, since «a peaceful abstinence no longer would secure them the benefits of non-contraband trade under international law.» In this way the Declaration of Paris would be abolished.

Van Dyke's conclusion was that «public opinion here (in Holland) looks to the United States for leadership in a firm united maintenance, by pacific means, of the common rights of neutral nations in commerce during the time of war.»[32] This reminder from the State Department's own official could not have been misunderstood, and the administration must certainly have had a clear view of what the other neutral nations expected from the United States.[33]

In July, 1915, the question appeared again, this time raised by Sweden in connection with the British request for rights of transit through Sweden to Russia. On this occasion the British had proposed to limit the importation of some American goods into Sweden. The Swedish minister had then made an inquiry as to the position of the United States. He wanted to know whether the two countries could make a uniform representation to the British Government in behalf of the rights of neutrals. The proposal was answered by Lansing, July 26, 1915, but the reply gave little information. He said he was unable to state what was the attitude of his government to this issue, but would be glad to discuss it later.[34] Nevertheless, The Swedish minister grew very optimistic and made haste to inform Lansing that he was looking forward to a discussion of this matter with him. He now hoped for «cooperation to the extent of uniform action».

Lansing's answer to this, however, was that if the British proposals would limit American exports to Sweden, and if that was done with the consent of the Swedish Government, «the United States would have no special grounds for objection,» but if the normal trade between America and Sweden should be affected he

---

[32] *Foreign Relations Supplement, 1915*, 148.
[33] By the end of the month, Van Dyke wrote still another letter in which he pointed out the harm which was being done to American trade within the Netherlands by the British Order in Council. March 25, 1914. *Ibid.*, 159.
[34] *Ibid.*, 486.

would give consideration to the matter.[35] (He gave no definition as to what he meant by normal trade, but it is likely to be interpreted as the pre-war trade.)

This could hardly be regarded as a satisfactory answer and the Swedish minister in his reply of August 10, stressed strongly that it was not so much the amount of trade that the Swedish Government objected to. What he considered to be the point was the principle involved: «Has a belligerent the right to limit the intercourse between two neutrals?» He further stressed that Sweden had not agreed to the British proposals, but refused to consider them. According to reports from the American charge d'affaires in Sweden,[36] the Allied interference with the trade between Sweden and America was of a very serious character. The British prize courts delayed their decisions unnecessarily long, and ships had been forced to unload their cargo as many as four times during one voyage.

It does not seem to have made any impression on Lansing who still avoided the real issue, and refrained from giving the least encouragement as to future collaboration. His comment was that he preferred to wait and see what position the Swedish Government would take before giving «even his informal views upon the matter».

He did, however, send the British Government a note in November, 1915,[37] protesting against the interference with trade. However, by that time nearly all export to Sweden was dependent upon special permissions granted by the British Government. These had to be obtained even before the articles could leave America. The Swedish minister, drew the attention of the State Department to the incongruity between Lansing's note of November 5, and the facts of the situation. He was very anxious to know whether any measures would be taken. Lansing's reply was in line with his previous statements and did not contain any explanation or comment. He merely told the Swedes that «due note had been taken» of the observations they had made.

The Dutch had the same experience when they wrote Lansing and referred to a case where a Dutch and an American ship had

---

[35] *Foreign Relations Supplement, 1915,* 500.
[36] July 29, 1915. *Ibid.,* 509.
[37] November 5. *Foreign Relations Supplement, 1915,* 616.

been unlawfully seized by the British and taken into Halifax. The Dutch had already made a special protest but thought the matter to be, in principle, of such importance that they asked for the opinion of the United States, who was in exactly the same position.[38] Lansing's laconic answer was that the State Department «has the matter under consideration, but is not prepared at the present time to announce its views.»[39]

The Greek Government, August 26, 1916, suggested to the State Department that a «joint and timely action of the neutral states» might perhaps bring the belligerents to accept a reference of such cases to an international authority offering every guarantee of impartial justice.[40] The Greek Government did not think that it could take the initiative in these preliminary negotiations and believed «that the United States is marked for that part».

The Department of State answered on September 11, that the United States had given «careful attention to the considerations» set forth by the Greeks, and even if it agreed in principle with the ideas of an international prize court, it did not think that the moment was opportune.

The State Department also called attention to the fact that the Hague Convention had never been ratified, and inasmuch as the Declaration of London had also been declared to be inadequate, the United States Government did not think it would help much to try to establish an international prize court at that time.[41] This was, of course, true, but it also implied avoidance of any positive action.[42] No more was heard of this matter.

Of course, the small neutrals did not constantly bombard the State Department with requests for collaboration, but practically each new violation of their neutrality brought forth new proposals. Thus when the British, in December, 1915, began to interfere with the overseas mail and repeatedly removed mailbags from neutral

---

[38] December 13, 1915. Ibid., 638.
[39] January 13, 1916. Ibid., 659.
[40] *Foreign Relations Supplement, 1916*, 692.
[41] Ibid., 694.
[42] Lansing told the Norwegian minister, Dec. 2. 1915, that there had been some talk of a semi-official league of neutral states for the purpose of preparing a peace, but let him know that he would not support such a coalition. Each government ought to act independently, Bryn to Ihlen, Norwegian Department of Foreign Affairs *(UD). P 2. B. 1/15. I.*

ships, the governments of the Netherlands and Sweden again turned to the State Department with urgent requests for information as to the attitude of the United States, and whether it would join them in protest. With regard to these requests, Van Dyke strongly advised his government that this was necessary for the dignity of the United States. It must make a strong protest, and, if it was disregarded, make reprisals.[43]

Lansing's answer, however, was as evasive as ever and did not indicate any positive action on the part of the United States.[44] Later, in January, he instructed Page to protest to the British Government because of its interference with the mail.[45] Even so, this protest could not have the same effect as if it had been sent immediately and simultaneously with those from the other neutrals.

On July 25, 1916, the Norwegian, Swedish and Danish governments sent a note to the British Government in which they protested to the proclamation issued by the British on July 7, (declaring the Declaration of London null and void). They maintained that these new rules adopted by the Allies, were not in conformity with the recognized rules of international law. Stressing the great importance of this step for all neutrals, they proposed that the government of the United States should make a similar presentation to the British and French Governments.[46] Like action was also taken by the Dutch.[47]

The British blacklisting measures raised new questions from Norway and Sweden as to the position of the United States.[48] In a letter of July 28, 1916, the Swedish minister declared that his government was «willing and ready, if such should be agreeable to the United States, to cooperate for the purpose of rectifying the unsatisfactory conditions which the British blacklisting practice had created.»[49]

Acting Secretary of State, Polk, did not go into the question of cooperation in defense of neutrality, but answered (August 1, 1916) that he had taken into consideration some individual cases without

[43] *Foreign Relations Supplement, 1915,* 737—740.
[44] He did refer to a letter of Dec. 9, 1915, which is not printed.
[45] Letter of Jan. 4, 1916, *Foreign Relations Supplement, 1916,* 592.
[46] *Ibid.,* 427, 435.
[47] *Ibid.,* 438.
[48] *Ibid.,* 415, 418.
[49] *Foreign Relations Supplement, 1916,* 425.

thereby waiving the principle.⁵⁰ As already stressed, this did not mean that the United States took no interest in what the other neutrals were doing. Except for the key question of defense of neutral rights, it kept contact and always wanted to be informed on the neutrals' position on detailed questions relating to their neutrality. Lansing, in August, 1915, sent a circular letter to the neutral European countries asking whether they had placed embargoes on arms and ammunition, and if so, whether it was done for preservation, for home use, or to prevent export to belligerents. The majority of these countries answered that they had embargoed the sale of arms and did so for all the reasons cited.⁵¹

In October, 1916, Polk sent a circular telegram to the diplomatic officers in neutral countries and asked what positions these governments had taken on belligerent war- or merchant ships in neutral ports and waters.⁵² Holland said she had forbidden belligerent war vessels within her ports since August 4, 1914, and that she retained the right to decide herself as to submarines. Van Dyke, who never missed an opportunity to express his views on neutrality, now took the occasion to communicate to the Netherlands' Foreign Minister that he would be glad if his and the United States Governments could cooperate in the entire submarine question.⁵³

By 1916 the efforts of the small neutrals had not met with much understanding and most of them appear to have given up hope of establishing a cooperation with the United States in a common defense of neutrality. There were, at least, few proposals from the Danish and Norwegian Governments by this time.

But Sweden did not give up. In spite of all the rebuffs and disappointments she had sustained, she went on trying with an admirable persistency. On January 24, 1916, her Foreign Minister sent a very serious and pleading note to the Secretary of State. He first recalled how many times the Swedish Government had proposed that through collaboration and cooperation, important rules of international law should be maintained and preserved against the violations of Great Britain. Nevertheless, these viola-

---

⁵⁰ *Ibid.*, 426.
⁵¹ *Foreign Relations Supplement, 1915*, 801—804.
⁵² *Foreign Relations Supplement, 1916*, 772.
⁵³ *Foreign Relations Supplement, 1916*, 773.

tions of existent rules had constantly increased until only a few now were observed by the British. He deemed the last violation, the interference with first class mail on neutral ships from one neutral country to another, to be particularly serious. He urgently appealed to the Government of the United States for cooperation for the purpose of seeking to bring about a «discontinuance of the violations of international law,» and asked whether «his excellency is willing to take appropriate action in cooperation with the Royal government (of Sweden) and eventually with the governments of other countries.»[54]

To this urgent appeal, Lansing merely answered that he had received the note from the Swedish minister,[55] and «had noted his remarks.» There was no further comment.[56]

In February,[57] Mr. Wrangel, the Swedish Minister in London, wrote to Colonel House and then reiterated the Swedish point of view. He stated that the Swedish Government viewed it as «the duty and inalienable right of all sincerely neutral countries to intervene... against every attempt» to render international law void and invalid. Mr. Wrangel went on to say that this was a serious effort on the part of Sweden to attain collaboration with other neutrals:

> Such a collaboration would be especially precious and effective if it could be established with the United States. This country is without comparison the most powerful and influential amongst neutrals... also with regard to the material relations, there exists between Sweden and the United States a common interest which has steadily been increased and will be of great importance in the future.

Pointing to this Wrangel expressed his regret and disappointment that the United States did not live up to the aims that it had set forth in its protest of November 5, 1915. Wrangel ended his letter with a new appeal to the United States for collaboration with other neutrals or «at least in parallel action» to help defend all the neutral rights and interests, and to «make the powerful contribu-

---

[54] *Foreign Relations Supplement, 1916*, 594.
[55] January 28, 1916. *Ibid.*, 594.
[56] As cited previously, Lansing had already sent a protest against the interference with the mail, but that was not the point of the Swedish note.
[57] February 14, 1916.

tion they are capable of to further the maintenance or the restoration of the law of nations.»

This note gives a very realistic impression of the unpleasant situation in which the small neutrals found themselves. Humiliated, harassed, and exposed to increasing pressure, they were desperately looking for aid from the only state that was capable of helping them.

Also the Foreign Minister of Spain in April, 1916, sent a request to the State Department asking whether the United States Government thought a joint protest on the part of the neutral powers would be effective against the torpedoing of neutral vessels. Lansing replied that the State Department was giving «sympathetic consideration» to the Spanish note, — but nothing more was done.[58]

Cooperation for Mediating a Peace.

By the middle of 1916, the neutrals seem to have given up the hope of establishing any effective defense of their neutral rights. Most of these rights had been so persistently violated that the damage was almost irreparable. At least it could be safely predicted that the Allies were not likely to release their hold on the neutrals' foreign trade and economy until the war was over.

It, therefore, seemed natural that the neutrals as their only salvation should concentrate their efforts for bringing the war to an end as quickly as possible. But the assistance of the United States was necessary in this matter, just as it was in the question of protecting neutral rights.

In May, 1916,[59] the United States ambassador to Spain communicated to the State Department the views of the King on this subject.[60] The King of Spain thought that at last the time had come for the neutrals to mediate between the belligerents. There might now be a chance for peace as both sides were tired of the war. He admitted that England might be opposed to such a movement, but yet she could not resist the influence of the United States and the Vatican, supported by sentiment of the other

---

[58] *Foreign Relations Supplement, 1916,* 229—230.
[59] May 11, 1916.
[60] See page 144 for the King's first proposal.

civilized countries. He wanted as soon as possible to have the President's views on this question.[61]

The issue of Wilson's mediation has been widely debated in later years. Borchard has commented about Wilson's chances for mediating a peace. He thought that, «his (Wilson's) helpfulness as a mediator was hardly desired and limited to his aid as a belligerent.» He said in effect that because of the unneutral position taken by the United States, it had to fail when it tried to mediate because it no longer could not expect to gain confidence with the neutral powers.[62]

On September 19—22, 1916, the Scandinavian ministers met in Christiania to discuss the situation.[63] In the first place, they agreed that their commercial policy ought to be carried out in wider collaboration. They also considered whether to invite the neutral European nations and the United States to a conference for the purpose of discussing questions of mutual interest. For various reasons this was postponed, and instead the Swedish minister was authorized to take the matter up verbally with the different neutral nations.[64] Thus, on the 17th of October, 1916, Sweden, through her legation in Washington, invited the United States to join the Scandinavian countries, Spain, Switzerland, and Holland in a conference of neutrals. However, the Secretary of State, after having conferred with the President, declined to participate.[65]

On the same day, December 1, 1916, the Swedish minister had an interview with Lansing, and now verbally invited the United States to participate. Lansing then told him that after a conference with the President «it had been concluded to be inadvisable for this Government to participate in the proposed conference,» partly because of «our geographical location,» which makes the problems proposed for discussion so different from those of the «countries contiguous to the belligerents that there would be no common grounds for discussion.» He also pointed to the near relations to the American republics which were not included as possible participants and that it has been «our policy, heretofore, and it seemed

[61] *Foreign Relations Supplement, 1916,* 28—29.
[62] *Ibid.,* 43.
[63] Oslo was at that time called Christiania.
[64] *Foreign Relations Supplement, 1916,* 694.
[65] *Foreign Relations Supplement, 1917,* 56.

to be a wise one, to act independently of other countries..., although as far as possible identically with them.»[66]

For more than two years the small neutrals had repeatedly and steadfastly proposed a collaboration with the only country that might be able to save them. During that period the State Department had neither replied in the affirmative nor in the negative, but constantly avoided the issue. But two months *before* the German declaration of the unrestricted submarine warfare, it finally cast off the mask and declared its definite unwillingness to collaborate with the other neutral countries.

It may be a bit far-fetched to interpret this as indicating that by December, 1916, the United States had already made up its mind to leave the path of neutrality for good. Nevertheless, it does seem to indicate some change of policy. Technically, there was nothing to prevent the United States from maintaining the same evasiveness which previously had characterized its stand as to neutral collaboration. It might have said it would want it later. It could have taken collaboration into serious consideration or have asked for more details, but instead, its attitude gives the impression that the government did not think it worth while to play under cover any longer, so it gave a flat refusal which left little doubt about its stand so far as the neutrals were concerned.

It is worth noting that when President Wilson in the middle of December, 1916, made his famous offer of mediation to the belligerents it was enthusiastically supported by most neutral countries, who again expressed their preference for uniform action. The Norwegian Government sent a special note of congratulation to the President for his peace note and declared that it stood ready to cooperate with him in any action he might take regarding these proposals.[67] But again Sweden took the lead to promote neutral cooperation and went so far in her efforts to make the other neutrals support Wilson's note that it even caused some irritation in Norway and Denmark.[68]

The Allies were strongly opposed to Wilsons proposal: Neither the English nor the French wanted mediation at that time. Lloyd George's motto was, «Fight to the finish», but there is evidence that the Allies feared Wilson's attempt to have the other neutrals

[66] *Foreign Relations Supplement, 1916*, 696—697.
[67] *Foreign Relations Supplement, 1916*, 112.
[68] Gihl, *Svenska utrikespolitikens historia*, IV, 245—246.

join in cooperation for peace. Some of the neutral governments were told that the Allies would resent affirmative anwers to Wilsons note. Such a league of neutrals, headed by the USA, might put pressure on the Allies, but hardly on the Germans, and the British and French consequently feared that such a mediation might be more advantageous for Germany, than it would be for themselves. They therefore managed to scare some of the neutrals from supporting the proposal.

On December 20, 1916, Harald Bryn, the Norwegian Minister in Washington wrote to the State Department saying the Foreign Minister of Norway had informed him that Switzerland and Holland had accepted an invitation from the Scandinavian Governments to a meeting for calling a conference of neutral powers. Incidentally, Spain, possibly due to the influence of the Allied powers, had not accepted and he understood that the United States would probably not accept.[69]

This extremely cautious assertion of a fact already herein established,[70] gives an indication that the Scandinavian neutrals had been encouraged by Wilsons action for peace and were reluctant to believe that the refusal to meet with other neutrals, which the United States had given on Dec. 1, could be definite. But what little hope these countries might still have left was soon to end.

Cooperation for War.

Immediately after the German renewal of the unrestricted submarine warfare, Wilson made a belated effort towards cooperation with the other neutrals, but on different grounds. On February 2, 1917, he said in his cabinet that he did not want to see either side win, and that he still believed in peace without victory. He went on to say that he «would like to see neutrals unite,» and that it might be possible to coordinate the neutral forces.[71] On February 3, 1917, the State Department notified the neutral countries that because of the German declaration of unrestricted submarine

---

[69] *Foreign Relations Supplement,* 1916, 697. This was confirmed by the Spanish minister who stated that Spain would take only such course as England and France desired.

[70] *Ibid.,* 696.

[71] Notter, *Foreign Policy,* 614.

warfare, it would sever diplomatic relations with Germany. Further, «he (the President) thinks it will make for the peace of the world if the other neutral countries can find it possible to take similar action to that taken by this government.»[72]

Shortly afterwards Wilson worked out «the four Bases for Peace», which, he declared, should be the first foundation for discussion among the neutrals in case they should take joint action. This in fact, constituted Wilson's first draft of the Covenant of the League of Nations. He intended the neutrals to join in this covenant while they were still planning practicable cooperation for the protection of their rights.[73]

This action came much too late, as cooperation under such conditions and at that time could not be acceptable to the neutrals.[74] For more than two years the United States had consistently refused to cooperate. Now the opportune moment had passed by and the European neutrals no longer felt any desire for common action, not only because it was too late, but because it was meant for a different purpose.[75]

The neutrals had wanted to establish a league for the maintenance of their neutral non-belligerent status. What Wilson wanted was exactly the opposite thing. He wanted cooperation for war. It is hard to see how such collaboration could be expected, and the small neutrals did not hesitate in giving their answers. On February 6, Wilson's offer was declined by Denmark and Spain, by Sweden and the Netherlands on February 8, by Switzerland on the 10th, and by Norway on February 13.[76] None of them wanted a cooperation that would bring them into a war which they desperately struggled to keep out of.

Wilson did not, however, make this distinction clear when he addressed the Congress on this matter: «We have asked for the cooperation of the other neutral governments to prevent these depredations, but so far none of them has thought it wise to join us in any common course of action.»[77]

[72] *Foreign Relations Supplement, 1917*, 108.
[73] Notter, *Foreign Policy*, 619—620.
[74] Seymour, *Intimate Papers*, Vol. II, 445.
[75] Gihl, *Svenska utrikespolitikens historia*, IV, 253—255.
[76] Seymour, *Intimate Papers*, Vol. II, 116—130.
[77] Address to Congress, requesting authority to arm merchant ships, February 26, 1917. Baker and Dodd, *Public Papers*, Vol. II, 421.

Seen on the background of the desperate efforts made by the small neutrals during the 1914—1916 period, Wilson's statement sounds hypocritical and hardly fair. It was certainly not fit to give a true picture of the real issue. Wilson's proposal would give them war instead of peace, and thus there could be no common ground for cooperation between the United States and the European neutrals.

Latin American Attempts to Cooperation.

The course taken by the United States in its relations to the Latin American countries makes an interesting parallel to the efforts of the European neutrals. In November, 1914, the Argentine Government turned to the State Department for information on its stand as to the British contraband seizures. Lansing answered immediately and presented very complete information on this issue. The United States objected to the British definition, and held that if a neutral vessel carried articles to a neutral port it could not be held responsible for what happened to them later. It was also the opinion of the Government, that a belligerent might have a right to exercise visit and search when done simultaneously and on the high seas. There was just reason for complaint if the neutral ship was taken into port.[78]

The Argentine minister was evidently very much pleased and encouraged by this. He answered the same day that this was exactly the position which his government would take. He therefore suggested «a close understanding between our two governments» for the maintenance of this doctrine. He believed that each should keep the other informed of the progress in every case and «adopt uniform interpretations and methods of procedure.»[79]

This was, however, not quite what the State Department had in mind. Bryan hastened to say that in spite of the fact that the United States and the Argentine Government seemed to take the same position in this matter, he did not think they should extend this to a joint action: «It is understood to be impossible to make joint representation to the British Government in particular cases.»

[78] *Foreign Relations Supplement, 1914*, 433.
[79] *Ibid.*, 434.

If the Argentines meant that representations should be made «separately, but in harmony with each other,» the United States would be glad to cooperate.[80]

About the same time it was reported to the State Department from Lima that the Peruvian Government believed that «the moment has arrived for the American Republics to take joint action to guarantee the inviolability of their trade routes by keeping them in all their extent free from the effects of hostilities between belligerent naval forces.»

Notes to the same effect were sent from the Chilean and Argentine Governments.[81] They both hoped that the American republics could get together and establish a neutral zone along the American coast. This arrangement with the belligerents was to be made by the Pan American Union. The question was taken up by the Pan American Union at its meeting in December, 1914, and the governing board adopted a resolution to the effect that a special commission of nine members should be appointed. The Secretary of State was appointed chairman of the committee. The commission was to study «the problems of the present European war,» and make suggestions to the governing board. The immediate problem involved was to find «a better definition of the belligerent and neutral rights».

In its whole setup the commission gives the impression of lacking serious intentions. It appears from the notes of the Latin-American ministers that there was an urgent need for some remedy against the belligerent practices that might become effective immediately. There was a need for practical measures, not for definitions. Even the aim of the commission «to study the problems» of the war signify that no applicable solution could possibly be reached within a reasonably short time.

It is likely to have been a measure for delaying decisive answers and the attitude taken by the State Department reminds very much of the evasiveness shown by the United States in its relations to the European neutrals. The matter would have been different if the commission had been appointed to study the establishment of a neutral zone along the coast or other practical issues instead of the «problems of the war». The South American countries

[80] *Ibid.*, 435.
[81] *Foreign Relations Supplement, 1914,* 436—438.

probably had the same feeling because all the republics continued to suggest effective measures to the State Department.

Shortly after the resolution was adopted, the Venezuelan Government presented a new memorandum. The proposal went further than the others as it suggested that the task of defining neutral rights and duties under these new conditions «should be entrusted to a congress of neutrals summoned for this purpose». The conclusions reached were to be submitted to a congress of all nations and embodied in international law. This congress might establish a new duty for the neutrals, namely, «that of jointly mediating in conflicts of such magnitude as the present one». The initiative of that Congress belonged to «the nations of America,» and it was suggested that the lead be taken by the United States.

This memorandum is among the best predictions telling how the practice of the belligerents would ultimately destroy the whole principle of neutrality, if they were not checked in time. As contraband was extended to include almost everything, the sovereignty and integrity of the neutral would be affected. «Neutrals cannot remain indifferent to the world-wide economic losses that will probably result from the present European war if it should last indefinitely. ... All will suffer equally, even though some countries may seem for the moment to profit by the war.» The Venezuelan Government arrived at the conclusion that in opposition to the active right of the belligerents arose the right of the neutrals to unite and organize. Instead of their previous passivity, «they should take effective and beneficent action in behalf of their own security.»

It was further suggested that the solution must be a *league of neutrals* for the defense of freedom of commerce and navigation. The duty of neutrals to unite should be established, and the American nations, due to their special position, were called upon to perform this duty.[82]

There could be no doubt as to the soundness and logic of the argument presented in that note. If, therefore, the United States had seriously wanted to preserve neutrality as a leading principle in world politics for themselves as well as for other nations, it ought to have accepted the proposal and done something about it.

---

[82] For the full text see *Foreign Relations Supplement, 1914*, 447—450.

That it did not do. A month later, January 13, 1915, the State Department informed the Venezuelan Government that the memorandum had «been read with deep interest and will receive the considerations of this Government.» The suggestions which had been presented by the Peruvian and the Chilean Governments were politely referred to the Pan-American neutrality commission.

This adds to the impression that the establishment of the commission was a fine tactical maneuver. It gave the United States the opportunity to transfer the responsibility for taking measures to an outside body which was completely in the hands of the Secretary of State, and was likely to accomplish just as much as he wanted it to do. The commission thus became a burial ground for unwanted proposals.

This diplomatic manoeuver seemed for a while to have put a stop to the Latin American efforts at cooperation. The only exception occurred during the *Sussex* crisis when the situation was very critical and a break between the United States and Germany was expected. The Brazilian Government suggested that before any American power decided to take aggressive steps towards one of the belligerents, a conference of the leading American States should be called at Washington, in order to reach an agreement on submarine warfare and other subjects that had become acute through the actions of certain belligerents. «Such a conference would solidify continental relations and convince Europe that the interests of the American powers are identical.»[83] The Secretary of State, Lansing, answered April 6, that he appreciated the friendly suggestion which had received «our sympathetic consideration.»[84]

After the United States had severed diplomatic relations with Germany, its attitude to the Latin-American republics changed radically. The State Department now tried to convince them that it did not think «such a conference would serve any useful purpose at that time.» The further correspondence of this period reveals how the United States feared a South American block of neutrals led by Argentina. To prevent this it tried by all means to induce the Latin American countries to enter the war.

Thus we find the same pattern here as we found in the United

---

[83] *Foreign Relations Supplement, 1916*, 217.
[84] *Ibid.*, 223.

States' dealings with the European neutrals. It apparently feared a working American neutrality just as much as a European one. The line of action was the same in both cases. The United States refused to collaborate with the neutrals as long as their aim was to stay out of war, to maintain neutrality and preserve the peace for the countries concerned. But it was extremely eager to cooperate and make them join in common action when the aim was exactly the opposite, when the point was to get into the war instead of staying out of it.

The Unnatural Neutral.

All this must leave us with the impression that the United States did not want to strengthen the principle of neutrality; on the contrary there are reasons to believe that it did not want a workable neutrality. We always have to take into consideration the traditional policy of isolation which has been a dominant trait in the United States foreign policy for more than a hundred years. The persistant refusal to collaborate may have been due to the traditional reluctance to make foreign commitments which might deprive the United States of its complete freedom of action, an aim of which that country has never lost sight. There may also have been a fear that those small and weak neutral nations some day might become a liability to the United States instead of an asset. They were all situated quite close to the center of belligerent activity and no one could foretell how and when they were to be involved. Those countries were also weak economically as well as militarily, and intimate collaboration might lead to some kind of dependence which might go farther than the United States would wish itself.

However, we can not exclude the possibility that the United States would actually have wanted to save and reinforce neutrality as a principle, if it had not been for fear of unforeseen commitments. But viewed on the background of the neutral proposals and their formulation, this does not seem likely. In fact, none of the proposals from the small neutrals went so far as to involve a commitment. In most cases they suggested that the United States join them in protest, which might mean a protest to the same effect as those made by the other neutrals, a common neutral protest, or just that the United States would protest at all which it very often was reluctant to do, regardless of the fact that its rights as a neutral were flagrantly violated.

Wrangel, speaking for Sweden, limited his appeal to mean «collaboration at least in parallel action.» In other cases the small neutrals just wanted to make sure that they could count on the «sympathetic attitude of the United States» to the steps they had taken or were about to take in order to defend their rights. Even that moral support was at times denied them.

Such actions could hardly be called commitments and none of the belligerents could justly blame the United States for protesting against their violations of its alledged neutral rights, whether the protests were made by single-handed action or in collaboration with other neutral states that were in the same position. Even so United States apparently did not want the active collaboration which was the only thing that might effectively have checked the belligerents from interfering with the neutrals in their domestic as well as their foreign affairs. Of course, the neutrals were mostly small and inadequate in strength, taken one, by one, but some of them had great merchant marines, others raw materials and a domestic production of great value to the belligerents. The dependence on imports was their weakest point, but the United States might easily have provided them with necessary commodities. In this way the most important means of pressure might have been taken out of the hands of the belligerents. Without the economic weapon, they would have been thrown back on the threat of military invasion and naval blockade as the only means of coercing the neutrals to obey their commands. Such means might have proved too hazardous for general use.

Together with the United States the neutrals might have formed a formidable league. With their enormous combined bargaining power they would certainly have exerted great influence on the duration and extent of the war. But by taking a strict, impartial attitude they could hardly influence the outcome of it. This latter consideration seems to have been the decisive point in the policy of the United States as a neutral during the First World War.

The Wilson Administration probably realized this very clearly. These men knew that if the United States should keep the position that its dominant economic strength entitled it to, it would have to join the war, if it proved that the Allies were unable to defeat the Germans without direct help from the Americans. To strengthen the status of neutrality in general would, therefore, be to work against their own interests. Thus the traditional policy of isolation was not the main obstacle blocking cooperation. If the United States had been reluctant to accept the European proposals for common defense of the neutral rights because it feared entanglement in European affairs, its attitude to the Latin-American cooperative efforts ought to have been different, and as we have seen the European as well as Latin-American neutrals got the same treatment. If the Administration had seriously wanted to make neutrality work, it is extremely hard to see why they consistently rejected the only way that gave some hope of success.

The small countries' persistent proposals for cooperation must, therefore, have been a great nuisance to the State Department. Knowing what was Lansing's real purpose,[85] we must admire the skill with which he avoided all such issues, and put the dangerous questions into a nebulous future.

Whether this policy was wise or not, is a debatable question. Who can tell whether the United States would not have gained a much greater influence on the postwar development if it had been heading a strong neutral league, instead of being a last-minute belligerent? The fact is, however, that the coolness of the United States during the neutrality period made the small neutrals extremely suspicious of its intentions. After February, 1917, it had lost its position as the natural leader of the neutrals and its influence with them was limited to what could be demanded by economic pressure.

President Wilson said in his war message that «neutrality is no longer feasible or desirable where the peace of the world is involved and the freedom of its peoples, and the menace to that peace and freedom lies in the existence of autocratic governments, backed by organized force, which is controlled by their will, not the will of the people. ... We have seen the last of neutrality under such circumstances.»[86]

From then on the United States turned against the neutrals with no less severity than the other belligerents. Before America declared war, the neutrals had been able to get along by obtaining

---

[85] See page 125.
[86] Baker and Dodd, *Public Papers*, Vol. III, 11. *När Demokratien bröt igjenom.*

from the United States what was refused them by the Allies. After April 6, 1917, they were completely at the mercy of the belligerents and had to accept unconditionally the terms offered. The American pressure in order to stop all exports to Germany actually brought the Scandinavian countries on the verge of starvation.[87]

The unneutrality policy of the United States made impossible a timely and efficient common defense of neutral rights; its war entry in 1917 dealt the final blow to neutrality during the First World War. This must be accepted as a fact, and no general statement can be made as to whether it was good or bad. The main point is that the United States now was a major power and therefore could not remain neutral. Instead of being a means of necessary protection, neutrality had become «intolerable». The United States had grown to become a world power with economic entanglements in most parts of the world. Its industrial and financial setup was no longer built for home comsumption, but for meeting a world demand.[88] This is obvious today, but it also held true as early as 1914. To avoid a depression, export trade had to be continued.

The British ambassador to the United States, Mr. Spring-Rice, wrote to Grey on November 21, 1915, «The brutal facts are, that this country (the United States) has been saved by the war and by our war demands from a great economical crisis,» and further, August 13, 1916, «The reason why there is not an embargo on arms and ammunition is not sympathy with us, but the sense that the prosperity of the country on which the administration depends for its existence would be imperiled by such a measure.»[89]

The men in the Wilson Administration have over the last 30 years been repeatedly accused of having led the country into a war that could have been avoided and for having betrayed the cause of neutrality. At times they have been characterized as being hopelessly inadequate as diplomats. That may hold true in some respects but not when it came to the basic aim of their policy. From the viewpoint of the United States, whose interests they

---

[87] Keilhau, *Norge og Verdenskrigen;* Thulstrup, *När Demokratien bröt igjenom.*
[88] See page 120.
[89] Spring-Rice to Grey, Seymour, *American Diplomacy,* 46.

were chosen to defend, they did what they had to do, and their policy was basically sound. The economic side of the question has been touched upon already, but also politically they took the necessary steps. For more than a hundred years the prosperity and security of the United States had been dependent upon the British naval and financial supremacy. If Germany won, this would have been broken, and no one could foretell what place the United States would be able to find for itself in a new continental system under a German aegis. For that reason alone, the Wilson Administration was justified in doing what it did.

In addition to these reasons came the emotional ones which affected the administration as well as the American people. Page and House were practically on their knees in admiration for the British Empire; Wilson was closely tied to the English traditions and cultural ideals; Lansing was perhaps the one with whom the sentimental arguments carried the least weight. British propagandists did a good job and the American people were sentimentally inclined to be pro-British.[90]

This does not mean that the statesmen of the small countries did not have their definite sympathies; but there was an essential difference in their international status. They could not afford to be influenced by their personal sentiments. Their path of neutrality was too narrow, and impartial dealings with both sides were their only hope.[91]

The American people had been progressing ever since the time of their independence. On that occasion they had won self-determination for themselves and they pointed to it with justifiable pride. The Americans were told how they had fought to free themselves, how they had expanded all over the continent and how they had preserved their unity in the Civil War. Since then they had gone on expanding, even beyond their own continent, and they were still dizzy with the enormous industrial development which had brought America up among the top producers of the world. All in all, it was a marvellous record of successful progress. No American in 1914 had ever had the slightest feeling of national defeat. The Americans had advanced, progressed, and won, ever since their short history began. They had the confidence, the belief in them-

---

[90] Millis, *Road to War.*
[91] Gihl, *Svenska utrikespolitikens historia,* IV. 73.

selves that success always gives. How could it be expected that a people so conscious of their own power and creative capacity should bow to the humiliations and depredations that a status of neutrality necessarily would involve?[92] There can be no doubt that the American people as a whole wanted to stay out of war, but they were not prepared to take the sacrifices that such a privilege would have necessitated — and they wanted to have their say as to the outcome of the war.

The attitude of the Scandinavian peoples was different. *Their* history had not been a flashing race of almost explosive expansion. For more than a thousand years it had been a story of ups and downs, and their recent history had included numerous defeats. The Norwegians had to go some nine hundred years back to look for any glorious triumphs in the way of foreign policy; the Swedes and Danes to the sixteenth and seventeenth centuries. They knew only too well that they did not possess their freedom because of their drive and expansive force, but by the grace of a specially balanced system and owing to extremely favorable circumstances.

As persons, as individuals, they had their dignity and a victorious tradition. In this respect they felt unconquered and equal to anybody, but not as great powers. They, therefore, realized that their continued existence as nations would imply sacrifices and humiliations. But they were willing to take them rather than risk further losses of sovereignty and a possible incorporation in a foreign system. So they clung to the illusions of sovereignty and neutrality though the real basis for these no longer existed.

*

World War I proved that during a general conflict, neutrality could no longer be applied as a working political principle. The process of economic and political inter-dependence had gone too far. The great countries could not afford a neutral policy because it would hurt them more to be completely outside than to be inside the conflict. By being strictly neutral, they would lose the influence to which their great-power position entitled them. The small countries would have profited on a strictly neutral policy, and they sincerely wanted to maintain it, but as long as the neutrality

---

[92] «Neutrality is a hard way for at proud and emotional people.» Morrissey, *American Neutral Rights*, 206.

laws were not backed up by force, they had to yield to pressure. In the case of the small states the strictness of their neutrality policy became dependent upon their status of sovereignty. None of them was sufficiently sovereign to live up to the rules of impartial neutrality.

The natural solution for all the neutral powers which separately were too weak, seems to have been cooperation, in order to prevent the belligerents from violating their rights. This was clearly realized and it was attempted. However, it did not materialize because the United States, the only great neutral, refused its support. It did so for good reasons, but will nevertheless have to take a great responsibility for having consistently wrecked the attempts that were made to preserve neutrality on a cooperative basis.

No one can tell whether neutrality might have been saved by such cooperation of great and small neutral states. But all the countries that declared themselves neutral in World War I, would have made quite a powerful combination had they got together in a group with the United States as their leader and the supply base for their various needs. It might have constituted the strong third group, which is so necessary to the balance. Who knows whether the United States had not been in a better position to influence world affairs if it then had put itself at the head of a «neutral league» whose demands were backed up by force?

III. The Inter War Period 1919—1939

1. Neutrality under the League Covenant

The First World War left neutrality in a sad shape. The principle had fallen so completely into disrepute that very few thought it might ever be restored to what it had been before. This feeling was particularly strong in the period immediately after the war, when the helpless submissiveness of the neutral states still was vividly remembered. As time went on, however, the traditional neutrals tended to forget the brutal lesson of 1914—1918. Through the twenties and thirties, there were an increasing number of attempts made to revive neutrality as a political principle, polish it up and bring it back to its former dignity.

There are writers like P. M. Brown, who still maintain that after 1918 «the basic principle of neutrality remained unchanged,»[1] but most others seem to have taken the opposite view. Newton D. Baker drew, from the experience of the First World War the conclusion that «belligerents will respect neutral rights only so far and so long as they do not interfere with their chances of success in the war. ... Whenever the danger of losing a war becomes sufficiently great, the rights of a neutral will be sacrificed even to the point of adding an ally to the enemy.»[2]

Fenwick said the First World War had shown that the institution of war as it was understood at the Hague in 1907, «could not be restrained and kept within legal bands. ... neutrality was in itself no protection for the small state.»[3] Joseph L. Kunz

---

[1] P. M. Brown, «Neutrality», in *American Journal of International Law*, 33 (1939) : 727.

[2] Newton D. Baker, «Why We Went to War,» in *Foreign Affairs*, 15 (October, 1936) : 26.

[3] Fenwick, «The Inter-American Neutral Committee,» in *American Journal of International Law* (1941) : 40.

took Wilson's point of view when he said that the «law of neutrality
... broke down in the world war and did not protect the neutrals.
... Neutrality is no more possible in fact and no more desirable
in law.» [4]

The famous Greek expert on international affairs, N. Politis, is perhaps the one who most consistently has stressed the destructive influence of the First World War on neutrality: «The conflagration of 1914 showed the absurdity of the absolute right of war and of neutrality. ... The catastrophe of 1914 dealt a death blow to neutrality by demonstrating that war is no more a private matter between belligerents, but that it henceforth necessarily concerns all states.» [5]

This will indicate that Wilson has achieved a substantial following to his statement that neutrality was no longer feasible or desirable. In fact, Wilson stands as the central figure in this period of transformation, where an old ideology had to give way to a new. This new theory was in reality the old Grotian conception of the just war, which was now revived and claimed to be the leading principle in world politics. In the interests of humanity and civilization, no state could in the future declare itself to be neutral and disinterested. War was considered a crime and the state who started it was the criminal. No member of the world society could be justified in saying he did not care when a crime was committed next door. Such things could only happen in a lawless anarchy; in the civilized world of the twentieth century this was no longer to be tolerated. Every single state should now have the obligation of executing police power over nations that were found guilty of aggression, and who tried to improve their position by making war on their neighbors.

The consequence of such a system would mean the abolishment of neutrality. As Wilson put it: «The nations of the world must get together and say, 'nobody can hereafter be neutral as respects the disturbance of the world's peace for an object which the world's opinion cannot sanction'.» [6] He made this statement in October, 1916, and after having stressed that neutrality was intolerable, he went on to say: «Just as neutrality would be intolerable to

---

[4] Joseph L. Kunz, «Covenant of the League of Nations and Neutrality,» in the *American Society of International Law Proceedings* (1935) : 36—42.

[5] Politis, *La Neutralité*, 22, 90, 92, 97.

[6] Baker and Dodd, *Public Papers*, Vol. II, 381.

me if I lived in a community where everybody had to assert his own rights by force and I had to go around my neighbors and say, 'Here, this cannot last any longer, let us get together and see that nobody disturbs the peace any more'.»[7]

This was the basic principle upon which the League of Nations was founded. However, in discussing the League in relation to neutrality, we must make a very clear distinction at the outset, namely, what the League was meant to be, and what it actually *was*.

The League was supposed to include all the nations in the world and if all these states had given it their whole-hearted support, neutrality would have died then and there. But, unfortunately, it did not work out that way. The discussion of the League of Nations period will, therefore, necessarily have to build on theories more than on facts.

When the League started its activity in 1920, it did not count potential states as Germany, Russia and the United States among its members. Germany and Russia were not even invited; while the United States let President Wilson down, returned to its traditional isolation and refused to become a member. Thus, the League of Nations from the very beginning lacked the universal character which would have been necessary to make it work. This condition was improved somewhat when Germany was admitted in 1926 and Russia in 1934, but the United States still stayed outside, and when some of the greater states such as Japan and Germany broke away from the League in the thirties, it never had a substantial chance of success.

However, the failure of the League is not exclusively due to such external causes as great and influential states remaining aloof. It might as well have been caused by the internal weaknesses within the League itself. A unanimous agreement as to how and when the League apparatus should work was unfortunately never reached. As uniform action by all not always could be guaranteed, there still remained a possibility of actual neutrality.

The Covenant of the League of Nations did not even mention the word neutrality, but it was tacitly understood to be non-existent under the League system. However, the question appeared in 1920,

[7] *Ibid.*, 381.
[8] Speech by Mr. Balfour, League of Nations, *Official Journal*, No. 1 (Londcn, 1920), 57.

when Switzerland applied for League membership, but without giving up her status of permanent neutrality.

This controversial issue was discussed at the third public meeting of the Council held in London, February 13, 1920.[8] It was realized that in the first place, «complete neutrality in everything, economic and military, is clearly inconsistent with the position of a member of the League.» On the other hand, it was recognized that Switzerland was in a unique situation, based on a century-old tradition which had even been incorporated in the Law of Nations. It was thus believed that Switzerland «would not stand aside when the high principles of the League have to be defended.» Therefore, the Council unanimously carried the resolution that «while affirming that the conception of neutrality of the members of the League is incompatible with the principle that all members will be obliged to cooperate in enforcing respect for their engagements,» it was recognized that Switzerland's perpetual neutrality was compatible with the Covenant.[9]

Thus it was strongly stressed that Switzerland was to be the only exception to the rule, and that neutrality in all other cases would be incompatible with the League system. By this official statement, it was resolved, once and for all, that no member was allowed to stand aloof and remain outside the actions that the League sooner or later would have to take. But even so there might be doubts as to when they should step in and the extent of participation. The Covenant had mostly been composed in broad and general terms, and there was ample room for discussion of the details.

Article 16 and the Extent of Sanctions.

The most debated of all the provisions was the famous Article 16, which dealt with the sanction's question. It ran as follows:

---

[9] *Ibid.*, 58. Switzerland had already on January 20, presented her application for membership in the League to the Supreme Council of the Paris Peace Conference. Her point of view was obviously favored by the Great Powers, but on Clemenceau's suggestion, no decision was taken, and the matter was referred to the League. Incidentally, Switzerland got a special prolongation of the time limit in order to facilitate her entrance in the League as an original member. *Foreign Relations,* The Paris Conference, Vol. IX, 1919, 907—911.

Should any Member of the League resort to war in disregard of its covenants under Article 12, 13, or 15, it shall *ipse facto* be deemed to have committed an act of war against all other Members of the League, which hereby undertake immediately to subject it to severance of all trade or financial relations, the prohibition of all intercourse between their nationals and the nationals of the covenant-breaking state, and the prevention of all financial, commercial or personal intercourse between the nationals of the covenant-breaking state and the nationals of any other state, whether a Member of the League or not.

It shall be the duty of the Council in such case to recommend to the several governments concerned what effective military, naval or airforce the Members of the League shall severally contribute to the armed forces to be used to protect the covenants of the League.

The Members of the League agree further that they will mutually support one another in the financial and economic measures which are taken under this article in order to minimize the loss and inconveniences resulting from the above measures, and that they will mutually support one another in resisting special measures aimed at one of their number by the covenant-breaking state, and that they will take the necessary steps to afford passage through their territory to the forces of any of the Members of the League which are co-operating to protect the covenants of the League.[10]

The question whether this and the other articles of the Covenant, (particularly Articles 10 and 15) excluded neutrality, became a matter of heated discussion between the international lawyers for more than twenty years. The Polish professor, Ehrlich said, «There is in my opinion no neutrality under the regime of Article 16 of the Covenant.»[11] Quincy Wright declared that «members of the League cannot be neutral, but must take effective action to safeguard the peace, and if war develops, must give moral if not physical support to the victim of aggression.»[12] Borchard put it

---

[10] For the full text of all the 26 articles of the Covenant, see League of Nations, *Official Journal*, No. 1, 3—11; *International Conciliation Documents*, 1928, 414—420; and League of Nations, *Constitution* (Boston, 1919).

[11] Ehrlich, «Collective Security,» in *International Studies Conferences*, 1936, 437.

[12] Wright, *American Society of International Law, Proceedings*, 1930, 88—89.

this way: «The theory of the Covenant that a war or a threat of war anywhere, is a matter of concern to the whole world, ... necessarily excludes the conception of neutrality. ... disinterestedness, non-participation and impartiality are by definition ruled out.»[13] On the other hand, international lawyers as Jessup, maintained that «... it is quite possible that members of the League may remain neutral.»[14]

With so much dissension on this vital issue, it became imperatively necessary to find a clear interpretation of the Covenant and of Article 16 in particular. The questions were, who is going to decide when the sanctions that Article 16 provides for shall become applicable, and in case they are going to be made effective, what are the exact obligations of each member?

If these questions were not satisfactorily solved and defined, sanctions were likely to be applied in a different manner and at varying times by the members of the League. This tendency appeared already on the first meeting of the Assembly, November—December 1920. During this first session, the Danish, Norwegian and Swedish Governments proposed the following amendment relating to Article 16:

> At the request of a Member for which the applications of the above provisions might entail serious danger, the Council may authorize this Member to maintain intercourse, in such measure as the Council shall decide, with the Covenant-breaking state.[15]

This position is clearly understandable on the background of what had happened to these countries only two years earlier. The pressure to which they had been exposed from both belligerent sides, made them realize better than anyone else that to break off relations might be easier said than done. The Council, however, refused to adopt the proposal.

In August, 1920, Mr. Tittoni, the Italian delegate, made a report to the Council of his views on Article 16. He characterized this as being essentially a matter of blockade, and thought it clear that

---

[13] Borchard, *Neutrality*, 247.
[14] Jessup, *Today and Tomorrow*, 115.
[15] League of Nations Assembly, *Reports and Resolutions on the Subject of Article 16 of the Covenant*, Doc. A, 14 (1927) : 12.

«the states Members of the League of Nations who declare the blockade have the right to render it effective against all states, including those who are not Members of the League, but they have not the right to force the states who do not form parts of the League to declare the blockade themselves.» His main point was that an International Blockade Committee should be appointed to study the question of Article 16, and make proposals for an organization for the use of it. This was adopted by the Council, August, 1920.[16]

This committee was appointed shortly afterwards, and a year later, August 28, 1921, it submitted its report to the Council. In the foreword, the committee members stressed the great complexity of the problem, and pointed out how difficult it would be to apply economic sanctions on a universal scale: «So long as great exporting countries remain outside the League, the application of Article 16 in its entirety would not merely meet with great obstacles, it might even put the states Members of the League in very embarrassing situations.» For this reason the committee thought it best to deal primarily with measures on a limited scale.

It was then stated that «the unilateral action of the defaulting states cannot create a state of war, particularly as this state of war would be a mere fiction as regards most members of the League.» Consequently, those relations with the defaulting state which were not ordered severed by Article 16, might be continued. Likewise, the cutting off of the food supplies should be considered very drastic and only used as an *ultimo ratio*.[17]

Even more important were the opinions which the committee formed as to who should decide whether the Covenant had been violated and whether the members then ought to adopt the measures laid down in the Covenant. It found that this was the duty of the various members of the League:

> It appears difficult indeed, to make it obligatory for a free and independent nation to accept the opinion either of the Council or the majority of the Members of the League, when the issue is the adaptation of measures of such importance as those prescribed in case of a violation of the Covenant.[18]

[16] *Ibid.*, 11.
[17] League of Nations Assembly, *Reports and Resolutions*, 17.
[18] *Ibid.*, 17.

This illustrates the principal weakness of the League. It attempted to achieve international solidarity without reducing the sovereignty of the member states. The report of the committee indicates that such a combination of aims was impossible, and the attempt was bound to fail. According to the proposal of the committee, each state would be free to decide for itself when it would act and which measures it wanted to apply. It was, however, recommended that the decision taken by the Council should carry great weight and there should be given «the widest possible publicity» of the reasons for the decision. This might convince the member states of the necessity of a common action and «the public opinion in the country which has been declared a covenant-breaker will also be aroused, and that in consequence, a new political orientation may be adopted, thus making a return to a normal situation possible.»[19]

Article 16 provided that severance of relations should ensue immediately when an act of war had been committed by a state against any of the members. This was recognized by the committee, which admitted that any state could take preliminary measures if it considered it desirable. But the members were agreed that it did not mean at once, but at «the earliest possible moment at which unanimous action could be secured,» and that this would lead to an action which would «in the strict sense of the word, be immediate.» In short, the Council should fix a date on which common action should be taken. All states were to be treated with the «most absolute impartiality» in the carrying out of sanctions. The committee felt, however, that some exceptions might be made in line with the amendments proposed by the Scandinavian governments. It was, therefore, recommended to make such in cases when «members can show that the facilities demanded are essential for their economic or political security...»[20]

As to what extent relations should be severed, the committee thought that states being not directly in the war ought not to sever diplomatic relations completely with the covenant-breaking state. Consuls and subordinate diplomatic representatives ought to remain in the first instance. The Member States should further take

---

[19] League of Nations Assembly, *Reports and Resolutions*, 18. This does not show any great understanding of the totalitarian tendencies in the thirties.

[20] League of Nations Assembly, *Reports and Resolutions*, 19.

effective measures to prohibit all commercial dealings with «residents» of the defaulting state. As to these matters, the committee pointed at the extreme difficulty in prescribing in detail the exact measures to be taken. Humanitarian relations ought, however, to be continued during a conflict. Nor did the committee think that personal relations needed to be totally prohibited.[21]

The committee fully realized the significance of non-member states. It thought it very important that every possible effort should be made to arrive at arrangements «which will at least ensure their passive cooperation with the measures to be taken.» It believed that such agreements could be made without too much difficulty, but gave no indications as to how it should be done.

The report of the International Blockade Committee is especially important as it expressively emphasized the point that a state of war does not automatically follow an act of war by a state violating its obligations. This had been decided upon early in the history of the League, but so far it had not been explicitly formulated.[22]

The committee finally stated that as the League of Nations did not include all the nations of the world among its members, Article 16 should not be so rigidly applied as would have been proper had the League been universal. The committee did not view the situation as it *might* have been, but took the facts into consideration as they actually were. As a consequence, the provisions of Article 16 had to be modified.

The report from the International Blockade Committee was referred to the Third Committee of the Second Assembly, and in September, 1920, presented to the Assembly by the rapporteur of the Third Committee, Mr. Carlo Schanzer. On nearly all points the Committee agreed with the earlier report. It stressed more strongly the difference between acts of war and a state of war.[23] An act of war on the part of the covenant-breaking state gave to all the other League members a right even to declare war against it. But, «the unilateral act of the defaulting state is not... sufficient to create a state of war.» The (Third) Blockade Committee went on to say that «the fundamental idea inspiring the

---

[21] Ibid., 20—21.

[22] Willard Hogan, *International Violence and Third States Since the World War* (Chicago, 1941), 5.

[23] League of Nations Assembly, *Reports and Resolutions*, 32.

Covenant is the avoidance of war.» Consequently, it would not seem rational to attribute to the defaulting state «the power of determining automatically a general state of war throughout the world.»

Concerning the very important point as to who was going to decide when the Covenant had been violated, the Committee followed the same pattern: «It is the duty of each of the Members of the League to ascertain and to decide whether a breach of the Covenant within the meaning of Article 16 has been committed.» Thus the Council had no authority to make a binding decision for the member states, but could only give them advice. Each of them was to decide for itself.[24] For the rest, the report was largely a restatement of the earlier ones. On October 4, 1921, a resolution containing all these statements and interpretations was adopted by the Assembly and thus made a part of the League legislation.[25]

*

There appears to have been no more work done on this matter until 1926, when the Preparatory Commission for Disarmament made proposals to the Council that something ought to be done to facilitate the meeting of the Council in case of emergency. It was also proposed to investigate the question of an efficient communication between the League Council and all the different countries, and, when it had decided who was attacked, how the necessary financial and economic help could be given as rapidly as possible. The Commission suggested that the Council ought to consider whether organizations for regional assistance ought to be established. This would mean more speedy and effective help in case Article 16 was to be applied.[26]

These proposals were made in relation to a memorandum from the Finnish Delegation. The Finnish Government proposed that the Council should undertake the examination of special arrangements for the benefit of «states unfavorably placed, owing to geographical or other exceptional circumstances.» By a reduction of armaments agreed to by them, they might be compensated in order to meet their requirements for security.

[24] *Ibid.*
[25] *Ibid.*, 42.
[26] League of Nations *Report of the Preparatory Commission for the Disarmament Conference to the Council, Doc. A, Vol. 14, 1927*, 54—56.

This Finnish proposal was indeed a frank and open statement and it exposed obvious gaps in the League system. It was clearly pointed out that a small state did not have the raw materials, nor the war industry needed to provide all the implements it would have to apply to meet an aggressor. It would, therefore, have to store great amounts of war materials, which could not exactly conform with the current drive for disarmament, or it would have to buy all these articles from abroad when the emergency actually was there. The Finns then very logically drew attention to the fact that most small states had difficulties in getting foreign loans even in times of peace and that their position was much more difficult in time of war. As a solution they suggested that, before a war broke out the Council guaranteed or set aside financial means for small states that were attacked. They also added, with unmistakable reference to Russia, that «the greater the disproportion between the small states and the aggressor, the greater should be the first installment of the financial assistance to the victim of the aggression.»[27] Proposals to the same effect were made by other delegations, but no positive action in this direction seems to have been taken by the League.

On behalf of the Preparatory Commission, M. de Brouckère of Belgium, in 1926 made a very thorough analysis of the report from the International Blockade Committee. He went along with the previous reports in admitting that the unilateral action of the defaulting state cannot create a state of war, but raised the question as to the general validity of this doctrine. As a consequence one would have to admit that a country could resort to war without there being a state of war. Undoubtedly, it would be a somewhat strange and illogical situation.[28] On the other hand, it would have been interesting to have had the opinion of the League as to what would happen if the aggressor had declared war as his first move.

M. de Brouckère warned strongly against the evasiveness in the League's first dealings with the aggressor, and drew attention to the importance of war prevention. The League should not wait until the crime was committed. Such inactivity was against the

[27] League of Nations *Report of the Preparatory Commission*, 57.
[28] (This actually happened in the thirties when rather extensive wars were fought without a declaration of war. Some countries then preferred to assume that a state of war did not exist.)

whole spirit of the Covenant. As soon as there appeared an actual danger that an act of war might take place, it was the duty of the League to take action.[29]

M. de Brouckère did not object principally to the adopted interpretation that «it is the duty of each member of the League to decide for himself whether a breach of the Covenant has been committed,» but he thought that the opinion of the Council should carry «unquestionable authority». This could not be avoided if the Council had been summoned from the early stage of the conflict. He also pointed at the serious consequences for a state that illegally abstained from taking action.[30] M. de Brouckère was definitely against the halfway measures that had been suggested, — and in part adopted by the Assembly. He maintained that diplomatic and consular relations had to be severed altogether, not only partially. The Council ought to take time to investigate an incident thoroughly before it made any definite decision, but when the decision was made the sanctions should be applied to the fullest extent. No state «could shirk the duty of applying certain economic sanctions on the ground that these would constitute acts of war with the state against which they were directed.»

M. de Brouckère's conclusion was an earnest warning to the League. If it did not prepare for cases that sooner or later were bound to occur, it might lose confidence and authority. It could not hope to become a permanent organization if all measures had to be improvised while the struggle was already going on. Certain preparatory work would be indispensable if effective use should be made of the economic weapon.

As already mentioned, M. de Brouckère gave this report in 1926, and the Assembly ought to have seen his point and the justification of his criticism. If the Assembly had wanted to make the League into what it was intended to be, and thought it possible, the logical consequence would have been what M. de Brouckère suggested, and not the half-hearted and fumbling steps that were actually taken. However, the proposals of de Brouckère do not

---

[29] League of Nations *Report of the Preparatory Commission*, 68.

[30] *Ibid.*, 68.

[31] «Legal Position Arising from the Enforcement in Time of Peace of the Measures of Economic Pressure Indicated in Article 16 of the Covenant, particularly by a Maritime Blockade,» in *Doc. A. 14, 1927*, V, 83—89.

seem to have caused any principal change in the League's attitude to those questions.

On May 17, 1927, the Secretary General submitted a report to the Council on this issue.[31] It dealt particularly with enforcement in time of peace of the measures of economic pressure related to Article 16; further, with the relations between the members themselves, and also to the third states not belonging to the League. It was a highly legalistic discussion and did not bring out any proposal for positive action in case a war broke out. One of the statements ran as follows, «From a League point of view, the existence of a state of war between two states depends upon their intention and not upon the nature of their acts. Accordingly, measures of coercion, however drastic, which are not intended to create, and not regarded by the state to which they are applied, as creating a state of war, do not legally establish a relation of war between the states concerned.» This shows the theoretical character of the report, and its remoteness from practical politics.

There is left to mention only the «Memorandum on Articles 10, 11, and 16 of the Covenant,» which was submitted to the Assembly in 1928 by M. V. H. Rutgers.[32] This followed much the same lines as de Brouckère's report. It was a severe criticism of what the League had done to solve the problem of Article 16, pointing out that in spite of the long period of years that had elapsed since the League started discussing this question, nothing but provisional measures had been adopted. It went on to say that if a situation should arise which made the application of Article 16 necessary, «the decision of the different countries would not depend on interpretations, however authoritative, or on the deduction of lawyers; the great question would be whether the principle of Article 16 was or was not a living reality.» Rutgers, therefore, wanted the League to work out plans to meet the eventualities. He did not think they could be elaborated on in all details, but he wanted general plans made which would facilitate the detailed planning when an emergency arose. He stressed strongly the point of the Preparatory Commission regarding the improving of direct communications between the Council and all countries, and also supported the Finnish proposal for financial guarantees to small countries. The report, however, was not followed by any resolutions or actions.

[32] League of Nations, *Official Journal*, 1928, 670—686.

Neutrality Lives On.

During eight years, this was as far as the League got with the measures that should abolish neutrality. In spite of the clear points made by M. de Brouckère and M. Rutgers, and the obvious need for more planning and preparations, «no further steps were taken by the League» to make Article 16 a working principle until the question actually became controversial in October, 1935.[33] Through all these fifteen years the issue had been drifting and nothing was done to settle it. When action had to be taken, there were no plans and what was to be done had to be improvised. No more documentation should be needed to tell that such halfway measures could not be sufficient to shut out neutrality. On the contrary, in this period, neutrality showed a stronger claim to life than the League itself. It is hard to see how the principle of neutrality could be seriously affected under such circumstances.

In the first place, there was the existence of the non-members, the United States, Brazil, Germany, Russia, Japan, and some lesser states, who were all outside the League. Regardless of how eagerly the League tried to include them in its calculations and establish some kind of cooperation, these states were completely outside the control of the League.[34] On the other hand, even the control that the League exercised over its own members tended to be rather illusory. If a violation of Article 16 had automatically obligated the members to take action against the aggressor, or if the Council had been allowed to decide, neutrality might have been out as far as the League members were concerned. But according to the resolution of 1921, there was an essential difference between *acts* of war and a *state* of war. As the members also were free to judge and decide for themselves what constituted a violation of Article 16, there seemed to be ample room for neutrality, even within the League itself. Some states might decide that a state of war existed and start applying sanctions, but if a state decided that there was no war going on and did nothing, then what about its status? This question was the source of endless discussions among the international lawyers throughout the whole League period.

The treaties and conventions made in these years show better

[33] Jessup, *Today and Tomorrow*, 114.

[34] *Ibid.*, 115. «The Covenant of the League, a treaty to which they are not parties, could not affect them or the possibility of their future neutrality.»

than anything else that traditional neutrality was far from dead. The first world war was hardly over before the powers got together in a new attempt to regulate the relations between belligerents and neutrals. The International Air Navigation Convention of 1919 did not make any reference to Article 16, but prescribed that in case of war its provisions would not interfere with the traditional freedom of action for belligerents and neutrals.[35] Similar reservations were found in the statements of freedom of transit made at the Barcelona Conference in 1921 and the International Waterways Convention of the same year.[36]

During the Russo-Polish War in 1920, Germany declared her neutrality and in 1923, the Permanent Court of International Justice discussed her neutral duties very seriously. Nobody suggested that neutrality was no longer a tenable position.[37]

In the course of the Greco-Turkish War[38] in 1921, the Allied Governments issued a collective declaration of neutrality.[39] When the Turkish Straits were regulated by the Treaty of Lausanne, July 24, 1923, no changes were made in the traditional system. The treaty had also provisions for the right of free passage for neutral shipping.[40] In the second part of the treaty, the Turkish neutrality was dealt with at great length and reference was even made to the Hague Convention of 1907, concerning neutrality during maritime warfare.[41]

February 6, 1922, statesmen and experts on international affairs from nine countries met in Washington. Among those were most of the great powers, as the United States, Great Britain, France and Japan. In Article 6 of this Nine-Power Treaty, the signatories bound themselves to respect scrupulously China's right as a neutral power in the wars in which she was not a participant. On the other hand, China declared that she, as a neutral, would observe the rules of neutrality.[42]

---

[35] Article 36. It was never ratified. Cohn, 62.
[36] *Ibid.*, 62.
[37] Jessup, *Today and Tomorrow*, 118.
[38] Greece being a member of the League and Turkey not.
[39] Hogan, *International Violence*, 11.
[40] League of Nations, *Treaty Series*, XXVIII, 702, 1924, 116.
[41] In the Montreux Convention, July 20, 1936, which superceded the Treaty of Lausanne, neutrality was again recognized.
[42] League of Nations, *Treaty Series*, XXXVIII, 702, 1924, 283.

At the official conference, held in the Hague in 1922 subsequent to the Washington Conference, the most prominent lawyers of the world took part. They met for the purpose of supplementing the rules of neutrality made at the Hague in 1907, by drafting regulations of the newest means of communication, such as radio and airplanes.[43] The President of the Conference was the famous American international lawyer, John Bassett Moore. He said about the conference that «the idea that the law of neutrality had become obsolete was never broached.»[44]

There were also signed a great many bilateral «neutrality treaties» during the twenties and thirties. All these indicated that neutrality still was possible and could be taken into consideration. They were mostly merely defensive agreements and provided that in certain circumstances the parties would remain neutral or observe the rules of neutrality. Their differences should be settled by conciliation and juridical measures.[45] To this category belong many of the treaties which Soviet Russia made with neighboring states in the middle of the twenties.

During the Chaco War between Bolivia and Paraguay, Argentina, Brazil, Chile and Peru in 1933 declared their neutrality in spite of the fact that three of them were members of the League.[46] The neutrality legislation of the United States in the thirties may also be regarded as manifestations of the neutral principle. However, the seriousness of the neutral intentions and the hope for success may be illustrated by the Anglo-American agreement as to neutral damages.

The United States in 1926 tried to get compensation for the immense property losses which were inflicted upon it by the Allies before the United States joined the war as a belligerent. Great Britain then put up a claim for services which she had given to the American Navy in 1917 and 1918, and was willing to give up that in return. By the Executive Agreement, made in May, 1927, England refused to pay anything for damages caused by her violations of neutral rights. Incidentally, she went even further

---

[43] It did not reach decisions of any significance to neutrality.
[44] Moore, «Appeal to Reason,» in *Foreign Affairs*, II (July, 1933) 560—563.
[45] For the texts of those, see League of Nations, *Treaty Series*.
[46] G. G. Wilson, «War and Neutrality,» in *American Journal of International Law*, 27 (1933) : 724.

than that. During the First World War she had justified her curbing of the neutral rights on the grounds that it was necessary to make reprisals against the illegal practices of Germany. Now she professed openly in the Agreement that she reserved to do the same thing over again in a future war. The United States reserved the right to protest.[47]

It is hard to point at any attempts in this period to reestablish neutrality on a general world basis. In this respect the Havana Convention of 1928 is probably the most important one. It was namely the only multi-lateral instrument, formulating rules of maritime neutrality, which was adopted after the First World War.[48] This convention had, however, a rather limited scope and was of a strictly regional character as it was ratified only by the United States and some of the smaller Latin American countries.

It is important to stress that except for this Havana Convention, being limited to a particular area, no significant general agreement was made to strengthen and reestablish the principle of neutral rights and duties.[49] The accepted legal system of neutrality had been thoroughly broken down during the First World War, and even if we cannot point at decisions that formally abolished those rules, we must also admit that nothing was done to maintain them by new general legislation. No attempts were made to learn from experience and consequently to reinforce and improve the system of neutrality. This would seem to have been the natural reaction if there had still been a firm belief in neutrality as a sound political principle. The fact that so many neutrality treaties were concluded all the same, does not prove the vitality of traditional neutrality in general, but is rather an indication of the ideological confusion of the period.

[47] The paragraph runs as follows: «That the right of each government to maintain in the future such position as it may deem appropriate with respect to the legality or illegality under international law of measures such as those giving rise to claims, is fully reserved, it being specifically understood that the juridical position of neither government is prejudiced by the present arrangement.» Borchard, *Neutrality*, 282—285.

[48] Also called «Convention on Maritime Neutrality adopted on the Sixth International Conference of American States held at Havana, January 16, to February 20, 1928.» For details, see James Brown Scott, «The Sixth International Conference of American States,» in *International Conciliation Documents*, (Worchester, 1928).

[49] Hogan, *International Violence*, 13.

2. *The Pact of Paris*

By the end of the twenties the world at large appears to have realized that the League and the provisions of the Covenant did not bring about such a revolution in international relations as had been expected. The League did not abolish neutrality; it did not unite all nations; it did not create a new world order. Even the most ardent believers in the League could not help seeing that the League of Nations was a somewhat faulty instrument which would need a great deal of strengthening before it could be made to work smoothly and efficiently. Thus, a great many idealists were at that time searching for something that might fill in the gaps which the Covenant had left open. This fact may explain the world-wide attention and great expectations that were attached to the so-called Pact of Paris (the Kellogg Pact).

This agreement was, from the beginning, not meant to change the world order, and even as an international, multilateral pact the vagueness of its provisions seemed to make its influence very limited so far as war and neutrality were concerned. Seen on the background of the whole period it is sometimes hard to understand why it was taken so seriously and given so much consideration. However, as in the case of the League, the discussions around the Pact of Paris were primarily of a legal and theoretical character and did not materially affect the political decisions.

In 1927, a movement for the abolition of war had gained a considerable momentum in America and according to Bailey, it was Professor James T. Shotwell, one of the most ardent agitators of this movement, who gave the French Foreign Minister, A. Briand, the idea of a French-American pact.[1] In April, Briand suggested a bilateral treaty with the United States,[2] and on June 20, 1927, he

[1] Bailey, *Diplomatic History*, 707.
[2] Shotwell, «The Pact of Paris,» with Historical Commentary in *Text of Treaty and Related Documents*, (Worchester, 1928), 24.

presented the official draft of the treaty, which provided that France and the United States should denounce war as «an instrument of national policy.» [3]

This French proposal could apparently not have created a great enthusiasm in the State Department as six months elapsed before the administration answered. It must be admitted that their position was not an easy one. They could, of course, politely refuse to sign such a treaty, but it would make a bad impression on the rest of the world if the United States refused to accept a French offer of friendship, which did not imply more than a common denunciation of war. On the contrary, doubts might be raised as to the peaceful intentions of the United States if it would not bind itself to abstain from war as an instrument of national policy. There was already much bitterness in the European countries because the United States had wrecked the hopes for making a working League by staying out of it completely. This was a touchy point even within the country itself, and a new expression of extreme isolationalism was likely to be severely criticized, and give more drive to the interventionalist movement.

On the other hand, the signing of such a French-American treaty, would be contrary to the American tradition in foreign policy. Since the days of Washington, the administrations had been warned not to sign treaties with European countries for fear that they should develop into commitments which might deprive the United States of its freedom of action. From the French side, the proposal was definitely meant as an attempt to drag the United States into the sphere of the League and secure American support of it.[4] It might have meant the first step of a development that eventually would lead away from neutrality, and in time, obligate the United States to take sides in European conflicts.[5]

It took half a year to find an answer to this question, but from the State Department's point of view, it was worth the while. The solution was an expression of considerable diplomatic skill, and showed great psychological insight and statesmanship on the part

---

[3] *Ibid.*, 464 in *International Conciliation Documents.*

[4] Moore quotes Paul Boncour, Briand's great friend, as having said that «the Kellogg Pact was for Mr. Briand, before all else, a means to draw the United States, the decisive factor in the Allied victory, into the League of Nations.» Moore, «Appeal to Reason,» in *Foreign Affairs,* II (July, 1933) : 554.

[5] *Cohn,* 91.

of the administration. In his answer of December 28, 1927, Mr.
Kellogg expressed his appreciation of the French suggestion, but
stressed the point that such a treaty would have much greater
importance if it were extended to include all the principal powers
and was not limited to the United States and France only. He was,
therefore, willing to conclude a «treaty among the principal powers
of the world, open to signature by all nations condemning war and
renouncing it as an instrument of national policy in favor of the
pacific settlement of international disputes.»[6]

Thus, by making the proposed bilateral treaty into a world
settlement, the obligations would then be shared by a great many
states instead of binding two in particular. Further, by proposing
a general repudiation of war, it gained the support of all the
interventionists and the friends of the League, and partly made up
for the coolness it had shown so far.[7]

It is important to note that public opinion played a great part
in this. During the last half of 1927, the United States' government
was exposed to considerable pressure from the American public,
working through newspapers and speakers.[8] Thus, it would have
been hard to turn the French proposal down completely without
a satisfactory explanation. The idea of outlawing war was well
framed and caught the imagination of the American people.

The suggestion was favorably received by the other principal
powers, especially after Mr. Kellogg had explained the treaty in
a speech to the American Society of International Law. The State
Department sent a note to other foreign governments on June 23,
1928. Here it interpreted in detail the treaty provisions and pointed
out the numerous reservations. Mr. Kellogg first emphasized that
«there is nothing in the treaty which restricts and impairs in any
way the right of self defense. That right is inherent in every
sovereign state and is implicit in every treaty.»[9] He further stressed
that there was no inconsistence between the proposed treaty and
the League Covenant. As to the treaties of Locarno, he maintained

---

[6] The Secretary of State to the French Ambassador, Claudel, *International Conciliation Documents*, 1928, 465.

[7] *Cohn*, 91.

[8] Bailey, *Diplomatic History*, 708.

[9] Note of the Government of the United States to the Governments of Australia and Belgium, June 23, 1928. Shotwell, *The Pact of Paris*, 60—64.

that this anti-war pact would actually mean a double assurance and work to insure that they would not be violated. Nor did he think that the pact would prevent treaties of neutrality from being concluded.[10] Probably the most important statement was that «there can be no question as a matter of law that violation of a multi-lateral anti-war treaty through resort to war by one party thereto would automatically release the other parties from their obligations to the treaty breaking states.»

During the spring and the summer of 1928, most powers declared their satisfaction with the proposal and the Pact of Paris was finally signed on August 27. The purpose of the treaty was stated in such general terms that the whole Pact could be expressed in two small articles. The parties declared that they condemned «recourse to war for the solution of international controversies, and renounced it as an instrument of national policy.» Further it provided that the solutions of conflicts that might arise among them should «never be sought except by pacific means.»[11] The terms of the treaty are thus extremely vague, and there are no specifications beyond the basic principle. It is almost unnecessary to point to the fact that the broader the statement is, the more room there will be for varying interpretations.

It is interesting to note what a great difference of opinion there seemed to be as to the influence of the Pact on neutrality. As this status is meaningless and unimportant except in and during a war, an effective abolition of war would imply that there would be no more use for neutrality. Many of the contemporary writers, therefore, held that together with the League, the Kellogg Pact had ruled out neutrality.[12] In their opinion it meant a turning point in modern history,[13] as it had made neutrality an impossible status. Statements were frequently made to the effect that «the Kellogg

[10] Shotwell, *The Pact of Paris*, 62.

[11] For the full text of the treaty see *International Conciliation Documents*, 1928, 521: League of Nations, *Report of the Committee for the Amendment of the League of Nations in Order to Bring it into Harmony with the Pact of Paris*, Doc. A. 8, (Geneva, 1930), 30.

[12] Charles Warren feared that it would «be impossible to remain neutral in any war resulting from a violation of the League Covenant or the Kellogg—Briand Pact.» Warren, «Troubles of a Neutral,» in *Foreign Affairs*, 12 (March, 1935) : 377.

[13] Shotwell, *The Pact of Paris*, 12; «Neutrality and National Policy,» in *Outlook*, 151 (April 17, 1929) : 620.

Pact alone had made neutrality illegal,»[14] and has «ended the duties of neutrality.»[15]

Secretary of State, Henry L. Stimson, in January, 1932, presented his nonrecognition policy regarding *de facto* situations resulting from contraventions of the Pact of Paris. His interpretations of the implications of this policy suggested that with war outlawed by the nations of the world, there could be no neutrals and consequently, no neutral rights. In his famous «punctillo speech,» August 8, 1932, Stimson said that the «existence and lawfulness of war had given birth to neutrality,» but the war of 1914 had demonstrated that it was impossible to keep modern warfare within strict bounds:

> War is no longer the principle around which the duties, conducts and rights of a nation revolve. Hereafter, when two nations engage in armed conflict, either one or both of them must be wrongdoers, violators of the general treaty. We no longer draw a circle around them and treat them with the punctillos of a duelist's code. Instead, we denounce them as lawbreakers.[16]

This is quite close to the League point of view and supports the conclusions that many writers have drawn from the Pact. If it did not completely rule out neutrality as such, it at least did away with the impartial version of that principle. But it would not be true to say that this view was generally accepted. A good many distinguished scholars have consistently held that the Kellogg Pact did not affect neutrality and did not at all exclude it. If it had any effect, it was only of a formal character.[17]

The objections have mostly been raised on the fact that the Kellogg Pact did not include all wars and had been accepted with so many limitations that there actually was little force left in it. John Bassett Moore drew attention to the point that the British Government had accepted the treaty upon «the distinct under-

---

[14] Quincy Wright, «Neutrality and Neutral Rights Following the Pact of Paris,» in the *Reference Shelf*, 10, No. 7, 235; «League and Neutrality,» in *Congressional Digest*, Vol. 15, 9.

[15] Bradley, *Can We Stay Out of War?*, 214—215.

[16] *New York Times*, August 9, 1932, 2.

[17] H. M. Spitzer, «Small Nations and the Economic and Social Council,» in *World Affairs*, (June, 1946), 133.

standing that it does not prejudice their freedom of action.» He also pointed to Mr. Kellogg's own statement in a public speech, May 1, 1928, that every nation «alone is competent to decide whether the circumstances require recourse to war in self defense.»[18]

Three outstanding American experts on international law, Jessup, Fenwick and Borchard have also emphasized that as the Pact permits wars of self defense, it has a great number of limitations, and even lacks the machinery for enforcing what restrictions it might have left.[19] Jessup holds that even if the Pact pretends to make wars illegal, «a state is free to regard or disregard a breach of the treaty if it thinks fit and if it wants to.»[20] As it was stressed in Congress, the treaty had «no teeth,» and would lose its force if violated.

Borchard goes so far as to imply that the Pact has strengthened the position of war instead of weakening it, as it permitted wars of self defense, which actually would include practically all wars. «Now by a world treaty nearly all wars obtained the stamp of approval,» while they previously had been considered something like a disease, neither legal nor illegal.[21] The famous Danish international lawyer, George Cohn, wrote that «the laws of war and consequently of neutrality, were completely unchanged by the Kellogg Pact as to legal validity, and remained in force as before.[22]

As conditions were in the thirties, it may be said that so far as practical politics are concerned, the Kellogg Pact had very little effect on neutrality. Neither could that be expected with the vague formulation of the Pact and the numerous reservations that were taken. But this does not mean that it could not develop into something real. The possibility seems to have been there, if only earnest efforts had been made to make it work.

In 1929, the Labor government in England headed by Ramsey McDonald proposed that the Covenant and the Kellogg Pact should be harmonized in order to fill in the gaps in both.[23] This was

[18] Moore, «Appeal to Reason,» in *Foreign Affairs*, II (July, 1933), 552—553.
[19] Fenwick, *American Neutrality*, 26.
[20] Jessup, *Today and Tomorrow*, 116.
[21] Borchard, *Neutrality*, 293, 298.
[22] *Cohn*, 93.
[23] League of Nations, *Records of the Tenth Ordinary Session of the Assembly; Minutes of the First Committee*, (Geneva, 1924), 24.

proposed in the League Assembly and supported by a great number of states. In this connection, the Delegate of Peru made a rather important statement pertaining to neutrality. He maintained that prior to the Kellogg Pact, the states had had the right to declare themselves neutral. However, after the signing of the Pact, they had lost this right and were, therefore, bound to defend the obligations they had taken on. He, consequently, proposed that the nations should agree upon an amendment to the League Covenant providing that no state should have the right to remain neutral.[24]

This Peruvian proposal, which if adopted would have completely ruled out neutrality on a legal basis, raised serious doubts in the so-called traditional neutral countries. They thought such action to be extremely dangerous. The northern neutrals, therefore, decided not to support the proposals. The Danish delegate maintained that the Kellogg Pact had not abolished war, and if a war broke out, the rules of the Hague Conventions as well as the League sanctions would be in force. If a plan for a combination of the systems should be worked out, fundamental changes had to be made in both. In this connection, the Dutch and the Scandinavian Governments made the significant distinction between moral and economic, and purely military sanctions.[25] They were doubtful as to the application of the latter.[26]

This position of the small northern countries was bitterly attacked by other powers, especially by Great Britain and Belgium. Not until 1930, was a commission for harmonizing the two systems appointed, and in spite of the fact that the question appeared every year in the Assembly, no satisfactory solution was found.[27]

The International Law Association at its Budapest Conference in 1934 had adopted some Articles of Interpretation to the Kellogg

---

[24] *Ibid.*, 11.

This statement was in accordance with the official view held in the British White Book of 1930. The British Government maintained in 1929, that «as between members of the League there can be no neutral rights, because there can be no neutrals.» Quoted by Quincy Wright, «League and Neutrality,» in *Congressional Digest*, Vol. 15, 9.

[25] This distinction was introduced by Switzerland in 1920.

[26] League of Nations, *Records of the Tenth Session*, Doc. C. 499, (1929), 12—15.

[27] See League of Nations, *Report of the Committee for the Amendment of the Covenant to Bring it in Harmony with the Pact of Paris*, Doc. A. 8, (1930), 1—31.

Pact. Whereas formerly the obligation of neutrality had arisen automatically at the outbreak of war, this could no longer be the case if the Pact were violated. According to those articles of interpretation, «each state would, as regards the Pact, be free to determine for itself whether it would or would not perform the duties of neutrality.»

There was, however, at the Association's conference in England in 1946 a general agreement that legally the Kellogg Pact was still in force.[28] This statement, made after the second War, is very interesting, and may indicate that the Pact perhaps still have some significant influence on international law, even if its practical value so far, has not been impressive. On the whole, the Pact of Paris can hardly be said to have had any *direct* affect either on war or on neutrality, at least not in the first instance. It may have aroused hopes in the beginning, but they did not last very long. The statesmen all over the world seem to have denied it a real place in their policy, and no evidence can be found that it directly changed the political course of any country.

But, the Kellogg Pact was important in one respect, as it may be said to have formed the starting point for a closer cooperation between the United States and the League[29] and morally as well as legally, it has undoubtedly had some importance. The treaty must be seen as an expression of the change that gradually took place in people's minds in their relations to war. It had begun to dawn upon humanity that wars were waged for different reasons, and that the moral arguments on both sides did not always carry the same weight. In some cases, it seemed as if the neutrals had an obligation to join what might be called the «right side». This sentiment had come into existence with Wilson's condemnation of neutrality as an undesirable principle in conflicts between the right and wrong forces in society. This was in fact, nothing but a revival of the theory of the just cause of war, and both the Covenant and the Kellogg Pact were reintroductions of the same idea. In this connection, Wright said that, «international law has thereby been restored to the Grotian foundations, and freed from the inconsistencies which the idea of neutrality gave to the late

---

[28] International Law Association, *Report of the 41st Conference*, Cambridge, England, 1948, 40.
[29] *Cohn*, 102.

eighteenth and nineteenth centuries. ... under the Pact, partiality is permissable for a neutral state against a violator.»[30] Politis held the same view, «... under the Pact of Paris impartiality is no more conceivable.»[31] This shows that the principle of impartial neutrality had become doubtful on the basis of morality, as it already was from a political point of view. It must be kept in mind that as the Kellogg Pact officially declared war to be a crime, and had this incorporated in international law, it took on great importance as a legal basis for convicting war criminals. The notion of war guilt was strong even after the First World War,[32] but as no legal basis could be found for a trial of those who were held responsible, nothing was done. What opinion one may have on the Nürnberg trials following the Second World War, they no doubt were of great importance and created a fateful precedent for future war-makers — and the legal background was to a great extent provided by the Pact of Paris.

As far as neutrality goes, the Pact prepared people's minds for the justification of a partial attitude which meant an exclusion of the classical or impartial neutrality. This concept lost its moral support and justification, because no one could be disinterested in a war between right and wrong.

---

[30] Wright, «League and Neutrality,» in *Congressional Digest*, Vol. 15, 9; Wright, «Neutrality and Neutral Rights,» in *Reference Shelf*, 10, No. 7, 235.
[31] Politis, *La Neutralité*, 130, 146.
[32] *Foreign Relations*, The Paris Peace Conference, IX (1919) : 888.

3. Revision of the Concept of Neutrality

In the early thirties it become evident that the world had not, after all entered upon a new era. During the decade that had passed since the end of the First World War, great attempts had been made, but the goal of lasting peace was still far ahead. The great expectations occasioned by the League and the Kellogg Pact had not in turn been lived up to. No wonder then that many international experts started looking backward to see what could still be used of the «old stuff» which had been condemned in 1919. In this rather unstable period, the craving was for *security* above anything else. It was, therefore, natural that the principle of neutrality should once again become the focus of public interest. The more so since throughout the period, it had been persistently applied in spite of all prohibitions and condemnations.

Very few, however, had the moral courage to insist upon the former strict and impartial concept of neutrality that had been codified at the Hague Conventions. On the contrary there was a widespread belief that this classical conception of neutrality had undergone profound changes. «In theory, as in practice, neutrality is at present an idea in active evaluation.»[1] Even though it was agreed that neutrality was possible within the League itself, it was felt that it could not be of the same prewar quality. M. de la Pradelle, the French delegate, said that «for the members of the League of Nations it is a matter of conscience. The last world war proved that strict impartiality is practically impossible,» and further, «neutrality subsists but the system of 1907 is obsolete.»[2]

---

[1] Paul de la Pradelle, in the «Evaluation of Neutrality,» a memorandum submitted to the eight members of the League of Nations Conferences of International Studies held in London in 1935. Recorded in *Collective Security*, edited by Maurice Bourquin (Paris, 1936), 404. It also has reports from the Seventh International Studies Conference in Paris, 1934.

[2] Paul de la Pradelle, «Evaluation of Neutrality,» 406—408.

On the same occasion, the British expert on international relations, H. Lauterpacht, stated that «under the Covenant there is no room for neutrality in the established sense. ...absolute impartiality is... a denial of the existence of a true legal community among states.»[3]

These statements, and many more to the same effect, were made at the two International Studies Conferences held in Paris and London in 1934 and 1935. All of the principal countries were represented at those conferences and it seemed to be the concensus of opinion that neutrality ought to be revised. Though impartial and passive neutrality had proved to be an impracticable principle, it was thought that by giving up these two very essential elements of neutrality, an efficient means to keep countries out of war would still remain. It must be admitted that the practical results of these efforts were rather negligible and went little beyond theory; yet as a phase in the development of the concept of neutrality these theories deserve further discussion.

The delegate of Norway, A. Raestad, at the Paris Conference in 1934, characterized neutrality at that time as being of three different kinds. First, the old traditional neutrality which might as well be called the Swiss neutrality since Switzerland was the only country that officially advocated the old passivity and inviolability of territory; secondly, the qualified and new neutrality, and finally, the American neutrality which he classified as being modified or inconsistent. Whatever it was, in his opinion it could no longer be called traditional neutrality.[4]

Swiss Neutrality.

Regardless of what might be said about the Swiss position, one cannot help admiring the remarkable consistency and steadfastness of the Swiss in claiming respect for their century old permanent neutrality. They managed to have their way at the Peace Conference of Paris in 1919, and in the League Assembly, 1920, and they were not inclined to change their point of view during the thirties.

---

[3] H. Lauterpacht, «Neutrality and the Covenant of the League,» in *Collective Security Conferences*, 412—414.

[4] A. Raestad, memorandum, *Collective Security Conference*, 150—152.

It should be noted that the Swiss did not speak generally about the maintenance of traditional neutrality, nor were they concerned about the principle itself. As long as they were allowed to apply it within their own country and have it respected, they seemed to care less about what systems the rest of the world might adopt. The Swiss Professor, D. Schindler, said at the London Conference that Swiss neutrality was not occasional, but a permanent institution, and it was incorporated as such in the Federal Constitution. He further said that, «it has nothing in common with the neutrality which is dictated exclusively by considerations of expediency.» [5]

It must be kept in mind that even though the Swiss were exempted by the League from military sanctions, they were still expected to carry out the economic ones. It would, therefore, be difficult to classify their neutrality as being strictly impartial. D. Schindler consequently put it very diplomatically and guarded himself by saying that «it (Switzerland) is not indifferent, but it tends to be impartial».

The Swiss have presented three justifications for their insistence on this privileged position among the world's small nations. Their claim of a legal right to remain permanently neutral has been restated many times since 1815, and from a strictly judicial point of view there can be no question as to its validity. However, it is after all a treaty provision like so many others, and in view of what happened to similar treaties during the last decades, the traditional point does not seem to carry much weight. This was clearly realized in 1914, when Belgium and Luxembourg had just been overrun. *Das Genferblatt,* one of Switzerland's leading papers, said on August 5, 1914:

> Die Vorgänge in Luxemburg und Belgium bedeuten für die Schweitz ernsthafte Präzedensfälle. Doch bestätigen sie nur die alte Wahrheit dass alle papirenen Neutralitätserklärungen in Konfliktsfälle wertlos sind, und dass der ungerüstete Kleinstaat das Schlactfeld der Grossen wird. [6]

---

[5] Memorandum by D. Schindler, *The Perpetual Neutrality of Switzerland,* 420.

[6] Peter Alemann, *Die Schweitz und die Verletzung der Belgischen Neutralität im Weltkrieg 1914,* (Buenos Aires, 1940), 64.

There seems to be more to the theory that Swiss relief to prisoners and wounded is of such importance that the whole world would benefit by guaranteeing the Swiss neutrality. There is also much logical force in the point D. Schindler brought out in his memorandum, drawing attention to the fact that «Switzerland, being right in the center of Europe, would risk complete annihilation if involved in a modern war.»[7] Of course, that is the risk which all of the small states would have to run, but Schindler seemed to think that the other countries were not so exposed as his own. It might hold true for the northern neutrals, at least when viewed in the middle thirties, but Schindler seems to have overlooked the First World War and the extremely difficult position of Belgium and Holland, Those states were as likely to be near the theater of war. He thought, however, that the «mere necessity of allowing a right of passage through her territory to the armed forces would be enough to expose her to this risk» (of complete destruction).

This idea does not give the same solid impression as Schindler's reference to the domestic situation in Switzerland. Knowing that the Swiss people are actually composed of three different nationalities, he had a good point when he stated that «neutrality is one of the essential conditions of internal peace of the Union and consequently, of the independence of a nation made up of elements which differ in language and culture.» The First World War showed the dangerous elements that were latent in the sympathies and antipathies of the different nationality groups.[8] This caused great difficulties, even when the country was neutral, and was likely to become extremely dangerous when the country had to enter a war.

The «New» Neutrality.

The new or qualified neutrality became quite a popular theory in the thirties. Its fundamental principle was that instead of being passive and impartial, neutrality should be active and partial, and

[7] Alemann, *Die Schweitz und die Verletzung*, 421.

[8] See Alemann, *Die Schweitz und die Verletzung*.

[9] «Neutralité et Société des Nations,» in Munch ed. *Les Origines et L'aeuvre de la Société des Nations*, II (1924) : 152.

work through cooperation of neutral states. The leading spokesmen of this neo-neutral cooperative version were Phillip C. Jessup and the Danish scholar and diplomat, Georg Cohn. In 1924, Cohn presented his ideas in «Neutralité et Société des Nations,» which has later been called the Danish Treatise.[9] This theory did not become generally known until in the thirties, and is to some extent related to the Argentine Anti-War Pact of 1933, which carried out the same idea.

This pact, also called the Saavedra Lamas Treaty after the Argentine Foreign Minister, was in some respects a counterpart to the Kellogg Pact. The signatures of more than thirty nations were affixed to it and thus gave it a general character.[10] Its primary aim was to coordinate the system of neutrality with the sanctions system. It also condemned wars of aggression, but went further than that and included the Stimson Doctrine of January, 1932, which provided for non-recognition of territories won by conquest. The Saavedra Lamas Treaty can, therefore, be called an attempt to incorporate parts of the Covenant, the Kellogg Pact, and the Stimson Doctrine, and to combine these into a new version of neutrality.

The three first and most important articles of this treaty read as follows:

> The high contracting parties solemnly declare that they condemn wars of aggression in their neutral relations or in those with other states, and that the settlement of disputes or controversies of any kind that may arise among them shall be effected only by the pacific means which have the sanctions of international law.

> *Article II*
>
> They declare that as between the high contracting parties territorial questions must not be settled by violence, and that they will not recognize any territorial arrangement which is not obtained by pacific means, nor the validity of the occupation or acquisition of territories that may be brought about by force of arms.

---

[10] According to Cohn it was first meant as a bilateral pact between Argentina and Brazil. Cohn, 134.

Article III

In case of non-compliance by any state engaged in a dispute with the obligations contained in the foregoing articles, the contracting parties undertake to make every effort for the maintenance of peace. To that end they will *adopt in their character as neutrals a common and solidary attitude;*[11] they will exercise the political, juridical or economic means authorized by international law; they will bring the influence of public opinion to bear, but will in no case resort to intervention, either diplomatic or armed, subject to the attitude that may be incumbent on them by virtue of other collective treaties to which such states are signatories.[12]

The foregoing articles seem to imply that Argentina wanted to establish a neutral league, whose objective would be, not only to keep out of war, but also to use its influence to prevent or restrict wars. This was not a new idea in the politics of Argentina. The proposals made by the Argentine Government in 1917, providing for a neutral league with or without the United States, are essentially based on the same idea. [13] However, these proposals were not so elaborate and comprehensive, as they did not take into consideration the theories of the League and the Kellogg Pact.

This treaty provides the fundamental basis for the new conception of neutrality. Dr. Cohn's theory of neo-neutrality seems to be fairly well defined in principle, but is not convincing when it comes to application.[14] Cohn maintained that the theory of collective opposition to aggression had been defended merely on moral grounds, and consequently, some might think that neutrality was immoral since it did not try to check the aggressors. To this he said that «when emotions are appealed to in a purely scientific discussion, it is often a sure sign that arguments are lacking.»[15] Instead, he held that the mere fact that a neutral state is able to keep its territory out of war is in itself so important that the moral

---

[11] Italics supplied.
[12] For the full text, see *Treaty Series, No. 906,* 14—18. Also, Q. Wright, *Neutrality and Security,* Appendix, 233—240.
[13] See page 108.
[14] Georg Cohn, *Neo-neutrality.*
[15] Ibid., 342.

and political considerations which call for neutral participation in the war, lose their force by comparison with it.[16]

The neo-neutrals were not supposed to make any distinction between different kinds of war. «It (neo-neutrality) rules out and disqualifies war, morally and legally, regardless of its motives and causes, whether it is a war of aggression or of defense.» There should no longer be an obligation of impartiality and the neo-neutrals should take no stand as to which of the two parties was right.[17] Neo-neutrality would thus be partial, but as the aim was to bring the war to an end as soon as possible, the neutrals would discriminate in the way they saw fit in order to restrict and stop the war. Apparently they would not feel obliged to help the defender in all cases.

Cohn is vague on this point, and seems to be suggesting the abolishment of war by denying the existence of it, a point of view very close to the essentials of the Kellogg Pact. He actually turned the League system of aggressors and sanctions upside down. While the League members had an obligation to join in a war against an aggressor, the neo-neutrals would be correspondingly obligated to stay out of all wars, «The fight should be against war, and not neutrality».[18] «The first and most important duty of a neutral is to keep its own people out of war.»[19] This sounds very much like the doctrines of the nineteenth century liberalism. If each individual strives to improve his standards of living, inevitably conditions must be better for all members of the world society, as nobody would work against his own interest. Thus, if every state would strive to remain out of war, there would be no wars. This is a delightful theory, but extremely hard to transform into a workable system.

In spite of the fact that Cohn stressed the high moral and ethical duty of keeping one's country out of war, he did not overlook the possibility of a war breaking out all the same. In that case it should be the aim of those countries, not at war, to bring the war to an end as soon as possible. A neutral council should assemble to decide on the means to be used. The idea was that the war should

---

[16] *Ibid.*, 281.
[17] «It does not recognize the two parties to the war as having equal rights, nor one as having greater rights than the other.» Cohn, *Neo-neutrality*, 282.
[18] *Ibid.*, 288.
[19] *Ibid.*, 185.

be localized within the smallest possible area and checked by economic sanctions. If this did not prove sufficient, (and here is Cohn's dilemma) military sanctions might be applied, «but with no obligation of the states to extend military sanctions.»[20] All the same, there would be an armed interference in a localized war, which could not help it from extending and expanding.

To get out of this Cohn said that no action might take place through a declaration of war, or by the individual states, as was prescribed by the League system. Instead, the neutral council should establish an international police force consisting of voluntary contingents from the neutral countries. This seems to indicate that neo-neutrality carried out to its logical consequence, would result in a system which exercised the same functions as the League and with principally the same means. Quincy Wright in commenting upon this theory has stated that:

> Neutrality is said to have demonstrated its value in history as a means of localizing war, discouraging war, keeping out of war, and regularizing international relations. It is difficult to prove that neutrality has served any of these purposes except the last. Far from discouraging war, neutrality... has tended to encourage aggression of the strong against the weak. Neutral rights have themselves provided the basis for disputes which have drawn nonparticipants into war.[21]

In spite of its apparent faults, this neo-neutral theory is interesting as an expression of changing attitudes towards neutrality. It must be seen as an effort to systematize and tie together the many loose ends of the period. The League, as well as the Kellogg Pact, was in existence, but neutrality was still a living principle. The Stimson Doctrine was the last innovation in the fight against aggression. The Argentine Anti-War Pact, and the cooperative and neo-neutral theories upon which it was based, tried to unite these tendencies and consolidate them into one system. It must be realized, however, that the basic idea behind these efforts did not originate from the Danish Treatise of 1924, as maintained by Cohn, but from the neutral attempts at cooperation during the First

---

[20] Cohn, *Neo-neutrality*, 287.

[21] Quincy Wright, «The Present Status of Neutrality,» in *American Journal of International Law*, 34 (1940) : 409.

World War. Cohn thought his principle of neo-neutrality was fundamentally new as its purpose was not to protect neutral rights but to prevent and restrict wars. He, therefore, maintained that it was widely different from the qualified neutrality,[22] and the collective cooperation of neutrals which had been advocated by Jessup. Cohn's reason for this distinction is that they both take traditional neutrality as their starting point, with stress on its economic aspects, while neo-neutrality does not.[23]

Neutral Cooperation Once More.

Philip C. Jessup, however, seems to make the same basic points, namely, that «the primary objective of a neutrality policy should be to keep out of war.»[24] In addition to that purpose, the aim should be to «frame a policy which will aid in preventing the outbreak of war or of limiting its scope and duration if it does occur.»[25]

Jessup made no secret of the fact that he thought the only way by which this aim could be reached was through neutral cooperation. To point out that purpose, he went back to the seventeenth and eighteenth centuries when the neutrals first united in defense of their rights. It was his conviction that these armed neutralities failed because of the «political jockeying» of the period which made neutrals and belligerents shift roles incessantly, and because «in no case was there a real solidarity of neutral interests.»[26]

From the study of these early centuries, Jessup thought he had found proofs that «where the neutrals have been able to rally sufficient naval or military power, they have succeeded in persuading the belligerents to come to terms.»[27] He then followed up the attempts at cooperation throughout the nineteenth century and finally pointed out the failure of the United States to cooperate

---

[22] Qualified neutrality is a rather vague term. It has been used largely to describe the position of a country who stays out of war and still favors one side.

[23] Cohn, *Neo-neutrality*, 323.

[24] Jessup, *Today and Tomorrow*, 156; Jessup, «The Birth, Death and Reincarnation of Neutrality,» in *American Journal of International Law*, 1922, 786.

[25] Jessup, *Today and Tomorrow*, 156.

[26] *Ibid.*, 161.

[27] *Ibid.*, 162.

with the other neutrals during the First World War. He went on to say, however, that since the United States had signed the Argentine Anti-War Treaty, he thought and hoped it would not make the same mistake again, but next time cooperate with the neutrals and check the belligerents, or perhaps even prevent the outbreak of war.

Jessup's idea of neutral cooperation was, for the most part, in line with the armed neutrality leagues of the eighteenth century, with the significant distinction that they should not use arms. In Jessup's opinion, the neutrals should prevent the belligerents from violating their rights by using their combined economic and financial power. By cutting off the sources of supplies, the neutrals would be able to shorten wars. However, such a policy had definite drawbacks because it would lead to enormous armaments in time of peace and would expose the small, rich neutrals to the danger of being swallowed up by great belligerents needing supplies.[28]

The main point in Jessup's theory was that for the neutrals, the question would be «profits or peace». For centuries controversies had arisen from the urge of the neutrals to expand their trade in time of war, while the belligerents wished to restrict it or use it for their own benefit. The neutrals, by insisting on their rights to make profits, would inevitably be drawn into the war or have their rights violated. The solution then seemed to be that in order to stay out of war the neutrals would have to sacrifice their profits. In the long run this system would pay because they would keep the peace. Without the neutral resources to aid the belligerents, the wars would be limited in time and space.[29]

Jessup has set forth a great many detailed illustrations in support of this theory, and although he realized that well founded objections might be raised and that his plan was likely to meet great practical obstacles, he still thought that the system could work even if the League system of sanctions should be applied. His proposal was not entirely in line with the view maintained at the Paris and London conferences in 1934 and 1935, as Jessup thought of a neutral cooperation even in case of effective League actions against an aggressor.

[28] Jessup, *Today and Tomorrow*, 182.
[29] *Ibid.*, 180—206.

Maurice Bourquin said in his final report at the closing of the London conference that the utilization of a neutrality system «would not, of course, take place except in the absence of a determination of the aggressor.»[30] He further stressed the necessity of relaxing the rigid system of 1907, to what neutrality had been in the earlier centuries, elastic, flexible, and with a full opportunity to discriminate between the belligerents.

The essential question is, would it still be neutrality? Quincy Wright said in 1936: «Probably the term neutrality in this connection should be abandoned, for the object is not impartiality, but keeping the country out of war.»[31] Thus, according to Wright the mere object of staying out of war at any price is not sufficient to entitle a state to use the term neutrality. This distinction is important for the status of nonbelligerency which will be discussed later.

Borchard did not think much of this «new neutrality», for it was his belief that «it makes confusion worse confounded».[32] Further, it is dangerous as it may lead peoples to think they can escape the consequences of hostility and participation. Borchard put his finger on the neo-neutral's sorest spot when he stated that «economic neutrality is a paradox». Like Wright, he did not think that this new interpretation deserved the name of neutrality.[33]

Fenwick points out that neither in the Argentine Anti-War Pact nor in the Buenos Ayres Conference of 1936, was there a suggestion of a common attitude of neutrality as a means of practicing the American Republics as a body against the effects of war in other parts of the world. He implies that in spite of much talking, little had been done in order to meet an actual threat of war.[34]

Thus, there is no unanimity as to the benefits of this kind of neutrality. There is definitely something appealing to common sense in the assertion that if the neutrals should hope to have the least chance of remaining neutral, they must reach the full extent

---

[30] Bourquin, «Final Report,» in *Collective Security Conferences*, 455.
[31] Wright in *Polity*, (February, 1936), 8. Quoted by Borchard, 256.
[32] Borchard, *Neutrality*, 286.
[33] *Ibid.*, 258.
[34] Fenwick, «The Inter-American Neutrality Committee,» in *American Journal of International Law*, 35 (October, 1941), 12—40.

of active cooperation. That was the lesson from the First World War.

On the other hand, the fact that the neutrals thought arms could be replaced by economic sanctions sounds unrealistic in twentieth century politics and has probably caused many cooperationists to take a skeptical attitude. It should also be emphasized that these theories never continued beyond the treaty stage and no serious endeavor was made to apply them in practical politics.[35]

[35] For a concise discussion of the different theories see Llewellyn Pfankuchen, *A. Documentary Textbook in International Law*, (New York, 1940), 854—857.

4. Neutrality without Rights

The American neutrality policy of the middle thirties goes along with neo-neutrality and the attempts to form cooperative neutral leagues. The American aim was no longer neutrality in the traditional and accepted sense of the term, even if the basic idea was the same. The Americans wanted to stay out of war and were willing to do almost anything to that end.

While the European and Latin American attempts at revising neutrality never reached beyond wishful talking on the theoretical stage, the Americans turned once more to the founding fathers and found the solution in municipal legislation. There seems to have been a general agreement throughout the United States that wars must be avoided. How this should be done became a central issue in American foreign policy all through the 1930's. There was a number of different fractions who all had their own ideas as to how the United States might be able to keep the peace during a general war.

The League had been a dead issue ever since the twenties,[1] but there was still a solid group of interventionists who thought that the best way to stay out of war would be to prevent it, and, therefore, join the League in its efforts to check aggression. There were two kinds of so-called co-operationists; one group believed in sanctions, while the other was opposed to any direct or indirect coercion.[2] Opposed to these were two fractions of isolationists. There was also a group of people who persistently believed in the strict neutrality of the pre-1914 model.

Of all these the ones who wanted to sacrifice neutral rights in order to stay out of war were the most influential.[3] Their argu-

---

[1] Charles A. Beard, *American Foreign Policy in the Making, 1932—1940* (New Haven, 1946).
[2] Fenwick, *American Neutrality*, 32.
[3] *Ibid.*, 32.

ments seemed logical and their reasons for giving up the rights were clear enough. They stated that twenty years earlier the United States had tried to follow a neutral course during a major conflict, but in spite of good intentions to stay out of war, it had nevertheless ended up as a belligerent with the losses and damages which would inevitably follow. They believed that during these three years, from 1914 to 1917, decisions must have been made, steps taken, in short, something must have happened which eventually led to direct participation.

In order not to make the same mistake over again, the logical thing to do was to analyse the 1914—1917 period and thus bring forth the reasons why the war entry at last became inevitable. Such an investigation brought out the crucial issues connected with the maritime commerce during the First World War, but a glance further back in American history seemed to indicate that in previous cases when the United States had been drawn into foreign wars, the reason had been its insistence on neutral rights and the freedom of the seas. Following this line of thought, the country ought to be able to stay out of wars if it gave up neutral rights and did not repeat the technical errors made by the Wilson administration. By keeping their money, goods, ships, and citizens out of dangerous contact with the belligerents, they thought no incident would occur which might draw them into the war. It was believed that this could be effected by municipal legislation.

However, since the insistence on rights had been perhaps the oldest and most essential item of traditional neutrality, abandonment of neutral rights would be of the greatest significance for the whole future concept of neutrality. Even though this idea was, in fact, a break with the traditional conception, it was, nevertheless, in accordance with the American concert of neutrality. It was, in principle, the same remedy which had once been used sucessfully by Washington and his successors. At the end of the eighteenth century, the United States had been in a similar situation. They wanted to isolate themselves, to mind their own business, and stay out of other people's quarrels. They realized that the more contact with the belligerents, the greater were the chances for involvement, so they voluntarily laid restrictions on their own citizens and decreased the war risks by enacting municipal legislation. They did not give up any rights, though by enacting the laws of 1794 and 1818, they imposed upon themselves duties and sacrifices which no other country required of them, but which they themselves thought necessary to keep their country out of war.

The neutrality policy of the late thirties seems to have followed the same basic trend, but it went much further. While the United States had previously limited itself to keeping belligerent activities out of its own territory, it now in addition forbad its own citizens to enter the belligerent zones and spheres. The 1930 politicians seem to have aimed at an isolation which was much more effective than the one attempted by the founding fathers.

It is hard to see how the United States could have hoped for good results by such a policy. Jefferson's embargo had proved a failure 130 years earlier in an almost rural world as compared to the interrelation of the 1930's. Still embargoes were attempted. True, these embargoes were not general, but were limited to the strictest contraband, arms, and war implements, but the developments 1914—1918 had shown that sooner or later everything was likely to be classified as contraband. The Italo—Ethiopian conflict in the fall of 1935 disclosed the need for extensive embargoes and the flexibility of the definition of war implements.

It is well worth noting that the opposition and the discussion that arose around these legislative efforts in the thirties, was not so much concerned with the embargoes themselves as whether they should be applied impartially to both belligerents, regardless of who was at war; or whether the President should be authorized to impose export prohibitions when and against whom he thought fit. This question became the main issue in the making of American foreign policy during this period. All parties seemed to agree that the United States should stay out of the wars that apparently were brewing in Europe. The great controversial question was how this could be done. Was it possible to prevent wars from breaking out by helping the League to check the aggressor, or should all efforts be concentrated on keeping America out of war regardless of what might happen to the rest of the world?

The beginning was made in 1933 when Senator Borah introduced a resolution on an embargo on arms. According to this resolution, the President could, when he found that a conflict between nations was about to develop, proclaim an arms embargo. It is important to note that this embargo was not to be applied equally to all nations, but only to such country or countries as the President might designate.[4]

Such partiality was obviously incompatible with a neutral status according to the accepted rules, and after the bill was passed it was severely criticized as being dangerous to the peace of the country. To meet this criticism, the State Department sent a memorandum to the House Committee on Foreign Affairs. This official statement of the United States Government, which was an emphatic denial that the resolution would mean any danger of involvement, gives a strong impression of the decline of traditional neutrality. It stated that «the developments of the past few years show that there is little or no practical danger involved and that the discussion is based upon almost medieval conditions which modern experience and realities have almost wholly replaced.» Further, it maintained that «much of the old conception of neutrality as a possibility is gone in the modern world, if great nations are involved in war ... war today involves blockade and the commerce of the neutral is as much under fire as are the participants.» It was also doubted whether a neutral was obligated to sell arms to a belligerent. To back up the statement, the State Department quoted such great international lawyers as Hyde and Oppenheim, and went on to say, «There is a general feeling among writers on international law that the rule of impartiality in supplying arms, if it ever was generally accepted, is subject to criticism.»[5]

This statement was made by the Hoover Administration, but the President-Elect, Franklin D. Roosevelt, also made statements in this connection that show his affiliation to these ideas. He is reported to have said on January 11, 1933, «I have long been in favor of the use of embargoes on arms, especially to nations which are guilty of making an attack on other natiōns ... that is, aggressor nations.»[6] When Roosevelt took over the administration, the Borah resolution was reintroduced, but by this time its unneutral implications had been widely exposed and propagandized and the resolution was accepted only after Senator Johnson's amendment had been applied to it. This provided that «any prohibition of export,

[4] Borchard, *Neutrality*, 305.
[5] *Ibid.*, 305—307.
[6] *Ibid.*, 308.

or of sale for export, proclaimed under this resolution shall apply impartially to all the parties to the dispute or conflict to which it refers.»

Thus impartiality, the most conspicuous part of the old neutrality, was reintroduced, and shortly afterwards it was applied to an actual situation as the United States proclaimed an impartial embargo on shipments to Paraguay and Bolivia in the Gran Chaco War in 1934.

The same year the so-called Nye Committee was appointed to make an investigation of the munitions industry. The committee brought out facts to prove that great fortunes had been made on the sale of ammunitions during the First World War, which indeed had been a profitable affair for a great many people. The findings of this committee received extensive publicity and became a new incentive to the growing demand for legislation that would keep the United States out of war. The developments in Europe also gave ample reasons for fear of new conflicts in the near future. Consequently, the Neutrality Act of 1935 was passed on August 31, and remained in force for six months.

This joint resolution provided for:

> the prohibition of the export of arms, ammunition, and implements of war, to belligerent countries; the prohibition of the transportation of arms, ammunition and implements of war by vessels of the United States for the use of belligerent states; for the registration and licensing of persons engaged in the business of manufacturing, exporting and/or exporting arms, ammunition or implements of war; and restricting travel by American citizens on belligerent ships during war.[7]

The embargo was mandatory but the President was not without influence as a great many of the most important prohibitions were dependent upon his proclamation. The President could, by proclamation, enumerate and extend the articles embargoed, prohibit American ships to carry arms, and citizens to take passage. He could also prohibit submarines from entering United States' ports or territorial waters, or have these used as bases for belligerent ships.

[7] Wright, *Neutrality and Collective Security* (Chicago, 1936), Appendix. For the full text see *Ibid.*, 240—246 or *Public Resolution, No. 67, 74th Congress.*

Still there is reason to believe that President Roosevelt found this act much too inflexible and would have liked provisions that made it possible for him to discriminate more markedly between the belligerents. In giving his approval to the 1935 Act, he said that he had approved it because it was

> intended as an expression of the fixed desire of the government and the people of the United States to avoid any action which might involve us in war. ... It is the policy of this government to avoid being drawn into wars between other nations, but it is a fact that no Congress and no executive can foresee all possible future situations. History is filled with unforeseeable situations that call for some flexibility of action. It is conceivable that situations may arise in which the wholly inflexible provisions of Section I of this act might have the opposite effect from which it was intended. In other words, the inflexible provisions might drag us into war instead of keeping us out.[8]

There is no mention of the fact that discrimination would mean unneutrality, and that was just what the act intended to avoid.[9] This seems to indicate that the ideals of traditional neutrality were in no great favor with the Roosevelt Administration. In his approval speech the President went on to say, «at the same time (as avoiding entanglements), it is the policy of the government by every peaceful means and without entanglement to cooperate with other similarly minded governments to promote peace.»[10]

This act was applied shortly afterwards when the Italo-Ethiopian War broke out, and on October 5, 1935, the President proclaimed an embargo on all of the most essential arms, including aircraft and war vessels. The same day he made a proclamation whereby he gave notice to all American citizens that they might travel on belligerent vessels only at their own risk.[11] In a statement to the press he said, «In these specific circumstances I desire it to be understood that any of our people who voluntarily engage in transactions of any character with any of the belligerents do so at their own risk.»[12]

[8] Department of State, *Press Releases*, XIII, August 31, 1935, 162.
[9] Borchard, *Neutrality*, 316.
[10] *Press Releases*, XIII, 162.
[11] *Press Releases*, XIII, 256.
[12] *Ibid.*, 256.

It is hardly necessary to point out that even if these measures were applied equally to both belligerents, in this case it hurt one more than the other, as the trade between the United States and Ethiopia was negligible. The embargo measures would, therefore, be primarily directed against Italy, the aggressor.

The two months following these proclamations constitute a very interesting phase in the history of neutrality. Through all of the previous centuries, the neutrals had continually fought with varying success to limit and reduce the contraband lists as much as possible. In the past their aim had been to have them include actual war implements and nothing else. None of this happened in the thirties. Instead, the administration of the United States tried persistently to extend the embargoes and get more and more articles included among the prohibited commodities. Few things show more clearly how far the American policy had wandered from the traditional neutrality.

As the act covered only actual war implements, no other prohibitions could be proclaimed, but from early October, Secretary of State, Cornell Hull, tried to discourage American businessmen from trading with Italy in articles that were essential for the war, even if they were not included in the embargo. On October 30, the President issued a warning against transactions of any character with either of the belligerents.[13] In an address by the Secretary of State on Nov. 6, he said he would like an embargo that went beyond just arms, ammunition, and implements of war. In this connection he stated that:

> Our foreign policy would indeed be a weak one if it began and ended with the announcement of a neutral position on the outbreak of a foreign war.[14]
>
> I conceive it to be our duty and in the interest of our country and humanity, not only to remain aloof from disputes and conflicts with which we have no direct concern, but also to use our influence in any appropriate way to bring about the peaceful settlement of international differences.[14]

On November 15, he reminded the American people of the statements made by the President and himself, proving it contrary to the interest of the United States to encourage trade with the

---

[13] *Press Releases*, XIII, 338.
[14] *Ibid.*, 367.

belligerents: «The American people are entitled to know that there are certain commodities such as oil, copper, trucks, tractors, scrap iron and scrap steel which are essentially war materials.» He further announced that trade in these articles would be: «contrary to the policy of this government as announced in official statements of the President and the Secretary of State, as it is also contrary to the general spirit of the recent Neutrality Act.»[15]

These actions were obviously taken with a view to the sanctions that the League was expected to apply against the aggressor. Soon after the outbreak of the war Italy had been unanimously declared to be the aggressor state, but sanctions were slow in coming into effect. There had been fear among the League members that sanctions would be made useless by the United States not being in the League, but on the contrary, the position taken by the Administration was very cooperative. In fact, its actions went even further than those taken by most of the League members.[16] A. Dulles says that nothing that the Americans did in the fall of 1935 was of such nature that it should hold the European powers back from acting as vigorously as they wanted to restrict the aggressor and maintain peace.[17] However, as sanctions were applied on a very limited scale by the European powers, the U.S. government, after a while, withdrew its demands on the American exporters.

As the 1935 act was to expire by the end of February, 1936, both conservative and radical groups began preparing for changes. Some pro-League peace associations worked out a redraft of the Neutrality Act, the main purpose of which was to facilitate cooperation with the League by giving the President greater discriminatory power. This was obviously what the administration wanted, and the bill which Senator Pittman introduced in January, 1936, gave to the President the discretionary power to embargo commodities other than arms and war implements. He would, in fact, be granted complete control over the American foreign trade during a war.[18] This caused such great opposition that the bill was not passed, but instead, the 1935 act was reenacted with some very

---

[15] Ibid., 382.
[16] Borchard, Neutrality, 321.
[17] Allen W. Dulles and Hamilton Fish Armstrong, Can We Be Neutral (New York, 1936), 74. For comparison, read Charles A. Beard, American Foreign Policy in the Making, 156—170.
[18] Beard, American Foreign Policy in the Making, 325.

significant changes. The Neutrality Resolution of February 29, 1936,[19] substituted for the words «that upon the outbreak, or during the progress of war» in the 1935 act,[20] the words, «whenever the President shall find that there exists a state of war.» The embargoes of the act would, therefore, be dependent upon the President's finding that a state of war existed.

Furthermore, two new sections[21] were added. The first provided for a prohibition on loans to foreign belligerents, which was a far-reaching innovation in the history of neutrality. The second stated that: «This act shall not apply to an American republic or republics engaged in war against a non-American state or states, provided the American republic is not cooperating with a non-American state or states in such a war.»[22]

This last section showed perhaps better than anything else the confused state of the 1930 neutrality. By excluding all American states from the provisions of the act, only the non-American states would be affected by the embargoes, which were to safeguard the United States neutrality. Under such circumstances, it would be extremely hard to maintain the illusion of impartiality.

The new Neutrality Act was to remain in force until May, 1937, but as it did not include civil wars, the Spanish Civil War required special measures to meet this new situation. The steps taken are particularly interesting since they signify a break not only with traditional neutrality but with the traditional American policy as well. The position of the United States on civil wars had so far been either to do nothing at all, or to support the recognized government by embargoing arms to the rebels only.[23] In the case of the Spanish Civil War, however, exports of arms to both the rebels and the recognized government were embargoed. It was meant as an attempt to treat both belligerents impartially, but as the nationalists were not recognized as belligerents, it was not traditional neutrality because this would require diplomatic recognition of both sides.[24]

---

[19] *Public Resolution*, No. 67, 74th Congress.
[20] For the text of the 1935 act see p. 161.
[21] 1-a and 1-b.
[22] *Treaty Information Bulletin*, No. 78, March, 1936, 7—8.
[23] See Bailey, *Diplomatic History* for the pre-World War I period.
[24] Llewellyn Pfankuchen, *A Documentary Textbook in International Law* 976—977.

The Joint Resolution of January 8, 1937, (also called the Pittman Resolution) which prohibited all exports of arms and war implements to Spain, was, therefore, a clear expression of the new conception of neutrality in the thirties. It was neutral primarily in the respect that it aimed at avoiding American involvement in war. It may also have had a wider scope, and can be interpreted as international cooperation in the sense that the United States thereby supported France and England in their non-intervention policy. By not interfering, the civil war might have been isolated, thus realizing the ideals of neo-neutrality,[25] If ever such policy was intended, it was made impossible by the effective intervention by Germany, Italy, and Russia.[26]

As the fear of a general war increased steadily during the late thirties, there seemed to be a need for more definite action to keep America out of the wars that seemed about to come. The previous neutrality legislation had been more or less temporary, and when the Act of 1936 expired, May 1, 1937, a new Neutrality Act was passed which was intended to lay down a permanent neutrality policy for the United States. It contained basically the same provisions as the two previous laws. The principle of impartiality was maintained, and the embargoes were to be applied to both belligerents, but the act was still inapplicable in cases where American republics were involved. Some of the provisions were mandatory while others required the proclamation of the President.

Among the most important mandatory provisions were the prohibitions on exports of arms and implements of war to any belligerent, when the President had found that war existed. American vessels were not allowed to carry such goods to any belligerent, directly or indirectly, (continuous voyage). Foreign loans were prohibited, except for short time obligations of a very normal character which the President might give in special cases. Appropriations for relief and humanitarian purposes were exempted from the money embargo. There was also a provision which permitted embargoes on articles and materials that could not be included in the arms and implements of war provisions. This clause, however,

[25] Pfankuchen, *A Documentary Textbook in International Law*, 976—977. See also Borchard, *Neutrality*, 335—337.
[26] *Press Releases*, April 1, 1939, 245—247. In April, 1939; the Franco Regime was recognized by the United States and the embargo was lifted.

was to expire May 1, 1939, as was the «cash and carry» clause, which permitted the President to prohibit American vessels from carrying articles other than arms and ammunition, and required sellers to transfer the rights and titles to the buyers before the goods could be shipped to a belligerent nation.[27] As in the earlier act, American citizens were forbidden to travel on belligerent ships, except in special cases. American ships were not allowed to carry arms and war implements, and they could not be armed. In addition to these inflexible prohibitions, the President might, if he saw fit, apply the embargo to civil wars, forbid submarines and armed vessels to enter American ports and territorial waters, and forbid the belligerents to use American ports as supply bases.[28]

A few months after this Neutrality Act had been enacted, the Sino-Japanese War broke out, July, 1937. No declaration of war, however, was issued by either side and the President chose not to declare that a state of war existed. The new act was, therefore, not applied and there was no declaration of traditional neutrality. The President stated officially that the American export trade with China and Japan had to be done at the traders' own risk,[29] but no general embargo was imposed.

The administration showed a partial attitude toward China, however, by indirectly facilitating loans for her, and in July, 1938, Secretary of State, Hull, warned airplane manufacturers against exporting bombs and aircraft to armed forces that used their airplanes for attack upon civilian populations. This warning proved very effective.[30]

Towards Non-belligerency.

The neutrality legislation of 1935—1937 became the major issue in American foreign policy during this period. It is important to stress that there was a general agreement as to the final end, to keep the United States out of war. The disagreement began when

[27] Fenwick, *American Neutrality*, 40.
[28] Pfankuchen, *A Documentary Textbook in International Law*, 978—979. For the full text see Public Resolution, No. 27, 75th Congress in *International Conciliation*, Doc. 1937, 610—621.
[29] *Press Releases*, September 18, 1937, 227.
[30] Pfankuchen, *A Documentary Textbook*, 980—981.

discussion over means was commenced. Even if there were diverging views on this point, there were very few who contended that the old traditional neutrality still provided the best solution.

An editor of *The New Republic* came to the conclusion that: «Neutrality is impossible if we follow the old line of trading with the belligerents and trying to maintain the freedom of the seas. Neutrality is possible only if we embargo virtually all trade with both parties.»[31]

Charles Warren, one of the great men in the field of American foreign policy, was among those who maintained that the United States could not rely on «neutrality alone.»[32] If it wanted to keep out of a war between great powers it would have to do more than remain technically neutral. He very logically pointed to the fact that since 1917 nothing was changed which might improve the conditions of a neutral, and that the same violations of rights were almost bound to happen again. «The belligerents' disregard of rights growing out of neutrality is very likely to drive the neutral straight into war.»[33] He thought that by placing all exports on a quota basis the United States would have means to restrain the belligerents. If they put a new article on their contraband lists, the United States would put the same article on a quota basis, that is, reduce the export of it to the normal peacetime figure.[34] He did not, however, seem to have any realistic view on the strength of the national economic forces, and talked very lightly about cutting down the excessive profits of war.

On the other hand, Jessup was of the opinion that neutrality is important chiefly within the economic field.[35] This view was shared by a great many of the American international lawyers, and the provisions of the acts gave the same impression. Jessup said that the Neutrality Act of 1935 was «in fact an abandonment of neutral rights and the price paid not to get involved in a new war.» The question was «profits or peace.»[36]

---

[31] *The New Republic*, November 27, 1935, 60.
[32] C. Warren, «Troubles of a Neutral,» in *Foreign Affairs*, 12 : 377 (March, 1935).
[33] Warren, «Troubles of a Neutral», 378.
[34] Warren, «Contraband and Neutral Trade,» in *Academy of Political Science Proceedings*, 16 : 189—194 (January, 1935).
[35] *Cohn*, 345.
[36] Jessup, *Today and Tomorrow*, 127—132.

Quite a few realized the significance of giving up neutral rights. This meant a sharp break with the past, both from traditional neutrality in general and from American neutrality in particular. As James Shotwell put it: «The neutrality law of 1935 is not the traditional neutrality of American history, but almost the exact opposite. ... the trend which is now dominant is toward isolation, as the earlier trend has been toward our insistence on our rights.» [37]

Allen W. Dulles took the same view and thought that the United States could not keep out of war and at the same time enforce freedom of the seas. The choice was between great profits with grave risks of war, or smaller profits with less risks.[38] Dulles thought that the United States should no longer insist on the alleged neutral rights of trade, but he did not agree with the government in exerting moral pressure on traders to keep them from exporting to certain belligerents. That, he said, should be subject to legislation.[39]

Borchard criticized the neutrality acts very severely, and showed point for point that they did not have the necessary elements of genuine neutrality.[40] He repudiated the theory that the war of 1917 was brought about by the American insistence on neutral rights, and he did not think that the Wilson Administration was very seriously concerned about neutrality at all.[41] On the contrary, the United States, he said, had surrendered neutral rights as early as 1915 and still got into the war.[42] Thus, the abolishment of neutral rights would not provide a guarantee to remain out of war. He thought the United States would be better off without making a new neutrality of its own, which actually was unneutrality. He did not go along with the House Foreign Affairs Committee that preferred «to regard its measures as a plan to keep the country out of war rather than an attempt to maintain strict neutrality.» [43]

Salvatore A. Catillo wrote in 1935 that «every line of the new proposed neutrality act breathes with the spirit of unneutrality» and that it actually meant the abandonment of the traditional «freedom of the seas» doctrine.[44]

[37] James T. Shotwell in *International Conciliation*, Jan. 1936, 5—6.
[38] Dulles and Armstrong, *Can We Stay Neutral*, 105.
[39] *Ibid.*, 109.
[40] Borchard, *Neutrality*, 304—343.
[41] *Ibid.*, 346.
[42] By yielding to the Allies.

This last point has been stressed by many writers. Americans have always pointed with pride at their century long struggle for that principle, and no wonder it must have been hard to give it up completely. On the other hand, there was no use in denying that in spite of traditions and old usage, conditions had changed. The principle was not quite the same before as after the First World War. Warren has drawn attention to the fact that freedom of the seas meant trade in goods that were not contraband. The neutrals did not advocate their right to trade in articles that were not on the free lists. Warren concludes by saying that «as everything became contraband, freedom of the seas as an American principle has no application whatsoever.»[45]

B. M. Baruch wrote in 1936 that there were no laws of civilized warfare, and to make a distinction between absolute and conditional contraband was artificial and apart from realism. He argued that the United States was «off on the wrong foot on this confused idea of neutrality». The neutrality legislation was impracticable and would not keep the country out of war. Speaking about the First World War he said:

> The lesson there is that when great nations are in an economic death struggle, they will respect no asserted rights of neutrals on the high seas which in any way threaten the victory of their arms, or which cannot be asserted and adequately defended by the neutral. ... The United States can still put its neutrality policy on the doctrine of the freedom of the seas, but unless we are going to fight for it, it will not be respected and if we say we are going to fight for it we can be a hundred percent certain... it will get us into war.[46]

His conclusion was that the neutrals had no rights at all on the oceans.

This surrender of the seas to the belligerents has often been characterized as one of the most unneutral features of this legislation and a definite break with impartiality. Then if the neutrals stayed away from the seas it would mean indirect support to the

---

[43] *Ibid.*, 341—342.
[44] Salvatore A. Catillo in *New York Herald Tribune*, December 30, 1935, (quoted in *The Reference Shelf*, 10, No. 7, 248).
[45] Warren, «Safeguards to Neutrality,» in *Foreign Affairs*, 14 : 301.
[46] B. M. Baruch, «Neutrality,» in *Current History*, 44 : 43 (June, 1936).

predominant naval power, and it would work to the disadvantage of the opposing continental state who had based its system on sea transportation by foreign (neutral) carriers. So with everything declared contraband, the neutral, impartial position had become almost impossible. The ex-Secretary of State, Henry L. Stimson, has expressed this dilemma very clearly. He said that:

> When the average man speaks of neutrality he often confuses it with impartiality. It may mean just the opposite. If the war involves a great sea power which controls the sea... it may mean that by remaining neutral we are in effect taking sides with that power against its opponents who do not control the sea. ... So when we say that the great mass of our people wish to remain neutral, speaking with exactness we do not mean that at all. We only mean that they wish to keep out of war — which is a very different thing.[47]

Stimson seems here to have touched the core of the so-called neutrality legislation of the late thirties. As so many have pointed out, the aim was not neutrality, but avoidance of war. The impartiality was gone, the passivity limited to certain areas, the neutral rights were given up, the doctrine of the freedom of the seas was abandoned. Actually, so little was left of the old conception of neutrality that it hardly deserved the name any longer. Instead, many former neutrals had entered into the stage of confusion, panic, and fear, which might more appropriately be called *non-belligerency*. This status has one basic, simplified rule: stay out of the shooting war, regardless of how this may be done, as long as the vital interests of the country are not seriously endangered.

---

[47] Henry L. Stimson, *American Society of International Law Proceedings*, 1935, 121.

5. Small States search for Security

The Italo—Ethiopian War had given the United States a realistic impression of the immediate danger of a general European war and of the risk of involvement, but the Americans were not the only ones to learn from this experience. The world had been adrift for fifteen years as far as international relations were concerned. The League had raised hopes and disappointments, as had the Kellogg Pact and the disarmament conferences. All of these institutions had been attacked and defended, but up to the middle thirties only with words and theories. Nothing had been proved in either direction. The League might be able to handle aggressors' attempts to disturb the peace; the Kellogg Pact might check international law-breakers; and some day the world might reduce its armaments. Of course, people with realistic minds were skeptical about national security and could already point out numerous defects and faults in the system and prove in theory its unstable and incomplete construction. Yet there was also room for hope, and the faithful believers in the League organization were still justified in dreaming of collective security as being a reality.

The Italo—Ethiopian conflict was the great eye-opener for all who had put their faith in the efficiency of the sanctions system. There was a common realization that the League could not, after all, provide a basis for security.[1] Great and small, combined or single, realized that they had to look for other means to protect themselves against future dangers. The pattern became the old and familiar one. Greater states turned once again to the alliance system, while small and weak ones, like the Scandinavians started digging up the decaying remnants of traditional neutrality.

This political practice had been applied by the northern states

---

[1] A German comment was: «Der Schleier, der die Schönheitsfehler der Genfer Dame verdeckt hatte, zerriss.» Otto Schempp, *Der Neutrale Westen* (Leipzig, 1939), 6.

for more than a hundred years and it had admittedly served them well. The return to the old theory was therefore understandable, and could hardly have surprised any intelligent observer. The Scandinavian states had been among the sturdiest supporters of the League idea, but from the beginning they had been skeptical as to its effectiveness. There had always been a deep realization of the danger this might mean to their sovereign rights of freedom of action, and they were always on guard against being drawn into actions beyond their control which might endanger their independence and even their national existence. Therefore, they in 1920 attempted to amend Article 16 of the Covenant. According to this proposed amendment they would have been exempted from some of the strictest measures against the covenant-breaking state.[2] Shepherd S. Jones, in a special study of the Scandinavian states in relation to the League, said that: «The policy of the three Scandinavian states was founded upon the assumption that in view of their geographical and political positions, the advantages offered by a system of military and economic sanctions were outweighed by the risks involved for them as producers of security.»[3]

Consequently, they were severely criticized in the League Assembly for their selfish attitude and for not recognizing the obligation on the part of every state to contribute to the general peace. The Swedish delegate, Östen Undén,[4] answered that the Scandinavian states were as much animated by a sense of duty as any other state, but states could hardly be expected to make contributions to the security of other nations if to do so would imperil their own safety.[5]

Security through Alliances.

In the early twenties, some proposals were made by members of the Council to try to achieve security by military alliances. The Scandinavian states were, from the beginning, very much opposed to this. They advocated over and over again that such alliances

---

[2] See page 189, League of Nations, *Official Journal*, I, 6, 357.

[3] Shepherd S. Jones, *The Scandinavian States and the League of Nations* (New York, 1939), 217.

[4] Östen B. Undén has been Foreign Minister of Sweden since 1945.

[5] *Ibid.*, 227.

never had prevented wars and that «the contemplated defensive alliances might contain the germs of fresh conflicts of interest.» In the summer of 1923, the Council requested the opinions of the various governments on this issue. The Danish Government answered that military assistance could not be given on the ground that impartial neutrality was essential to the very existence and independence of Denmark. The note ran as follows:

> If her entry into the League and acceptance of the obligations of the covenant were not entirely in accord with the traditionally accepted meaning of neutrality, it was because she originally supposed that the League of Nations would very shortly include all the countries in the world, or at any rate all the countries of any considerable political or military importance.[6]

Denmark, moreover, never had accepted, nor would she accept, any obligation to employ military sanctions.[7]

The Swedish answer to the request of the Council was that individual governments should retain the right to determine whether military sanctions would be employed in cases contemplated in Article 16. The Swedes wrapped their opinion up in somewhat softer terms, but the point was essentially the same as in the Danish reply. As the League was not universal, the Swedes were not willing to undertake «international obligations possibly involving Sweden in warlike operations, which might appear to the nation to be in no way connected with the vital interests and independence of the country.»[8]

The Norwegian reply was a suggestion that to obtain guarantees of assistance a state must have lived up to its obligations of reducing armaments, furnishing exact information about its measures, and also must have accepted the principle of compulsory arbitration. This last point was strongly stressed by the Norwegian delegate, Dr. Chr. Lange, in various speeches and proposals.[9]

The invasion of the Ruhr (January, 1923) was in Scandinavia taken as proof of the inadvisability of making military commit-

---

[6] *League of Nations, Doc. A. 35*, 1923, IX, Part I (Geneva, 1923), 29.
[7] Jones, *The Scandinavian States and the League of Nations*, 227.
[8] *League of Nations, Doc. A. 35*, 1923, IX, Part I, 47.
[9] Jones, *The Scandinavian States and the League of Nations*, 230.

ments to defend treaty law, meaning thereby that justice as well as peace might be defeated. The Scandinavian notion was that there had to be a complete transformation of armies and navies into police forces. This was deemed necessary if there was ever to be a guarantee by the League or respect for treaties. However, the Scandinavian delegates, without modifying their stand on military cooperation, declared that they fully intended to cooperate loyally with other nations in applying economic and financial pressure.[10]

In discussions about the Geneva Protocol the same question was touched upon. The Scandinavian countries might have partially accepted the Protocol if the British had not rejected it, but they were not likely to ratify the sanctions provisions without the definite reservation that they would not be obligated to apply military assistance without their own consent.[11] [12]

Thus the Scandinavian countries were constantly on their guard against any suggestion to extend the sanctions system, and such attempts were sure to be met with reservation on their part. This attitude was evident in 1926 when the Finnish Government proposed a more extensive organization for financial help to a victim of aggression.[13] The three Scandinavian countries were not in favor of automatic or immediate help when a war threatened, but would make it dependent upon the Council's decision that such actions was necessary for the preservation of peace.

This point of view was brought into the discussions circling around the harmonizing of the Covenant with the Kellogg Pact.[14] Dr. A. Raestad, the Norwegian delegate, was strongly opposed to any extension of sanctions in that matter. He admitted that the question was very important, but maintained that it should be dealt with independently and not brought into discussions concerning the Covenant and the Pact.[15] In 1930, the Swedish authorities expressed the same view.[16] The Swedish Government found that instead of stressing the importance of the sanctions, the best way of rendering the system of security more effective would be to

---

[10] Jones, *The Scandinavian States and the League of Nations*, 233.
[11] See comment by Halvdan Koht, «Neutrality and Peace, the View of a Small Power,» in *Foreign Affairs*, Vol. 15, 1937, 283.
[12] Jones, *The Scandinavian States and the League of Nations*, 235.
[13] Se page 129.
[14] See page 142 ff.
[15] Jones, *The Scandinavian States and the League of Nations*, 239—241.

strengthen the preventive means which the League could use in time of crisis. Undén thought that the mere threat of sanctions would not be sufficient to prevent war if the governments and peoples of the quarreling states were not convinced «that sanctions would really be applied with the necessary efficacy.»[17] This view was also supported by the Norwegian Government. The Scandinavian states regarded the League as «an instrument for the prevention of war, rather than a criminal court for inflicting punishment on lawbreaking states.»[18]

This indicates that the Scandinavian states had limited aims in their cooperation in the League. It is, therefore interesting to examine their position during the Italo—Ethiopian conflict. When this war started the Scandinavian states were among those who most persistently urged the fulfillment of the obligations of the Covenant. At the Oslo Conference in August, 1935, they issued a communiqué in which they declared their «will to support every effort to guard the peace and maintain the legal principles of the League.»[19] There seems to have been a clear understanding of the implications of such a support. They realized fully that their status of traditional neutrality, to which they so often had referred, had to give way to their obligations to the Covenant. Undén publicly pointed out that Sweden's entrance into the League in 1920 had meant a decisive turning point in her policy of neutrality. He made the statement that «peace-loving people insisted now, not on neutrality in the sense of impartial passivity, but on the prevention of war or the stopping of hostilities by common effort.»[20]

In October, 1935, the three Scandinavian governments, without hesitation, accepted the proposals for applications of sanctions which the Coordination Committee had set up. These proposals included, among other provisions, embargoes on arms and war implements, financial measures and import prohibitions on Italian goods.[21] These governmental actions won the full support of the major political parties in the three countries.

---

[16] League of Nations, *Official Journal*, XI, 58, C, 101.
[17] *League of Nations*, Doc. 11 A. IC., 60.
[18] *Ibid.*, 41. Jones, *The Scandinavian States*, 243.
[19] *Ibid.*, 259.
[20] O. B. Undén, Speech at Uppsala, August, 1935; Jones, *The Scandinavian States and the League of Nations*, 260.
[21] League of Nations, *Official Journal*, Special Supplement, No. 147, 12—17

The Repudiation of Article 16.

As mentioned already, the failure of the League to take wholehearted and efficient action in the Italo—Ethiopian conflict caused great disillusionment in the Scandinavian countries and brought about a complete change in their attitude to the sanctions system. They had doubted its applicability before, as a means of punishment, but until 1935, they had believed in the League. They had repeatedly stressed their confidence in international cooperation as a means to achieve collective security by preventing the outbreak of war. There is reason to believe that they still put faith in that principle, but they now realized that theory and practice were two widely different things. The triumph of Mussolini and the humiliation of the League powers, together with Germany's nullification of the Locarno treaties, convinced the Scandinavian states that the League would not be able to guarantee them the security they wanted. On the contrary, it might involve them in conflicts which might threaten their existence as states. With so many powerful states outside the League, there was danger of a conflict between the Scandinavian states and the great states within the League. The latter might, in this case, use Article 16 as a means to force the small states into a war on their side. The small powers had entered the League of Nations hoping for general security in a universal League, but the League was not universal and was not likely to become so, and in a conflict, the system might work to the disadvantage of the small states. Thus they wanted recognition of the fact that they no longer considered themselves bound by the obligations of Article 16.

On July 1, 1936, the foreign ministers of seven of the small, «traditionally neutral» states, Denmark, Finland, Holland, Norway, Spain, Sweden, and Switzerland, signed a joint declaration which in fact meant a significant change in their foreign policy. This resolution declared that the parties had «exchanged views on the effects of current events on the organization and working of the League of Nations.» They had agreed on a good many points, one of which was that the recent developments and the increasing tendency to resort to force had «given rise in our countries to some doubt whether the conditions in which they undertook the obligations contained in the Covenant still exist to any satisfactory extent.»[22] The signatories of this declaration «did not think it right that certain articles of the Covenant, especially the article dealing with the reduction of armaments, should remain a dead letter while other articles are enforced.»

The small states did not intend to withdraw from the League or reject it, but they raised the question whether the principles of the Covenant were adequately applied. They further thought that «every effort should be made to ensure the success of the experiment», but they also had some doubt as to «whether the Covenant could be so amended, or its application so modified, as to increase the security of states which it is its object to ensure.»

They would consider any amendments, but they did not have much hope for such, and made it clear that their governments would have reservations to the application of sanctions:

> Though not forgetting that rules for the application of Article 16 were adopted in 1921, we would place it on record that, so long as the Covenant as a whole is applied so incompletely and inconsistently, we are obliged to bear that fact in mind in connection with the application of Article 16.[23]

On August 20, 1936, the foreign ministers of Denmark, Finland, Norway, and Sweden met to discuss a circular letter which the Secretary-General had sent out on July 4, 1936.[24] They then agreed on a common policy in reply to this in which they stated, more explicitly, essentially the same points put forth in the «seven-country declaration» of July 1.

[22] For the full text see League of Nations, *Official Journal, Special Supplement*, No. 154, 1936, 19.

[23] *Ibid.*, 19.

[24] This circular was an attempt to discuss the situation arising out of the Italo—Ethiopian conflict. The Secretary-General urged the members of the League to send proposals in order to improve the application of the Covenant:

2. Taking note of the communications which have been made on this subject.
3. Noting that various circumstances have prevented the full application of the Covenant.
4. Remaining firmly attached to the principles of the Covenant.
5. Being desirous of strengthening the authority of the League of Nations by adopting the application of these principles to the lessons of experience.
6. Being convinced that it is necessary to strengthen the real effectiveness of the guarantees of security which the League affords its members.

The Swedish Government pointed out that the lack of universality in the League was the main reason why it was not able to function in conformity with the Covenant. It was further emphasized that sanctions, military and economic, had to be made compulsory and applied in full, which they never had been. The Swedes made a point of the fact that in certain cases no sanctions had been enforced against the aggressor. In the only case where Article 16 had been applied, sanctions were imposed partially and by degrees. The Swedish Government concluded that if the League was to succeed, its chief aim should be to «ensure consistent and impartial application of the principles of the Covenant and to establish universal cooperation within the framework of the League.»[25] The same view was stressed by the other Scandinavian governments.

Sweden.

According to a League Assembly resolution of October, 1936, a special committee was established to study the application of the principles of the Covenant. In January, 1938, Lord Cranborne made a report on the question of universality of the League and how cooperation could be reached with the non-member states. In the general discussion which followed, Undén, the Swedish delegate, said: «I am forced to admit that, for the time being, the system of sanctions is suspended.» He then referred to several instances where others had expressed the same idea and went on to say:

> In my opinion, we cannot but recognize openly that, for reasons which are well known, the League is not capable of carrying out the program of the Covenant in its entirety.[26]

League of Nations, *Official Journal*, Special Supplement, No. 154, C.L. 124, 1936, VII, 6.

[25] League of Nations, *Official Journal*, Special Supplement, No. 154, 17—19. For the Norwegian point of view see Halvdan Koht, *Norsk Utanrikspolitikk fram til 9. April 1940* (Oslo, 1947), 13. For details on the Swedish stand on the Declaration of July 1, 1936, see Herbert Tingsten, *Svensk Utrikesdebatt mellan världskrigen* (Stockholm, 1944), 274.

[26] All of the members of the League sent their suggestions to the special committee in reply to the circular letters. They stressed various aspects; the lack of universality was probably the one that was most frequently mentioned and most sincerely meant. For the full text of the replies see League of Nations, *Official Journal*, Special Supplement, No. 154, 8—40 ᴎor a summary and discussion see Hogan, *International Violence*, 117—127.

The conclusion to be drawn from this consideration is that in practice, the League no longer possesses the characteristics of a coercive League corresponding to the provisions of Article 16 of the Covenant. By the force of events, without any amendment of the Covenant, a practice has become established whereby members of the League do not consider themselves bound to take coercive actions against an aggressor state.[27]

Mr. Undén stressed that this was the official view taken by his government, and not just his own personal opinion. But he was very anxious to point out that this should be recognized as a «loyal and legitimate interpretation» of the fact that conditions had changed, and made it impossible for the League to live up to the letter of the Covenant. He did not think that this would imply an abandonment of the idea of collective security. The League was not weakened by recognition of the fact that it actually was weak, but it would be an advantage to all states to make the distinction between theory and practice, and realize the limitations of the League instead of maintaining a «fiction of a system of automatic and obligatory sanctions.»[28]

This meant, in fact, that Sweden had given up all confidence in the League as a means of achieving security and had officially declared her intention to look for it somewhere else. She was not the only one. The small European states, one by one, soon made statements to the same effect.

Switzerland, Traditional Neutral.

Ever since 1920, Switzerland had been in a peculiar position among the League members, and could hardly be expected to give substantial support to the sanctions system. In her reply to the circular letter, September, 1936, she did not make any positive suggestions for reforms, but pointed repeatedly to the dangers in which the existing situation involved her. As the League was not universal, it might deteriorate from defense of international

---

[27] League of Nations, *Official Journal*, Special Supplement, No. 180, 9—10, (bound as *Publications, Political*, 1938, VII.)
[28] League of Nations, *Official Journal*, Special Supplement, No. 180, 10.

law to defense of the interests of a particular group of states within the League. The sanctions had been applied inconsistently or not at all, and the Swiss Government stressed particularly the difference between a small and a great power when it came to application of sanctions:

> For a small country, the application of Article 16 may be a matter of life or death.
> If notwithstanding the criticisms it incurs, Article 16 should be retained substantially in its present form, or if the risks it involves should be made still greater, Switzerland would be obliged to call attention once again to her peculiar position, which the Council of the League in the Declaration of London of February 13, 1920, described as unique. The Federal Council must in any case point out once more that Switzerland cannot be held to sanctions which in their nature and through their effects would seriously endanger her neutrality. That perpetual neutrality is established by age old tradition, and all Europe joined in recognizing its unquestionable advantages over a hundred years ago.[29]

During the general discussion following Lord Cranborne's report, the Swiss representative, Mr. George, spoke on the official attitude of the Swiss Government. Mr. George referred to the change in conditions regarding the League. He expressed the opinion that it was the belief of the Swiss that, «in a weakened League, we have no choice but to recover that full neutrality from which we only departed in 1920 in the hope that the League would become truly universal.»[30]

It was now the intention of the Swiss Government to revert to full neutrality. Mr. George stated that Switzerland had so far taken her share of the sanctions, but she could not do so any longer

> without the most serious danger to her neutrality, in a League from which two great neighboring powers have withdrawn. ... In our eyes these facts are decisive. They deprive differential neutrality of its political and psychological basis. They make the application of Article 16 by Switzerland impossible.[31]

[29] League of Nations, *Official Journal*, Special Supplement, No. 154, 29.
[30] League of Nations, *Official Journal*, Special Supplement, No. 180, 11.
[31] *Ibid.*

The Swiss representative continued to elaborate on this point, describing the Swiss neutrality as not being selfish, but as a necessity which had served the country well. Therefore, as the League had grown weak, the Swiss had to revert «by an instinct of self-preservation, to its traditional neutrality.»

The Swiss have always been able to convince others that their neutrality is of a very special kind, and they have succeeded in having this peculiarity recognized. Nor did they appeal in vain this time. On May 14, 1938, the League Council adopted a resolution which, in fact, recognized the Swiss claim to a privileged position within the League.[32]

During the same discussion in the Special Committee, January 31, 1938, Mr. Rutgers, the Dutch representative, stated that «There has in fact been a tacit, a *de facto* revision of the Covenant, and that as a result, the League ... is now nothing more than an optionally coercive body.»[33]

It is of interest to note the difference in the conclusions which the Swiss and the Dutch Governments drew from this fact. Mr. Rutgers, speaking for his government, stated that:

> The Netherlands Government has never desired, and does not now desire, a return to the old system of general neutrality when a war breaks out. It still supports the system of collective security. ... It may be said, for the moment, this obligation (to apply sanctions) is dead and buried; but it must not be forgotten that burial involves the idea of resurrection.[34]

Mr. Rutgers concluded by saying that «everyone for himself» seemed to be the present general motto in European politics.

These statements have a great significance as they show plainly

---

[32] The Council took note «that Switzerland, invoking her perpetual neutrality, has expressed her intention not to participate any longer in any manner in the putting into operation of the provisions of the Covenant relating to sanctions, and declares that she will not be invited to do so; and places on record that the Swiss Government declares its determination to maintain unaltered in all respects her position as a Member of the League, and to continue to give the facilities which have been accorded to the League for the free exercise by its institutions of their activities in Swiss territory.» League of Nations, *Official Journal*, May, 1938, 368—375.

[33] League of Nations, *Official Journal*, Special Supplement, No. 180, 14.

[34] *Ibid.*

that, with the exception of Switzerland, the small European neutrals had ventured upon a course which was neither collective security nor neutrality in the old sense. They seemed to seek a position where they could have one foot in each camp. In theory they were still members of the League, but in practice each of them had drawn a circle around its own territory, and declared its determination to stay within this as long as possible whatever might be going on outside. The incongruity of the new situation is perhaps best explained by the example of Belgium.

Belgium, «Realistic Neutrality».

Belgium, once a perpetual neutral, had been among the League members since the League was formed. Contrary to Switzerland, she had never asked for special privileges. On the other hand, however, she had in fact got extensive guarantees from the greater powers by the Locarno agreements in 1925, which granted her a substantial amount of additional security. Belgium was as much alarmed as other small states by the failure of the League to check the Italo—Ethiopian War; but she also had additional worries. Belgium had no doubt put more faith in the Locarno treaties than in the system of sanctions, and when Hitler, in 1936, sent the German Army into the Rhine Area, she felt that the old basis for her security was gone and that a new system had to be established along somewhat different lines. When attempts to bring about a substitute for the Locarno agreements were not successful in the first instance, Belgium also realized that «everyone for himself» was about the only possible solution. Consequently, she entered on a course which was characterized as «realistic neutrality».[35] It was pointed out that this did not mean that Belgium intended to return to the old pre-war conception of neutrality. On the contrary, she wanted to achieve an international status which permitted complete sovereignty and freedom of action, and yet she did not want to be too much bound by unilateral and collective obligations.[36] On July 20, 1936, the Belgian Minister of Foreign Affairs, Spaak, said in a public speech that it was his aim to con-

---

[35] Richard Whittier, «Belgium Emphasizes Security,» in *Contemporary Review*, 151 : 31 (January, 1937).
[36] Schempp, *Der Neutrale Westen*, 82.

duct the Belgian foreign policy in «the sign of realism». His conclusion was, «I want only one thing, a foreign policy exclusively and entirely Belgian.»[37]

The King, Leopold III (in a speech to his cabinet on October 14, 1936) said that, «the reoccupation of the Rhine, by breaking the Locarno agreements both in letter and in spirit, has placed us in the same international position as we were in before the war.»[38]

King Leopold made this speech in relation to a new law providing for extension of the term of compulsory military service, and his aim was apparently to prepare the people for an increase in armaments. He went on to say, «any unilateral policy weakens our position abroad, and gives rise, rightly or wrongly, to division at home.» He then repeated Spaak's statement by saying, «we must follow a policy exclusively and entirely Belgian. This policy should aim resolutely at placing us apart from the conflicts of our neighbors.»[39]

As a proof of the new policy, the term of military service was almost doubled, and other measures were also taken to strengthen the Belgian army.[40]

In this connection, the *New Republic* said that this time Belgium did not expect to get her neutral position guaranteed by an international agreement. «She will fortify her borders, maintain a comparatively large and mobile military force, and trust to luck. ... She will not place her reliance upon a system of security that no longer exists.»[41]

Even so, Belgium tried to get a new Western Alliance Pact to replace the Locarno Treaties. As a result of these efforts, on April 24, 1937, she was released from her obligations under the Locarno agreements and the Four-Power Agreement of March, 1936. France and England renewed their pledges to give assistance to Belgium in case of an attack. In return, Belgium promised to defend her borders against an aggressor, and gave assurance of her loyalty to the League Covenant.[42]

---

[37] *Ibid.*, 83.
[38] Hogan, *International Violence*, 116.
[39] Whittier, «*Belgium Emphasizes Security*,» 30.
[40] Schempp, *Der Neutrale Westen*, 85.
[41] «Belgium Returns to Neutrality,» in *The New Republic*, 88 : 340, (October, 1936), editorial.
[42] Hogan, *International Violence*, 116.

Whittier's comment on this new Belgian policy was that the Belgian statesmen no longer reposed confidence in collective security, but at the same time the obligations to the League «made it impossible to return to the simon-pure neutrality of before the war.» King Leopold, therefore, proposed the realistic neutrality which was conditioned to obligations. Belgium had learned, from recent developments, that treaties could still be violated. Spaak's idea was that by building up the armed forces, Belgium was doing more to preserve the peace than by merely relying on treaties.[43]

The Declaration of Copenhagen.

Due to her geographical location, Belgium was a somewhat special case, but with the exception of Switzerland and Spain, the policy of the small European states showed the same basic traits. There was, however, a recognition of the fact that even if each of them wanted no ties of obligation which might check its freedom of action, their position would be stronger if they could agree on some common principles. To that effect, the foreign ministers of Finland, the three Scandinavian countries, Belgium, Holland, and Luxembourg met in Copenhagen on July 23, 1938.[44]

The main object of this conference was to clarify the relationship of these states to the League of Nations. They all wanted to get rid of their obligations, but there was some discussion as to what extent. It is significant to note that proposals to follow the example of Switzerland got no support. These countries did not want a return to the old traditional neutrality. On the contrary, it was repeatedly emphasized that they had no intention to leave Geneva.[45] The seven states would continue to work for inter-

---

[43] Whittier, «Belgium Emphasizes Security,» 31. For details about the Belgian position see Schempp, Der Neutrale Westen, 63—91.

[44] Schempp, Der Neutrale Westen, 6—11. For further details see Tingsten, Svensk Utrikesdebatt mellan världskrigen, 298—300. These states have often been called the Oslo states. This term dates back to 1932 when Denmark, Norway, Sweden, Belgium, the Netherlands, and Luxembourg met in Oslo for the purpose of effecting a closer economic cooperation. It was later adhered to by Finland. Since 1934, a meeting of the Swedish, Danish, and Norwegian ministers has been an annual event.

[45] For a general discussion see F. Joesten, «Storm Over Northern Europe,» in Contemporary Review, 151 : 454—460 (April, 1937).

national cooperation and they thought it particularly important to do what could be done to bring about a reduction of the armament race by an international agreement.

Thus stressing the fact that their states would continue to work with the League of Nations, the signatories declared that their governments had decided to regard the sanctions system under the existing conditions and the way it had been applied in the last years, as being non-obligatory.

The ministers hoped this question would be discussed at the next meeting of the League and they repeated their willingness to do their share in solving this problem.[46] Shortly after the Declaration of Copenhagen, Poland, Estonia, and Latvia made declarations to the same effect.[47]

The Scandinavian countries were very anxious to stress that the step they had taken did not mean that they would follow a policy of isolation. There was a bitter fight over this issue in the Norwegian Storting. One of the representatives proposed that the Storting should make it official that Norway was to follow an absolute impartial neutrality policy in accordance with the traditional pattern. This proposal met great opposition, particularly from Koht, the Foreign Minister. A compromise was finally reached and the government declared that the neutrality of Norway should be valid only for those wars which *Norway herself* did not recognize as being actions by the League of Nations.[48]

The same problem existed in Sweden. From 1937, there had been an increased agitation for neutrality, not only for Sweden but for

---

[46] Damit. ihre Staaten ihre Mitarbeit in Völkerbund fortzetzen sollen, haben sie festgestellt, dass ihre Regierungen entschlossen sind, in ihrem Auftreten an der Linie festzuhalten die sie mit ihrer Erklärung gezogen haben, dass sie das Sanktionssystem unter den derzeitigen Verhaltnissen und nach der Praxis, die in den vergangenen Jahren angewendet worden ist, in seinem Charakter als nicht obligatorisch betrachten. Sie meinen übrigens dass dieser nicht obligatorische Character der Sanktionen nicht für eine besondere Staatengruppe besteht, sondern für alle Mitglieder des Volkerbundes. Schempp, *Der Neutrale Westen*, Appendix, 124. See also Torsten Gihl, *Neutralitätsproblem* (Stockholm, 1938), 85.

The declaration did not specifically mention the other articles of the Covenant as the right to cross the territory of «the League forces». However, the Dutch Foreign Minister said, in 1937, that permission for transit of troops was as important as the participations of sanctions.

[47] *Ibid.*, 89.

[48] J. C. Hambro, *Historisk Supplement*, 16; Koht, *Utanrikspolitikk*, 16.

the whole North. The idea was that the northern states should help each other to maintain their neutrality, yet they wanted no defense alliance. They feared that such action might be interpreted as being directed against any of the greater states. They also felt that the military weakness of Denmark made a northern defense pact impossible. She was so weak that «she could be taken by motorized troops within 48 hours.»[49] (This later proved to be a correct estimation.)

There was much confused talk about neutrality and the defense of it during the years 1937—1938, but as already pointed out very few spoke in favor of a return to impartial neutrality. The chief editor of *Arbetet,* a leading Swedish newspaper, said that «a genuine Swedish neutrality is impossible in any conflict to which Germany is a part.» He based this view on the German dependence on Swedish iron ore.[50] The Swedish Foreign Minister, Sandler, drew attention to the many variations of neutrality and stated, in a radio broadcast on March 20, 1937, that Sweden would like to be neutral, but, she could not obligate herself to a dogmatic neutrality in all cases. Sweden claimed for herself full freedom of action and prepared for a situation in which neutrality was neither possible nor desirable. «Our foreign policy aims at combining active membership in the League of Nations with a neutral attitude to the controversial interests of the great powers and a decided reluctance to engage in these.»

He later pointed out that the League of Nations had developed into a group of allies directly opposed to states being outside the League.[51] The major argument was almost identical with American isolationism and was, in essence, that Sweden must retain her full freedom of action and neither be bound by obligations to the League nor to strict traditional neutrality.

Sovereignty versus Collective Security.

The Copenhagen Declaration is important in two respects. In the first place because it was, in fact, a collective denunciation of the League by the small states of Europe. Yet, as far as neutrality is

---

[49] Tingsten, *Utrikesdebatt,* 327.
[50] *Ibid.,* 290—291.
[51] Tingsten, *Utrikesdebatt,* 279—281.

concerned, it was of even greater importance that they so emphatically refused to follow Switzerland in her return to traditional neutrality. The difference here is significant. On the part of Switzerland it was a positive action as well as a negative one, because she deserted the League in order to return to a clearly defined political status in which she firmly believed. But the other small countries were not so consistent. They knew what they were getting away *from* but not what they were getting into.

Schempp characterized the situation by saying, «dass der Entschluss zur Neutralität zugleich ein Aufstand gegen diesen omniösen Artikel 16 war.»[52] The main characteristic of the new neutrality policy was a return to individual freedom of action, which meant that Geneva had lost its authority.

The small European states were in the League, and at the same time they were out of it. They would go along with the League as long as they did not risk anything, but they had made it unquestionably clear that they might back out any time they felt their own interests were being endangered. In theory, they still believed in international solidarity and they still condemned all aggressive attempts to start a new war, but they apparently were somewhat uncertain as to which of the power-groups stood for the «right» cause. In spite of their sympathies and antipathies, they had learned that on both sides one could find motives that were far from being ethical and unselfish. There was a growing realization that beneath the peaceful surface of idealism and good faith were the cold and merciless realities of power politics. It had dawned on the small powers that none of the great nations would go to war for the sole purpose of defending international law and the ideals of humanity. On the contrary, the ensuing fight would be a question of extension or preservation of power. The League pattern was not going to be followed. The small states had joined the League with a vision of themselves, the sturdy small ones, standing firmly together with their big friends, their equals and League brothers, in an uneven fight against a single aggressor state who would not have a chance against the overwhelming superior force of all the others. The fight would have been short and with no great risks. They all hoped and supposed it would be fought far away

[52] Schempp, *Der Neutrale Westen*, 7.

from their borders, if it even got so far as to develop into an armed conflict.

Perkins says that one of the fundamental errors of the League was that, due to American and British influence, *it relied more on economic pressure than on military force*. This was in the traditional lines of those countries, but economic pressure is useless unless one is ever ready to fight to back it up.[53]

In the middle thirties the small states woke up to find that instead of a single aggressor fighting the rest of the world, the two sides in another war were likely to be quite evenly matched. The war might be long and destructive, it might endanger their independence and sovereignty, and expose their actual weakness. This they could not afford to risk, so they resolved to stay out. The tradition of a hundred years as spectators, the feeling of fear and necessity, easily choked what growing international conscience they might have developed during the past fifteen years, and so they returned to neutrality. The small states had put the emphasis on war prevention. They thought the League would stop the war before it began. This had been their main concern, and they had very vague ideas as to what *their* contribution would be if the war did break out. They could not send any expeditionary forces to help others. They could not even defend their own borders. In case of war some kind of non-participation thus seemed to be the only solution.

It cannot be overstressed, however, that the neutrality to which the small powers returned was not the traditional, impartial, and passive conception of the term. Since the First World War had wrecked all rules and left neutrality in disrepute, nothing had been done, on an international basis, to revive it. The fact that a landpower like Switzerland, with no maritime intercourse with other nations, still claimed to practice traditional neutrality, did not prove that it was applicable to any other power. The small states, therefore, by 1938, found themselves in a floating international position. They were members of the League and they were not; they were neutrals, but at the same time they adhered to a system of partial discrimination which, at least in theory, had abolished neutrality as such. The neutrality of the late thirties lacked most of the traits and characteristics of the legal and accepted concep-

---

[53] Perkins, *America and Two Wars*, 83. Italics supplied.

tion. As was the case with the United States, it had all boiled down to one single object, namely, to stay out of the war that was to come. Not conditionally, by insistence on rights and duties, but almost at any cost and by all means. To that purpose they had reserved their full freedom of action. Unbound by rules and obligations, they prepared to steer their course, through discrimination and compromise, in order to stay out of war. It was no longer neutrality; it was non-belligerency.

There are many intricate problems involved in the small states' desertion from the League, but the basic one is probably concerned with the sensitive question of sovereignty. To the small states sovereignty and security were regarded as very related subjects. The League had not attempted to do away with sovereignty as such. Only «military sovereignty», the right to dispose of their armed forces, was infringed upon as being absolutely irreconcilable with collective security for all. Neither the Covenant nor the Kellogg Pact curtailed sovereignty in a municipal sense, but limited it to the right of war. This was the sovereignty which the small states had given away and entrusted to the hands of the League. Security had for centuries been their aim, and neutrality had been their means to achieve it. When they joined the League in 1920, they knew perfectly well why they did so. They dropped neutrality as an antiquated implement, a policy which could no longer serve their purpose, and based their hopes on collective security. As the application of this principle before long became a threat to rather than a guarantee of security, they picked up the old disreputed neutrality in lack of something better. But this was to be applied in the old way only when it was convenient and when no other course was possible.

The Foreign Minister of Norway, Halvdan Koht, in 1937, wrote that all of the European countries have been brought into the political unity created by the League, which meant a change in their whole notion of neutrality. Since that time the problems of remaining neutral have not only become more difficult but they have also become quite different. Dr. Koht commented indignantly on some statements made by Litvinoff, the First Delegate of the U.S.S.R. The Russian representative spoke in 1936 with contempt for the small states which «strove to seek salvation in neutrality».

Litvinoff further reminded them that the recent lessons of violations of the neutrals and their rights ought to have made it clear to them that it was no longer sufficient to write the word neutrality on a frontier. Koht agreed that such criticism would have been perfectly justified if any of these countries had really planned to observe neutrality in the old sense of the word, but he emphasized, «that sort of neutrality had already become impracticable in essential respects during the world war, and with the organization of the League of Nations it had become absolutely unthinkable.»[54]

As the other small states had made statements to the same effect, the turning away from the League could not have been due to a new interest and belief in neutrality. The point is that the small states had based their entrance in the League on a misconception. They had been deluded into thinking that the aim of the League was to preserve a general peace equally beneficent to all nations. They hoped that the League would be a realization of the highest ideals of humanity and international goodwill. They had heard the ringing words of Woodrow Wilson inaugurating the era of collective security: small and great should stand together in shining armor; they should defend the good cause, and with the thunderbolt of heaven destroy the contemptible criminal who, driven by shameful and selfish motives, tried to corrupt the general peace.

It had taken them fifteen years to realize that the peace they were supposed to defend was not general at all, but of a very special kind. In fact, it was the victors' peace, and what they wanted to preserve was the *status quo*. By their victory in 1918, the Allies had gained what they wanted. They had put themselves on the top, and they were determined to stay there. It is no coincidence that the League was a part of the Peace of Versailles. In fact, *that* was the very peace it intended to guarantee, and the aggressors in the first place were the states that tried to upset the rules and provisions laid down in Paris in 1919. The Allies wanted no change. They had fought the war to get a favorable balance, and the League was to be one of the means to guarantee them the support of the other states to keep that balance intact. They had brought it about themselves, not as a natural development, but by force. Still they insisted that any attempt to change it should be

---

[54] H. Koht, «Neutrality and Peace,» in *Foreign Affairs*, 15 : 281.

met by armed intervention by all powers. They monopolized in advance the just cause for their own benefit, with disregard for open discussions as to what was universally right. War could no longer be of benefit to them; on the contrary, it might deprive them of what they already had. So they denounced war for all time. It was a futile attempt to preserve a situation that was in constant development.

C. Fenwick says in this connection: «There is little doubt that certain of the powers who appeared as its (the Covenant's) champions were more intent upon stability, upon retaining possession of the fruits of victory than they were upon readjusting international conditions to meet the demands of justice.»[55] Dealing with the failure of the League, he wrote in 1939:

> Equally disastrous was the inability of the leading statesmen and the public to understand that a world of law and order could not be built upon the conception of status quo, that something must be devised for the revision of the treaties of 1920. As no remedies were found, the rule of law gave way to the old right of self-help and the anarchy that inevitably attends it.[56]

The League was established to perpetuate a specific situation that was bound to change. It was not brought about by a just omnilateral agreement, but forcefully, as the result of a war. It, therefore, had to be artificial when applied to the future. Perkins states, «the abandonment of the Treaty of Versailles was a mortal blow to the system that had been set up,» and further, «that the absence of the United States could hardly fail to limit its actions, limited enough already.»

Still the League had given the appearance of a general world order for justice and peace. Peaceful and peace-loving were the nations that benefitted from the Peace of Paris. All others who might benefit by other arrangements were branded aggressors and criminals who tried to destroy the general peace of the «have»

---

[55] Fenwick, «Neutrality and International Organization,» in *American Journal of International Law*, quoted in *Reference Shelf*, 10, No. 7, 223.

[56] Fenwick, «International Law and Lawless Nations,» in *American Journal of International Law*, 33 : 745 (October, 1939).

nations. Thus the Italo—Ethiopian conflict was not the only reason for the growing distrust of the League in 1935—1936.[57]

It was the realization of these facts that made the small nations break out of the League in the middle thirties. The Allies had not lived up to their proclamations, nor were they able to enforce the system they had created. The most powerful of them all, the United States, was too confident of its own strength to believe or care for any European system, and France and England had been too occupied with their domestic situations and their internal problems to realize the approaching danger, even if it might have been possible for them alone to check the aggressors.

The British Prime Minister, Neville Chamberlain, made some important comments on the League in a speech in the House of Commons on February 28, 1938. His opinion was that the League of Nations, under the existing conditions, was not fit to provide collective security for any state. «In fact,» he said, «collective security does not differ from the old alliances of pre-war days which we thought we had abandoned.»[58] Consequently one should avoid deluding oneself, and particularly the small weak states, into believing that the League could protect them against being attacked. Chamberlain, therefore, thought that the states which remained in the League should not be burdened with obligations which they were not able to live up to.[59]

This left the neutrals with no illusions as to what they could expect from the League. After that speech they could have no scruples about leaving it. Great Britain had been the leader of the Allied coalition, and consequently, a leading factor in the League. Thus, when the British Prime Minister withdrew the guarantees and officially admitted the failure of the League of Nations as a trustee of security, the situation could not be changed, as far as war prevention was concerned, whether the small states stayed in the League or not. In short, they had much to lose and little to gain by staying.

Most of the small states were opposed to the developments in the dictator states and feared their aggressive intentions. Ideologically, they were on the side of the League group, and if these powers had been sufficiently strong and determined to check an aggressive

[57] Perkins, *America and Two Wars*, 111.
[58] Borchard, *Neutrality*, 378.
[59] Torsten Gihl, *Neutralitäts-Problem* (Stockholm, 1938), 87.

action, the smaller states might not have withdrawn. But England and France were obviously too weak to be strong maintainers of international law, and possibly even too weak to defend their own interests. This was clearly realized by the small states. They might have joined a great coalition to crush a mad, aggressive dare-devil in some distant area, but they would not risk their existence by joining in a war where the chances were fifty-fifty or even worse. They were not saints in international relations more than anyone else, and they did not pretend to be. They declined the honor of becoming martyrs. The small states were primarily concerned with themselves and their own eternal, insolvable problem of sovereignty and security. As long as there was peace at all, they did not care too much what kind of peace it was, whether just or unjust, provided the injustice was not done to them. The 1935 crisis showed them that this peace-system no longer worked. Instead of having the comfort of an overwhelming superiority on one side, the supposedly defeated part was now gaining strength, and if unchecked it would before long reach equality with the victors. The majority of the small powers sympathized with the Allied side, but not to the extent that they would risk their sovereign status to help them maintain the status quo and their particular peace system. Confronted with that possibility, they preferred to return to «watchful waiting»-and non-belligerency.

IV. From Neutrality to Non-Belligerency

1. *American Neutrality in World War II.*

The general European war which had been feared and anticipated all through the thirties finally came in 1939. It seemed, at first, to follow the traditional pattern of 1914. A certain group of countries issued declarations of war, while the smaller nations and the United States proclaimed their traditional neutrality. On the surface it might have appeared like a good old-fashioned war, with the three groups of states safely seated in their respective camps. But it could not be that way any more, and belligerents as well as neutrals knew this just too well. They realized from the outset that no matter how «phoney» the war might appear to be, it was, nevertheless, likely to become general in character. In the recent past there had been two general wars,[1] and the neutrals had lost them both. They, therefore, had substantial reasons for fearing the worst in the coming conflict. Since they had stripped neutrality of all ornaments and accessories and kept only the backbone of it, they hoped that this would prove sufficient to keep them out of actual war, which was the best they could hope for. There was no talk of rights and little talk of duties. To stay out of the shooting was their only aim.

It may give an impression of superficiality to attempt to deal with American neutrality in World War II in a small chapter. Some may even think it unnecessary to discuss it because the case seems so obvious. Yet, it would be unsatisfactory to by-pass it in silence, because this period gives a picture of neutrality at the end of its transitional stage, or perhaps the very loss of neutrality in the traditional meaning. It gives a striking illustration of the ambiguity and impracticability to which the status of neutrality had declined. A brief account of the main events and trends may, therefore, prove helpful to an understanding of the development.

[1] The Napoleanic Wars and World War I.

The prelude to the entrance of the United States into World War II has become one of the most controversial periods in American history since 1920. Our main concern is what happened to American neutrality during those years. Was the proclamation of September 5, 1939, an honest attempt to live up to the rules of neutrality, and if so, why did it fail?[2]

It is inevitable, in this discussion, to ask for the attitude of the Roosevelt Administration. Were the President and his advisers inclined to take an impartial view of the belligerents? The answer to this will have to be «no». Even long before the war, in 1934 and 1935, President Roosevelt and his Secretary of State, Cordell Hull, repeatedly made statements which showed their disapproval of the so-called aggressor nations. Yet at the same time as the President's Chautauqua and San Diego speeches, he maintained his firm resolution to keep out of war.[3] It was not until October 5, 1937, in his famous «quarantine speech» in Chicago that he, in plain and unmistakable words, discarded neutrality and pointed out the necessity of peace-loving nations to stand together against the aggressor states who were a threat to the general peace of the world and to international law and order.

> The peace-loving nations must make a concerted effort in opposition to those violations of treaties and those ignorings of human instincts which are creating a state of international anarchy and instability from which there is no escape through mere isolation and neutrality. ... the peace, the freedom and security of ninety percent of the population of the world is being jeopardized by the remaining ten percent who are threatening a breakdown of all international order and law.

Roosevelt's conclusion was that the health of the community must be protected by a quarantine of the aggressors.[4]

[2] Charles A. Beard has directed a deep-felt attack on President Roosevelt in his two books, *American Foreign Policy in the Making* and *President Roosevelt and the Coming of the War, 1941* (New Haven, 1948). Neither of these books, however, presents convincing proofs of obvious «war-guilt», nor do they disprove facts and interpretations which have been made in favor of the Roosevelt policy by writers such as Perkins, Millis, and Sherwood in their books.

[3] Beard, *American Foreign Policy in the Making*, 173, 183.

[4] *The Public Papers and Addresses of Franklin Delano Roosevelt*, Vol. 1927, 408—.

After the *Panoy* incident in December, 1937, the President made several statements to the same effect, but in somewhat softer and more indirect terms. He stressed the fact that whether Americans liked it or not, they «were a part of a large world of other nations and peoples.»[5] The implication was that this would necessitate cooperation and not neutral isolation.

In January, 1939, he spoke of the «storms from abroad» which challenged the three valuable American institutions of religion, democracy, and good faith. The God-fearing democracies could not let acts of aggression pass against sister nations. He did not say that Americans had to go to war against such aggressor states, but he indicated that «there are many methods short of war, but stronger and more effective than mere words, of bringing home to aggressor governments the aggregate sentiments of our own people.» He also commented on the neutrality legislation which, incidentally, never had enjoyed the whole-hearted approval of the administration.[6] He thought that the neutrality laws might operate unevenly and unfairly and «actually give aid to an aggressor and deny it to the victim.»[7] This idea was expressed not only in words but also in actions. Though the President was bound by the inflexible provisions of the neutrality acts, he was still able to discriminate against aggressor nations by not invoking the Neutrality Act. In the Sino-Japanese War of 1937, an embargo would have hurt China more than Japan, so the President did not find the existence of this war a necessity in bringing the inflexible provisions into effect.

The so-called moral embargoes had been used effectively for a short period during the Italo—Ethiopian War, and this new weapon had not been forgotten. In July, 1938, the Secretary of State placed a moral embargo on shipments of arms and aircraft to countries whose armed forces were «making use of airplanes for attacks upon civilians.»[8] These warnings were not neglected. Ever since July, 1938, there had been a reasonably effective embargo on arms, ammunitions, and implements of war.[9] In August, 1939, the State Department announced that there be «no further delivery to certain countries» of planes and equipment used for production of

[5] *Public Papers*, 541—549.
[6] Beard, *Foreign Policy in the Making*, 166.
[7] *Public Papers*, 1939, 1.
[8] Department of State, *Bulletin I*, 121.
[9] Borchard, *Neutrality*, 390.

aviation gasoline.[10] On the other hand, China was given a loan of twenty-five million dollars.

Thus, the Roosevelt Administration had given up neutral impartiality long before the great contest started. In words and actions it had given notice of the side on which it could be found, but this only indicated where the Administration itself would like to be. Unfortunately, it could not tell the future aggressors that the people of the United States would also line up against them if they should try to start something. On the contrary, the nation had expressed its opinion when it enacted the neutrality legislation, whereby the United States guaranteed that it would take great pains not to get into trouble. Every state was given a free hand to do what it liked as long as it stayed away from the American hemisphere.

Thus, the foreign observers had to make an estimate of what was decisive in forming the American policy. With the election system and party politics taken into consideration, one cannot help but wonder that they chose to disregard Roosevelt's warnings and to gamble on continued American isolation.[11]

Perkins said that «the culminating error of American post-war policy, however, came with the enactment of the Neutrality Acts...». He thought it to be an «extraordinary act of folly,» and maintained that it was, in fact, an active assistance to the German Fuehrer, in so far as the United States assured him that no help would be given to his enemies, England and France.[12]

Cash-and-Carry.

In January, 1939, the administration began making considerable efforts to change the neutrality legislation. Several bills were introduced in Congress to abolish the rigid and inflexible provisions and give the President the prerogative to discriminate against aggressors. One of those bills was sponsored by Senator Thomas, who stated that

---

[10] Department of State, *Bulletin I,* 714.

[11] The President repeatedly, in personal messages to the dictators, warned them against an aggressive policy and urged them to conduct a peaceful policy.

[12] Perkins, *America and Two Wars,* 115.

a neutrality that demands an impartiality calls for a dulling of every moral impulse. It insists upon erasing the line between good and evil. ... If neutrality means a crushing of world morality, it is better that we take sides and fight, because fighting for a right is better than passive submission to a wrong.[13]

In March of that year Senator Pittman introduced a bill providing for more flexibility, and in May, 1939, the President's proposals were brought forth in the Bloom bill. This bill did not propose a repeal of the whole 1937 act, but concentrated an attack on the arms embargo. In return, the President was willing to place all trade on a cash-and-carry basis and to establish combat areas which American ships and citizens were forbidden to enter, except at their own risk. The suggestion was actually a bargain between the President and Congress of an arms embargo for combat areas.[14] This did not save the bill from being severely amended and opposed. The House was not willing to lift the arms embargo entirely, but would consider lifting it so far as «implements of war» were concerned. No final decision was made, however, and the debate went on and on. In July, Congress decided to defer the matter until its next session. This was done in spite of urgent personal appeals from the President and the Secretary of State, who both argued that it might be too late, as a change in the laws after the war had actually started would be considered an un-neutral act.

In September, 1939, the President called a special session of Congress and the fight for the repeal went into its final phase. The administration now emphasized that the 1937 act was a departure from traditional neutrality which had served America well for centuries, while embargoes (referring to 1807) had brought difficulties. Roosevelt openly stressed the point that a lifting of the embargo would help the democracies win, while the establishment of a danger zone would mean a further guarantee that the United States would not be drawn in.[15] By skillful maneuvering of this

---

[13] Borchard, *Neutrality*, 396—397.
[14] By May 1, 1939, the cash-and-carry clause of the 1937 act had expired and American ships were free to go all over the combat zones.
[15] Bayley, *Diplomatic History*, 759—760; Borchard, *Neutrality*, 400—403; Perkins, *America and Two Wars*, 120—122; Beard, *Foreign Policy in the Making*, 224—230.

give-and-take policy, the President had the «Neutrality Act of 1939» enacted on November 3. On November 4, he proclaimed the state of war and revoked the embargoes proclaimed under the 1937 joint resolution.[16] From then on the belligerents could buy arms and war implements, but they had to come and get them and pay cash for what they got.[17]

Secretary of State, Hull, maintained that the repeal of the 1937 act was imperatively necessary to protect American interests on the high seas and to meet the «danger from lawless forces seeking world domination.»[18] The British, however, knew how to appreciate it. *The Spectator* said that United States neutrality «is strained all the time, in all practical matters, in our favour. ... Her neutrality act has been revised directly for our benefit. ... We should prefer America's active support to her neutrality, but if ever there was benevolent neutrality it is this.»[19] An American commentator added that Britain need not be afraid of having offended the United States by boldness, even at the expense of neutral rights; goodwill was too manifest.

Great Britain had ample reason to rejoice over the benevolence of American neutrality, for it was not limited to assurances of goodwill, but was expressed in actions as well. The President had, at the outbreak of the war, revived the hardly tenable distinction between belligerent merchantmen, whether armed for defensive or for offensive purposes. The Allied ships were supposed to be defensively armed and admitted to American ports. Completed war planes were flown to the Canadian border and the title of ownership was transferred. The planes were then pushed or pulled over the border and flown to the coast for shipment to the scenes of war.[20]

---

[16] Department of State, *Bulletin*, November 4, 1939, 453—454.

[17] For the full text of the 1939 Neutrality Act see *Public Resolution*, No. 50, 76th Congress, Chapter 2. Also printed in full in Pfankuchen, *A Documentary Textbook in International Law*, 986—989.

[18] C. Hull, «The Repeal of the United States Neutrality Act,» in *American Journal of International Law*, 1942, Vol. 36, 118. For further comments see E. Borchard, «War, Neutrality and Non-belligerency,» in *American Journal of International Law*, 35 : 622 (Oct., 1941); Q. Wright, «The Repeal of the Neutrality Act,» in *American Journal of International Law*, 1942, Vol. 36, 8—23.

[19] Editorial, «The Greatest Neutral,» in *The Spectator*, 164 : 616 (May, 1940).

[20] Borchard, *Neutrality*, 411.

The war between Finland and Russia, December, 1939, to March, 1940, did not result in an invocation of the provisions of the Neutrality Act. After the bombing of Helsinki, the President announced that the American Government and people had «for some time pursued a policy of wholeheartedly condemning the unprovoked bombing and machine-gunning of civilian populations from the air.»[21] Consequently, a moral embargo was invoked on aircraft and implements for producing aircraft gasoline. This applied to Russia, as it already had been applied to Japan. Nevertheless, a number of new naval fighting planes were released for export to Finland. Some time later, March, 1940, the Finn's were granted a large loan, from ten to thirty million dollars, for purchases of «agricultural surpluses and other civilian supplies.»[22] These acts were hardly within the sphere of legal neutrality but they can not be called extraordinary flagrant violations of neutral duties. The great turning point came with the fall of France in the summer of 1940.

All Help — Short of War.

From time to time throughout 1939 and 1940, Roosevelt had given evidence of his sympathy to the Allied cause. In January, 1940, he had implied that the United States had a duty to intervene abroad,[23] but after May, 1940, his pro-Allied statements got increasingly stronger and more determined, and the collaboration with Great Britain became closer. Roosevelt had been communicating with Winston Churchill since the beginning of the war,[24] and on May 15, Churchill cabled Roosevelt urging him to proclaim «a state of non-belligerency for the United States, which would mean supplying all kinds of aid, but no armed action.»[25] This sentiment was even more clearly expressed in Churchill's «never surrender» speech of June 4, 1940.[26] Roosevelt expressed his

---

[21] Department of State, *Bulletin I*, 686.
[22] Borchard, *Neutrality*, 417—419.
[23] *New York Times*, January 20, 1940, 2.
[24] Beard, *Foreign Policy in the Making*, 235. Already in 1940, Anglo-American staff negotiations had taken place. Walter Millis, *This is Pearl* 49—50.
[25] Robert E. Sherwood, *Roosevelt and Hopkins* (New York, 1948), 141.
[26] Ibid., 143.

reaction in his equally famous speech at Charlotteville, Virginia on June 10. On that day, Mussolini had made his rear attack on France, and Roosevelt shocked all America by saying, «the hand that held the dagger has plunged it into the back of its neighbor.» In this speech, he gave, for the first time, an unmistakable answer to all who had doubted what would be the future course of the United States. It meant maximum help to the democracies and military preparations to meet the consequences of this policy.

> In our American unity we will pursue two obvious and simultaneous courses; we will extend to the opponents of force the material resources of this nation; and at the same time, we will harness and speed up the use of those resources in order that we ourselves in the Americas may have the equipment and training equal to the task of any emergency and every defense.[27]

On June 13, the President cabled Reynaud, the French Premier,

> This government, as I have already stated to you and Mr. Churchill, is doing everything in its power to make available the material to the Allied Governments which they require so urgently and we are redoubling our efforts to do still more This is an expression of our support of and our faith in the ideals for which the Allied Governments are fighting.

Churchill tried to induce the President to give assurances which went beyond material assistance, but Roosevelt refused, saying he had gone as far as he could without the consent of Congress.[28] Hardpressed by Churchill, he stated that for constitutional reasons he could not give any assurance that the United States would declare war, no matter what the provocation, «short of direct attack upon the United States itself.» He made it clear, however, that if Britain fell, «he would do all that he possibly could, more than mere words, but short of war.»[29]

This sums up the key points and gives the realistic background for Roosevelt's' new policy. Faced with the possibility of having to stand alone against a hostile continent ruled by the ideology of

[27] Sherwood, *Roosevelt and Hopkins*, 143—144.
[28] *Ibid.*, 145—146.
[29] *Ibid.*, 148.

force, neutrality became meaningless and absurd. But Roosevelt was no dictator; he could not translate what he saw into immediate action. He was bound by the Constitution to wait until his point became obvious enough for Congress and the people to see it. The great majority of the people could not, or did not, want to see the point. They refused to look beyond the American horizon, or if they did, they were not inclined to draw logical conclusions from what they saw. The great majority stubbornly clung to the traditional policy of isolation, but were willing to take half-measures to a certain point and within limits.

A poll taken in the spring of 1940 (before the fall of France), disclosed that ninety-seven percent answered *yes* on the question of whether Germany was wrong in invading Norway and Denmark; but ninetysix percent answered *no* when they were asked if they thought the United States should fight Germany.[30] This indicated that practically all Americans would have liked to see the Allies win and Hitler defeated, but they were not willing to do anything about it themselves if it might result in a war.

The President, therefore, had to alter his tactics, and from then on he did not only urge help to the fighting democracies because it was a moral obligation and a civilized thing to do, but because it was absolutely necessary for the *security* of the United States. He might have used Wilson's words, «The Allies are fighting our fight,» — but he could no longer say that «our frontier is in France.»

In the meantime, while he waited for the people to realize this fact, he could do nothing but throw overboard the last battered remnants of neutrality and stretch his executive powers to the breaking point to give the Allies all possible aid «short of war». The period of undisguised non-belligerency began.

The year of 1940 was an election year, and the Republican candidat Wendell Wilkie, as well as Roosevelt, had unneutrality and maximum help to the Allies as a main plank in his platform. The candidates made almost identical statements of the necessity of aiding Britain.[31] Wilkie said, «I favor all possible aid to the Allies without going to war.»[32] Roosevelt took the same stand. This

---

[30] Editorial, *The Greatest Neutral*, 616.
[31] Beard, *Foreign Policy in the Making*, 270—320.
[32] *Ibid.*, 276.

indicates that by the autumn of 1940, the Americans had agreed and given their consent to unneutrality, but they were still unwilling to go to war. The strategy of the President was, therefore, concentrated on the theory that the best guarantee of peace would be maximum help to the Allies. After the election he admitted that there was danger of war but

> there is far less chance of the United States getting into the war if we do all we can now to support the nations defending themselves against attack by the Axis than if we acquiesce in their defeat. ... The people of Europe who are defending themselves do not ask us to do their fighting. They ask us for the implements of war.[33]

That is exactly what they were given in ever increasing quantities, and at the same time the United States began to prepare for its own defense.

From that time on, energetic steps were taken to strengthen the hemispherical defense. The colonies of Denmark, France, and Holland might provide excellent springboards for their new possessor if an attack should be attempted on the New World. The Senate, therefore, passed a resolution on June 17, 1940, which opposed transfer of territory in the American hemisphere from one non-American power to another. The Germans protested vigorously against this discrimination between non-American states.[34]

The cooperation with the Latin-American states became ever closer. In October, 1939, the Foreign Ministers of the American Republics had met and agreed on the hemispheric safety belt or the security zone around the Americas.[35] In July, 1940, in the Act of Havana they provided that territory belonging to European powers in danger of falling into unfriendly hands should be taken over and commonly administered by the American republics.[36]

---

[33] *Public Papers* vol. 1940, 633.
[34] Bailey, *Diplomatic History*, 765—766.
[35] Fenwick, *American Neutrality*, 126—135.
[36] Fenwick, «The Inter-American Neutrality Committee,» in *American Journal of International Law*, 1941, Vol. 35, 12—40.

«Dynamic Non-belligerency».

A further reinforcement of the hemispherical defense was achieved by the famous «destroyer deal» of September 3, 1940.[37] By this agreement the United States Government turned fifty over-age destroyers directly over to the British Government. In return, the British leased to the United States, for ninety-nine years, bases off the American coast from New Foundland in the north to British Guiana in the south. This act has been characterized as the United States' official and decisive break with what might be left of neutrality, even though Attorney General Jackson attempted to justify the deal from a legal and constitutional point of view.

The negotiations had gone on since July, 1940, when Churchill reminded Roosevelt of the first request for the destroyers which he had made on May 15.[38] Churchill's comment (1940) was, «the transfer to Great Britain of fifty overage warships was a decidedly unneutral act by the United States. It would, according to all the standards of history, have justified the German Government in declaring war upon them. [39] President Roosevelt put it this way:

> It is an epochal and far-reaching act of preparation for continental defense in the face of grave danger. Preparation for defense is an inalienable prerogative of a sovereign state. Under present circumstances, this exercise of sovereign rights is essential to the maintenance of our peace and security.[40]

Borchard stated that there was «no possibility of reconciling the destroyer deal with neutrality. ... It can only be explained by the legal fact that the United States is now ... and has been for some time, in a state of limited war.» He mocked the Attorney General's defense of the deal and maintained that «the concept of 'non-belligerency' like that of 'measures short of war' has no legal status.»[41] Essentially the same standpoint was taken by H. W.

---

[37] Perkins, *America and Two Wars*, 136; Millis, *This is Pearl*, 71.
[38] C. V. Easum, *Half-Century of Conflict*, unpublished manuscript, 864—865.
[39] *Ibid.*, 866.
[40] *Public Papers*, 1940, vol. 391.
[41] Borchard, «The Attorney General's Opinion on the Exchange of Destroyers for Naval Bases,» in *American Journal of International Law*, 34 : 690—697 (October, 1940).

Briggs,[42] while Quincy Wright found other judicial possibilities. He said that «if it (the United States) were neutral, the transfer of the destroyers to Great Britain would be difficult to justify,» on the basis of the Hague Convention. He doubted, however, that the United States actually was «neutral from the point of view of international law.» Since Germany had violated the Kellogg Pact, and other treaties, she was no longer a lawful belligerent. The United States, therefore, had the legal status of «supporting state.»[43]

Apart from such «legal niceties» there seems to have been a general agreement that the destroyer deal meant the final farewell to the neutrality of the United States. It was, however, not the only unneutral act in the summer of 1940.[44]

At Dunkirk, England had been stripped of nearly all her military equipment and was desparately in need of whatever she could get. In June, 1940, the Roosevelt Administration carried the «trade in» plan into effect. That is, the government turned over to manufacturers airplanes from their own supplies. These «obsolete» types were to be replaced by newer models. The private manufacturers then transferred the planes for immediate shipment to England.[45] The aircraft were fighters and bombers, new or used very little.[46] A great quantity of smaller weapons, rifles, machine guns, and 75 millimeter artillery with appropriate ammunition were likewise exported on this «trade in» or «surplus» basis.[47] American planes were no longer pulled or pushed over the border, but flown directly to Canada. Thousands of British pilots were allowed training facilities in Florida, and more than a hundred tanks (also obsolete) were sent from Illinois to Canada to be used for training the British tank units. British warships were allowed to make repairs of an extensive character in American shipyards. In August, 1940, neutral United States and belligerent Canada entered into an

---

[42] Ibid., 587.

[43] Quincy Wright, «The Transfer of Destroyers to Great Britain,» in *American Journal of International Law*, 34 : 680—689 (October, 1940).

[44] The American credits of Norway and Denmark were frozen on the day after the attack had been launched upon them. Bailey, *Diplomatic History*, 768.

[45] Ibid., 769.

[46] Easum, *Half-Century of Conflict*, 864—865.

[47] Ibid., 864—865.

[48] Bailey, *Diplomatic History*, 769.

actual defensive union when Roosevelt and the Canadian Prime Minister, Mackenzie King, agreed on setting up a permanent joint Board of Defense.[48] Whatever this was, it was not neutrality.[49]

In his letter to Roosevelt of May 15, Churchill had hinted at the situation which would arise when the British no longer were able to pay for what they received from the United States. Churchill had optimistically expressed his hope that they would get the materials just the same, and he was not disappointed.[50] In a series of speeches, the administration prepared the people for an all out help to the Allies. On the 29th of December, 1940, President Roosevelt, in one of his «fireside chats», stressed the danger to national security. He repeatedly emphasized the necessity of helping the fighting democracies. «The British are conducting an active war against an unholy alliance.»

> Our national policy is not directed toward war. Its sole purpose is to keep war away from our country and our people. ... But all our present efforts are not enough, we must have more ships, more guns, more planes, more of everything. ... We must become the great arsenal of democracy. For us this is as serious as war itself. ... There will be no «bottlenecks» in our determination to aid Great Britain.

What the President called for was a «dynamic non-belligerency» that would include all possible help to Great Britain and the fighting democracies.[51]

By that time Roosevelt had outlined his economic policy. He would not give England loans; he would «eliminate the dollar sign» and lend her and her allies the arms directly.[52] On January 6, 1941, he outlined this plan for Congress and asked for their approval. «They (the Allies) do not need manpower. They do need billions of dollars worth of weapons of defense.»

> Let us say to the democracies: «We Americans are vitally concerned in your defense of freedom. We are putting forth our energies, our resources, and our organizing powers to give

---

[49] Roosevelt defended his aid to the Allies by saying that it was no more unneutral than it was for Sweden and Russia to provide supplies to Germany. *New York Times*, December 30, 1940, 6.
[50] Easum, *Half-Century of Conflict*, 864.
[51] *New York Times*, December 30, 1940, 1.
[52] Bailey, *Diplomatic History*, 773.

you the strength to regain and maintain a free world. We shall send you, in ever increasing numbers, ships, planes, tanks, guns. This is our purpose and our pledge.»[53]

The issue of security became of overwhelming importance in the debate which followed; not only German attacks, but the danger from Japan also grew more and more evident.[54] The sad fate of the small European neutrals was effectively used as examples of states which relied only on neutrality without preparing for adequate defense. Secretary of State, Hull, stated in Congress that the United States was faced with the grim necessity of subordinating «the ideal of neutrality and the finer points of international law to the urgency of sheer selfdefense. ... Neutrality as we have known it is now definitely secondary to aid to the Allies.» As did Roosevelt, he referred to the small neutrals who had «the handcuffs clamped upon them before they could cock their gun.»[55]

The administration did not make its appeal in vain. It was explicitly stressed that it did not mean war. The Allies did not need American manpower, but they needed all the arms that America could produce. The American people did not want a war, but they wanted security, and if they could get it by giving material aid, this policy would receive their approval. Thus, after a long and bitter struggle, Congress passed a so-called Lend-Lease Act which put the huge productive capacity of American industry at the service of the Allies.[56] It also gave the President great discretionary powers as to which nation should be aided and with what.[57]

If the destroyer deal was called an indefensible unneutral act, there would be no adequate term left to describe the unneutrality of Lend-Lease. Bailey said that «it was more than an abandonment of neutrality, for neutrality had already been abandoned; it was an unofficial declaration of war upon the Axis...»[58] The more so, as the Lend-Lease Act was legally passed

---

[53] *New York Times*, January 7, 1941, 1; Raymond Phineas Stearns, «Pageant of Europe,» in *Sources and Selections* (New York, 1947), 953—954.
[54] See Millis, *This is Pearl*.
[55] *New York Times*, January 16, 1941, 1.
[56] Perkins, *America and Two Wars*, 138—142; Beard, *President Roosevelt and the Coming of the War*, 13—69.
[57] C. V. Easum, *Half-Century of Conflict*, 870—871.
[58] Bailey, *Diplomatic History*, 774.

by Congress, and thus constitutionally impeccable, while the destroyer deal was an executive agreement. Now there could be no doubt. The American people had, in clear and unmistakable terms, denounced the very idea of neutrality, and had given their approval to the course which the administration had followed since June, 1940. The people, through their chosen representatives, had given the government the «green light» to proceed on the road of non-belligerency.[59]

The most outstanding event in the period of unneutrality was no doubt the Atlantic Conference in August 1941, when President Roosevelt and Prime Minister Churchill, with large staffs of military and political advisers, met at New Foundland and agreed upon principles of common policy. The Atlantic Charter, one of the results of the conference, was a statement of war aims, substantially consisting of Wilson's fourteen points, but less explicit and not quite as clear and detailed in its terms. Article VI is perhaps the most notable. In this provision the non-belligerent United States agreed with belligerent England that «after the final destruction of Nazi tyranny «they hoped to establish a just and durable peace.»[60]

According to the traditional pattern, all this unneutrality and partiality would have resulted in a declaration of war from the opposing side, but the world no longer followed traditional patterns. On the contrary, Hitler seemed to have been willing to tolerate almost any act of unneutrality as long as the United States stayed out of the shooting war.[61] It was certainly not respect for

[59] March 30, 1941, sixty-five Axis or Axis-controlled ships were seized in American ports and in June all foreign owned merchant ships laid up in American harbors, were taken over. In April, the Red Sea was declared no longer to be a combat area, and American ships were free to carry supplies directly to the fighting British troops in the Middle East. Bailey, *Diplomatic History*, 777—779.

[60] *Pageant of Europe*, 956—957 gives the full text. For discussions of the conferences, see Sherwood, *Roosevelt and Hopkins*, 349—365; Perkins, *America and Two Wars*, 161; Beard, *President Roosevelt and the Coming of War*, 118—123, 452—483; Millis, *This is Pearl*, 125—127.

[61] The Nürnberg trials brought out facts to prove this. Grand Admiral Doenitz testified that Hitler took all precautions to avoid bringing the United States into the war. This statement was confirmed by the other German leaders. Grand Admiral Raeder testified that Germany urged Japan to take Singapore in March, 1941, in order to frighten the United States into remaining neutral. *New York Times*, May 9, 1946, 12.

international law which kept Hitler from warlike acts. The law of neutrality could not protect the United States more than it had protected Norway and Denmark in 1940.[62] It was the experience of 1917—1918, and the realization of the enormous American potential of materials and manpower which taught the Germans to be cautious. It must be admitted that they showed an admirable patience, and refrained from making issues of provocations which normally would have been considered extremely humiliating.

American naval patrols had been operating since very early in the war and naval vessels had patrolled «coastal waters» up to a thousand miles off the shore.[63] However, it was not until after the signing of the Lend-Lease Act that the question became controversial.[64] It would make little sense to make millions of tons of war equipment available for the Allies if this equipment would be allowed to be sunk by German submarines before it ever reached its destination. Secretary of the Navy, Knox, said, on April 24, 1941: «We cannot allow our goods to be sunk in the Atlantic. ... We must make our promise good to give aid to Britain. We must see the job through ...»[65] Similar statements were made by Cordell Hull.[66] In a radio address on March 15, President Roosevelt declared that he would maintain «a bridge of ships to Great Britain and Greece,»[67] but referring to the statements of Knox and Hull he denied that he had meant naval escorts for convoys, and stated that the United States warships and planes were engaged in patrol work which meant something else. He illustrated this by saying that there was the same difference between patrolling and convoying as there was between a cow and a horse.[68] By that time, however, April 21, orders had already been issued to United States ships on neutrality patrols, directing them to trail all Axis war

[62] Fenwick, *American Neutrality*, 4.
[63] Beard, *President Roosevelt and the Coming of War*, 100.
[64] Sherwood, *Roosevelt and Hopkins*, 367—383.
[65] *New York Times*, April 25, 1941.
[66] *Ibid.*,
[67] Beard, *President Roosevelt and the Coming of War*, 71—72.
[68] *Ibid.*, 97—98.
[69] Millis, *This is Pearl*, 71. By the beginning of April, 1941, Greenland was occupied by the United States, as a link in the defense of the convoys, and in July, American forces hat landed on Iceland with the consent of the Danish minister in Washington to protect the sea routes to Britain. Beard, *President Roosevelt and the Coming of War*, 113.

vessels, broadcast their positions, and shoot in defense of any American ships that might be attacked.[69]

There is too much evidence available[70] to doubt the fact that from April, 1941, and onward, the United States Navy and Air Force convoyed the Allied transports across the Atlantic. They traced and spotted German submarines and raiders, and broadcast their positions to the Allies. In some cases, this led to the sinking of the Axis ships. They also dropped depth charges on submarines. Yet, for a long time the Germans did not shoot back.[71]

The first inevitable clash between the naval forces of the two countries came in September, 1941, when a German submarine fired a torpedo at the U. S. destroyer *Greer*. The torpedo missed its mark, but according to reports the submarine could hardly be blamed for firing. The *Greer* had gone in search for the submarine, traced her, and in obedience to orders broadcast her position. The chase continued for four hours before the submarine turned and charged a torpedo at her attacker.[72]

This incident was characterized as German provocation. In a radio address on September 11, President Roosevelt branded it as «piracy legally and morally. ... These Nazi submarines and raiders are the rattlesnakes of the Atlantic. ... From now on, if German or Italian vessels of war enter the waters, the protection of which is necessary for American defense, they do so at their own peril.»[73] Shortly afterwards, the Secretary of the Navy announced that the «shooting at sight» order had been given. The American naval vessels on route to Iceland would be under orders «to capture or destroy ... Axis-controlled submarines or surface raiders in those waters.»[74] In October, the President asked for authority to arm the American merchant ships, and after the destroyer *Kearney* had been damaged in a battle with a submarine south of Iceland, Congress agreed. On October 27, 1941, the President announced that the «shooting had started», and on the same day Hull declared

---

[70] *Ibid.*, 69—119.

[71] The *Robin Moor*, an American merchant vessel, had been sunk in May, 1941, and as a result German and Italian assets had been frozen. Bailey, *Diplomatic History*, 779—780.

[72] Millis, *This is Pearl*, 149—150. The author makes the suggestion that the submarine was not aware of the *Greer's* nationality.

[73] *New York Times*, September 12, 1941.

[74] Millis, *This is Pearl*, 151.

that «the United States was abandoning international law as regards neutrality in favor of the law of self-defense.»[75] Nonbelligerency was at last made the official status of the United States. It did not enjoy it for long. Two months later, December 7, 1941, came the attack on Pearl Harbor, which abruptly ended the strange, intermediate status which the United States had had for more than two years.

It is impossible to discuss American neutrality in the Second. World War without comparing it to what it was in World War I. During and after the war of 1914—1918, a great many historians and writers on international law have maintained that the United States failed to remain neutral because of its inconsistency.[76] It had reached world preeminence in an economic sense, but refused to take the political responsibility which was a logical consequence of this position. This attitude was based on a misconception. Economic entanglement and involvement could not be combined with political isolation. The mechanism of world economy had become too complex to permit such a division. This was one of the reasons why the United States had to abandon neutrality in 1917.

If the world was economically interrelated in 1914, it was even more so in 1939. During these two decades, America had become increasingly dominant in the world's money markets and more entangled than ever. American experts on international law had always advocated that neutrality was in its essence «profits or peace».[77] If a neutral wanted the war profits, it would also have to accept its corollary, the risk of being drawn into war. The Neutrality Act of 1937 was an attempt to avoid entanglement, even if it meant cutting out substantial profits. It is very doubtful whether this legislation would have served the purpose even if it had been allowed to remain on the statute books. If applied to a longer period, no government would have been able to enforce it.

In the first war as in the second, however, it soon became evident that the question of neutrality was not entirely economic. It soon proved that ideological, political, and emotional factors were

[75] Bailey, *Diplomatic History*, 785—788.
[76] R. S. Baker, *Wilson, Life and Letters*, Vol. V, *Neutrality*, 26.
[77] Jessup, *Today and Tomorrow*.

equally important. The United States was dependent upon the rest of the world for more than markets and matters of finance. Wilson had strongly stressed the cultural ties that bound America to the Allies. The relationship in ideologies made an impartial attitude impossible. But Wilson also realized that this attachment to Great Britain was based on more than sentiments. He repeatedly pointed out the danger of a German victory and said it was a threat to civilization, and if Germany won, the United States would become a military nation.[78] Thus, to defend the American system and institutions, the United States was justified in sacrificing neutrality and if necessary enter the war.

Both Roosevelt and Wilson must have realized what the British naval dominance had meant for the United States. Sheltered by the British navy, the American republic had been developed. Without it, the Monroe Doctrine, and the freedom of the seas would have been a fiction all through the nineteenth century.[79] The system of naval protection had served its purpose already by 1914. By that time, the United States was unquestionably a world power, and before 1939, it ranked equal to Great Britain in naval matters. Thus, the dependence was no more unilateral, but now, as before, the two countries stood for the same ideology, the same kind of culture and civilization, and last but not least, for the same economic system. If Britain fell, the United States would have to defend itself by its own forces. What it previously had done in collaboration with Great Britain, — and its chances of successfully maintaining the balance, would be greatly reduced.

Faced with this possibility, the whole principle of neutrality became a matter of minor importance. It had been useful for a weak nation in the past, but was not applicable to twentieth century conditions. Too much was at stake. Therefore, in time of a national emergency, Roosevelt, as well as Wilson, decided to sacrifice neutrality. But, there should be no confusion as to their motives. They did not primarily want to destroy international law, nor were they thirsty for blood. When they wrecked the principle of neutrality and led the country into two disastrous wars, they did so because they were convinced it was necessary for the future

---

[78] See page 85.

[79] Walter Lippman, *U. S. Foreign Policy* (New York, 1943).

prosperity of the country and the people whose interests they were chosen to defend.

The American people had a vague feeling of this relationship, but they had no clear conception of its real importance. The average American was not accustomed to looking abroad for more than markets. They had grown into the habit of concentrating on their domestic problems and minding their own business. This was the case in 1939 as it had been in 1914. «The Americans agreed on two things, they wanted to keep out of war and they wanted the democracies to win.»[80] As those two aims could no longer be achieved at the same time, the Wilson and the Roosevelt Administrations had to lead the people first to unneutrality, and when that proved insufficient, to direct intervention by the American armed forces. The means they used were slightly different, but the basic argument was the same. The sovereignty of the United States, and the freedom and independence of its institutions were the great arguments used in their efforts to make the people see their points. Wilson was handicapped by a compact sentiment of isolationism, a greater indifference and ignorance as to foreign relations, strong pro-German elements, and a bitter anti-English attitude by the Irish. On the other hand he had the advantage of living twenty years closer to the nineteenth century idealism. He could, therefore, raise emotions by using ringing phrases, referring to high ideals in the abstract. The submarine warfare was an attack on humanity; the loss of American lives was a denial of the sovereign right to travel. The whole German campaign was a war against culture and civilization and aimed at making an end to freedom and democracy.

This last argument was effectively used by Roosevelt, but his appeals to humanity did not have the same force as they had two decades earlier, even though the bombing of civilians was widely resented. On the other hand, he could count on the existence of a solid and substantial group of interventionists and some general interest in foreign affairs, due to twenty years of discussions about international cooperation. But lofty phrases did not have the same appeal. The American people had gone a long way since 1917. War and depression had made them more skeptical of great words and taught them the value of hard facts. Roosevelt, therefore, had to

[80] Bailey, *Diplomatic History*, 759.

alter his tactics. Before the fall of France he had stressed the moral side of the question; aid to the democracies fighting for freedom and justice. After June, 1940, the emphasis was put upon national security and self-defense. Even so, the American people were reluctant to go to war. Isolationism was deeply rooted and until very late Roosevelt had to conduct his «warfare» as a campaign for peace. «Helping the democracies win is the best guarantee for peace.» The Americans rightly felt that neutrality was no longer a living force and an applicable principle, so they almost unanimously gave their consent to non-belligerency, but still they had to be attacked in order to realize its full implication, which was war.

2. The End of Norwegian Neutrality.

When the Second World War started, the small European neutrals fully realized that if neutrality had had a somewhat sickly appearance twenty-five years before, it certainly had not recovered in the meantime. Their attitude toward the whole problem had changed correspondingly. In 1914, the neutrals had protested vigorously against even the slightest violation of their rights. By 1939, they knew better. The Allies and Germans had both declared their blockades and counterblockades as early as September, 1939. War zones had been established across the trade routes, and by November, 1939, the Germans began strewing their magnetic mines which distinguished even less than the submarine between neutral and belligerent ships.[1] That the submarine campaign should be unrestricted seemed to be a matter of course.

At the same time, the Allies re-introduced their economic pressure system of the First World War, with strict rationing, the search in port, and all of the other measures which had made the neutrals submit to their will. The neutrals protested, but there was none of the frantic indignation which had characterized the situation in 1914. The protests were made largely for the sake of record. On the whole, the neutrals accepted the belligerents' infringements without appreciable protests or insistence on theoretical rights of trade.[2]

It will lead too far to follow up the sad story of each of the neutral countries in the Second World War. On the other hand it will be extremely difficult and also misleading to try to speak generally of the neutrality of all these small states taken as a group. Neutrality had long ago lost its international tinge, and had become a national conception which needed a special definition in each particular case. The neutrality of Portugal and Spain was widely different from that applied by, for example, Ireland and

---

[1] Bailey, *Diplomatic History*, 762.
[2] David L. Gordon and Royden Dangerfield, *The Hidden Weapon* (New York, 1947), 70 ff.

Sweden, and had to be dealt with in specific ways. Some writers have counted five European neutrals during the war and even refused to consider the Irish neutrality.[3] No attempt will, therefore, be made here «to put them all in one bag». Since Switzerland still claimed a status of permanent or perpetual neutrality, the small northern states will provide the best representation of old traditional neutrals. Scandinavian neutrality, particularly that of Norway, will therefore be given special consideration.[4]

Even before the Oslo states issued their Declaration of Copenhagen and denounced the sanctions system, the Scandinavian countries had taken steps to polish up their neutrality. On May 27, 1938, Denmark, Finland, Ireland, Norway, and Sweden met for the purpose of establishing common rules of neutrality. Denmark, Sweden and Norway had drawn up a set of neutrality laws in 1912 on the basis of the London Declaration. The rules upon which they agreed in 1938 were, with slight modifications, basically the same. There was a general hope in these countries that neutrality still might be an adequate measure. To some extent, there seemed to have been a difference in attitude between the administrations and the parliaments which reminds one of the American neutrality period. The representatives apparently were more in favor of a strict and impartial neutrality than were the governments who had the experts' knowledge of the impossibility of the task.

Thus, the Norwegian Storting on May 31, 1938, unanimously adopted a resolution stating that Norway would maintain perfect or strict neutrality in all wars that she herself did not regard as actions on the part of the League of Nations.[5] At the same time,

---

[3] Churchill in 1945 said of Ireland, that if it had become necessary, the British would «fast and violently have obtained what they wanted.» *New York Times*, May 14, 1945, 4. As it was, however, it would have been «more trouble than it was worth». Robert R. Wilson, «Questions Relating to Irish Neutrality,» in *American Journal of International Law*, 36 : 288 (April, 1942). See also R. Wilson, «The Neutrality of Eire,» in *American Journal of International Law*, 34 : 126 (January, 1940).

[4] The thesis originally included a chapter on Swedish neutrality as well, but as it had to be shortened, the detailed discussion of Swedish problems had to be left out.

[5] Halvdan Koht, *Norway, Neutral and Invaded*, (New York, 1941), 13; Finn Moe, *Norge i den nye verden* (Oslo, 1946), 22. Professor Halvdan Koht was Norwegian Foreign Minister, 1935—1941; Finn Moe has been the Norwegian delegate to the United Nations.

the Foreign Minister, Koht, said he was «fully convinced that in case of violations of neutrality, there would be no impartiality.» [6]

From the end of 1938, the belligerents to be showed an increasing activity in their courting of the neutrals. Great Britain had been very anxious to get a satisfactory naval arrangement and in the summer of 1938, the four Scandinavian Governments affixed their signatures to a naval treaty with England. This had apparently little practical value since it provided only for a limitation of naval armaments and the small northern navies could hardly be more reduced than they already were, but morally it had some significance. It was ratified by Norway on March 10, 1939. However, she became the only country to ratify the treaty, because shortly after Germany denounced it and the three other Scandinavian states consequently dropped their plans for ratification.[7]

In the spring of 1939, Germany offered non-aggression pacts with the northern nations.[8] These proposals were raised in connection with President Roosevelt's appeal of April 14, 1939. Roosevelt asked Hitler and Mussolini for assurances that they would not attack any of their surrounding countries.[9] These states, upon request, answered that they did not consider themselves threatened by Germany. On April 28, von Ribbentrop followed up his success by asking the Scandinavian states whether they were willing to sign non-aggression pacts with Germany. The Foreign Ministers of Norway, Sweden and Denmark gathered in Stockholm on May 9, but this time they could not agree upon uniform action. Norway and Sweden emphasized strongly the danger of alliances with the greater European states. They had already started cutting loose the obligatory ties that bound them to the League powers, and they did not want to establish new ones with the opposite side. They also remembered that a German-Polish non-aggression pact had been the initiation of a German orientation in that direction. A non-aggression pact would also necessarily weaken their contemplated neutrality policy and make its sincerity extremely doubtful. C. J. Hambro, the Speaker of the Norwegian Storting, said that Norway did not want any such guarantee since «a

[6] Koht, *Utanrikspolitikk*, 19.
[7] Koht, *Norway, Neutral and Invaded*, 11.
[8] *Ibid.*, 14—15.
[9] *Norway War Documents*, 22—25.

neutrality guaranteed from one quarter ceases to be neutral if the case arises».[10] The Norwegian and Swedish Governments, therefore, declined the offer.[11] Denmark, however, was in a different situation. Being the next door neighbor of Germany, she felt that she could not refuse to sign the non-aggression pact. She, therefore, signed the treaty without having many illusions as to the value of the guarantee.[12]

Denmark, however, did not consider that this seriously affected her policy of neutrality and she participated in the conference of the Scandinavian states which was held in Oslo on August 30—31, 1939. The day before the war broke out questions were discussed by the conference as regards «the carrying out of the absolute neutrality of the northern countries in case of a possible war in Europe». They also discussed how this could be facilitated by close economic cooperation.[14] The following day the Norwegian King Haakon VII, let it be known that «nous avons décidé qu'une stricte neutralité sera observeé par la Norvège pendant la guerre...,»[15] and that the neutrality rules of May 27, 1938, would be applied. Proclamations to the same effect were issued by the other Scandinavian countries.

The German reaction was immediate. On September 2, 1939 the Norwegians were told in plain words that if they did not live up to the letter of their neutrality proclamation the German Government would be forced to take any steps it deemed necessary to protect its interests. The British, however, remained silent for nearly three weeks. On September 22 the British minister in Oslo, Sir Cecil Dormer, finally told the Norwegian Foreign Minister that Great Britain would recognize Norwegian neutrality only as long as the Germans did so.[16]

The belligerents had previously taken no such reservations, and the fact that they did make their recognition dependent upon

---

[10] *Le Nord*, 1939, No. 2, 250.

[11] *Norway War Documents*, 2—3, 26. Norway actually had to choose between Sweden and Denmark and in this case the choice could not be doubtful.

[12] For details see Vilh. La Cour, *Paa vej mod Katastrofen*, Voll. III. *Som Sœden — Saa Høsten*, 145 ff.

[14] *Norway War Documents*, 27.

[15] *Ibid.*

[16] Johan Scharffenberg, *Norske Aktstykker til okkupasjonens forhistorie*. (Oslo 1951), 25, Koht's speech in the Storting, October 7, 1939.

certain conditions illustrates that the neutrality of the war was of a very special kind, not to be identified with the well-formulated, respected status it had enjoyed when hostilities began in 1914. The stress was now put almost exclusively on neutral duties, and the actions taken by the third power were drawn into what ought to have been a bilateral agreement. It may actually be defined as a sort of «conditional neutrality», which each of the belligerents was willing to respect only as long as it was respected by the other party.

The future of neutral Norway was accordingly to rest upon the decisions taken by the three concerned parties, Germany, Great Britain and Norway. Thus any step the Germans took toward Norway and her neutrality would automatically lead to Allied reprisals. On the other hand, if the western powers took any action that might give the German Government a good reason to believe that they would no longer observe the neutral code to the letter of the law, the Germans would feel free to counteract them. All parties seem to have understood that what counted were realities and facts, not international law. The crucial point was how this «conditional neutrality» was to be defined and interpreted. Who was to decide when and whether the neutrality of Norway was violated? As this question was not referred to a higher tribunal, it was left to each of the belligerents to decide when the acts of his opponent constituted a breach of Norwegian neutrality.

Norway, the third power, was thus sqeezed and threatened by both belligerents. Her position was extremely difficult and its precariousness and instability was clearly realized by all. The government was fully aware of the fact that the future of the country would to a great extent depend upon the means she found to defend her neutrality and how she applied them. One had to expect that, sooner or later, one or both of the belligerents would attempt to pull Norway over on their side and make her join the war or use her territory and resources to their own ends. If she wished to remain neutral, Norway would have to withstand such attempts. The vital question which the government would have to answer was where to concentrate the defense of neutrality. Was it primarily a military or an economic problem?

Speaking in the Storting September 8, the Foreign Minister, Dr. Koht said he did not think the risk of military violations was so great this time as it had been in 1914. On the other hand, he deemed the likelihood of violations of Norway's economic neutrality to be even greater now. From this basic calculation he found it expedient to concentrate the defense of neutrality on questions related to export and import. In matters of granting and refusing trade he thought it to be of major importance to deal impartially with the two belligerents. «Then we are absolutely irreproachable to all sides. No one can put any blame on us.» Great Britain had already made extensive claims on Norway's trade, and Dr. Koht made special reference to the threat that these meant to the «conditional neutrality» which Norway had been granted by the belligerents. If she were to accept the terms of trade, suggested by the British Government, «Germany would be justified in saying that this constituted a breach of her (Norway's) duties as a neutral, and Germany has explicitly stated that if we do not fulfill those duties that the Germans themselves think we have taken on with our neutrality, they will have a right to all sorts of counteractions on their part.» The Foreign Minister concluded by saying that if any of the belligerents could justly accuse Norway of practising a partial neutrality policy, such counteractions would be the inevitable result. In his opinion the Germans were likely to resort to some forceful means, for instance the torpedoing of ships, while the British probably would use economic pressure. Therefore absolute impartiality was a prime requisite in Norway's relations to the warring powers. The Prime Minister, Mr. Nygaardsvold, speaking immediately afterwards, gave his full support to the views laid down by Dr. Koht.

The lofty goal of such a policy was to make this neutrality equally advantageous to both belligerents. Were that aim attained, neither of them would be interested in destroying Norwegian neutrality. Whether or not it conformed to international law was a matter of minor importance. The contending powers would always have to evaluate the situation on a strictly realistic basis. Their decisions would be based on calculations of how much they could afford to lose compared to what they were sure to gain.

In the neutral camp the problem might be stated: How much can we give to one, before the other starts making objections.» The key-words to the answer were bargaining power and compensations. It was, of course, impossible to export equal quantities of all articles to each belligerent since they needed different things. But whatever the neutral gave to one, had to be counterbalanced with a corresponding amount of goods or services of similar priority rank to the other side. The vital point was to keep the two accounts fairly well balanced. In conformity with the reservations taken in the recognition of Norwegian neutrality, an unsatisfied belligerent would no longer feel obligated to respect Norway's rights as a neutral, and might try some sort of independent action. However, the «injured party» was likely to consider such a step very carefully, particularly if he were in urgent need of the articles he could still obtain from her or if Norway had at its disposal a military force, sufficiently strong to prevent the Allies as well as the Germans from violent actions. The decision would depend upon the belligerents' estimate of the risks, the costs and the gains.

During World War I the neutrality of Norway had been advantageous to the Allies as well as to Germany. Russia was then on the Allied side, and in the critical years up to 1917, enormous quantities of Allied provisions and war-implements had been necessary to keep her fighting. The supplies reached Russia either as transit goods through Norway and Sweden or by way of the arctic searoutes. The transport ships were then in a position to take full advantage of the protection offered by Norwegian territorial waters, and by keeping inside «the Leads» as the British called this sheltered corridor, they were safe from German submarine attacks for hundreds of miles. Naturally, the German freighters using the southern parts of this waterway, took the same advantage of Norwegian neutrality.[17]

The situation in 1939 was entirely different. As Russia was considered to be an ally of Germany, the northern route became of primary importance to the Germans only, who now used the long neutral corridor to their full and exclusive advantage. While the British were not interested in any part of it they still had some need for Norway's tonnage and nitrates, but from an Allied point of view, the maintainance of Norwegian neutrality was not of vital significance to their general warfare.[17] On the other hand, there is a substantial amount of evidence to show that Germany profitted directly and greatly from a strictly neutral policy. Hitler stated on several occasions that Norwegian neutrality was an asset to the German cause. Dr. Koht was «all the time convinced that

---

[17] *Nazi Conspiracy and Aggression.* Collections of documents published by the office of United States Chief of Council for Prosecution of Axis Criminality, VII : 800 (Washington, 1946).

Germany wanted us to stay out of the war.»[18] The Russians and the social democrats all over the world maintained that Scandinavian neutrality would definitely work to the benefit of Germany.[19] This general view has also been accepted by most Allied writers. Christopher Buckley wrote in his chapter on Norway: «... That the occupation of Scandinavia formed no part of Hitlers original conception is now certain. ... Hitler emphasised repeatedly that in his opinion the most desirable attitude for Norway as well as for the rest of Scandinavia would be one of complete neutrality.»[20]

The Germans definitely had quite substantial reasons for wanting to preserve Norwegian neutrality. First, Norwegian domestic products played an important part in Germany's war economy. Fish, herring and whale oil together with certain ores and minerals were almost indispensible, and as the Germans had been stock-piling these articles since 1936, the principle of «normal trade» which the Norwegian Government had chosen as a basis for its exports, was well adapted to German demands.

The Swedish iron ore was no doubt the most important single reason for Hitler to welcome Scandinavian neutrality. This question did not directly concern Norway, but as the Swedish ore during the winter months were sent by train to the Norwegian port Narvik and shipped from there to Germany, it became a grave problem which indeed threatened the neutral status of Norway. All the way from Narvik the ships sailed in Norwegian coastal waters, always keeping inside the three mile limit and never exposing themselves to the risk of being intercepted by Allied naval forces. Considering Germany's naval weakness, the uninterrupted use of this passage was of inestimable value to her. As long as these shipments were safe from Allied violations and as long as the Germans were allowed to carry on their normal, trade with Norway, there seemed to be no reason why they should want to disturb the status quo in Scandinavia. The only possibility for such a disturbance rested with actions taken either by Norway or the Allies.

---

[18] Halvdan Koht, *Frå Skanse til Skanse.* (Oslo 1947), *Norsk Utanrikspolitikk.* (Oslo 1947) p. 43.

[19] During the early stage of the war, they even whispered rumours of some sort of secret connection between those countries and the German General Staff! *Arbeideren* (Oslo) and *Het Volk* (Amsterdam) September 1939.

[20] Christopher Buckley, *Norway, Commandos, Dieppe.* (London 1951) p. 4.

The first alternative, that Norway by her own free will would give up her strict, impartial status, was probably never seriously considered by anyone. Hitler and his generals knew perfectly well that most Norwegians, privately and officially, disliked them and disapproved of their governmental system. But they were also convinced that this idealistic sentiment was not sufficiently strong and deep-rooted to make them give up their peaceful and comfortable neutrality to embark on a crusade against Nazism. Thus the initiative to alter the Scandinavian status quo would necessarily have to be taken by the Allies. This might of course be done by direct military intervention, but the British were thought more likely to use their economic and naval power in order to press Norway into denying the Germans the advantages that a strict observance of the neutrality rules seemed to call for.

But did the Allies really want to take steps that would mean the end of Norwegian neutrality? And even if they should so desire, could they carry them out? Was their own strength sufficient to overcome Norwegian resistance and a possible German counterstroke, and as far as that is concerned, would the Norwegians put up any resistance at all?

During the winter of 1939—40 the Germans were eagerly trying to find out the extent and character of the Allied plans against Scandinavia. Grossly simplified, their problem can be divided into a few detailed questions. The first they were likely to ask for was whether Scandinavian neutrality increased the chances for an Allied victory. If not, were those powers held back by respect of neutral rights, lack of strength to undertake an intervention, or could it be that the Allies feared Norwegian armed resistance?

First, would the disruption of Scandinavian neutrality work to the advantage of the Allies? There was no general agreement. Some of the German officers in charge of naval operations did not think that the British would be able to gain much from an occupation of parts of Norway, while Hitler and Raeder with the leading generals and admirals held that for strategic as well as economic reasons, an Allied intervention might be fateful to Germany and had to be opposed with all means.

It does not appear that the Germans at first knew quite how poorly the British were prepared for the war and how limited their resources were. They apparently had little doubt that the Allies were able to undertake offensive operations in the north if they wanted to. At any rate, it was certain that the British could gain a complete control over Norwegian territorial waters through use of their naval forces alone. So if the Allies could improve their chances of winning the war by starting something that would make Norwegian neutrality worthless to Germany, the German officers naturally wondered why they did not do it?

In the first place, there was the problem of international law and neutral rights. However, this was more formal than real. The First World War had demonstrated very clearly that the law could not give protection if it was not supported by force. It could never be a serious obstacle when vital issues were at stake. Besides, the British had recognized Norwegian neutrality only conditionally; and, provided some pretext could be found, they were free to determine when these conditions no longer existed.

The problem of public world opinion was of greater significance to the British, especially public opinion in the United States. The feeling of traditional neutrality was still alive in the average American and strict neutrality was still popularly believed to be the official policy of the country, even if the administration long since had discarded it. In World War I it took three years to swing the public opinion in America, and the British knew very well what serious consequences might be expected if it could be proved that Great Britain was bullying the small neutrals. From the first stage of the war the British were highly dependent upon American resources, and an open violation of the neutrality of Norway involved great risks and demanded careful consideration. Any Allied step against Norway ought to be camouflaged as a League of Nations action or have some other idealistic justification to make it acceptable to the Americans. Churchill realized this very clearly and made a specific point of it in the memorandum he wrote in December 1939.

> The effect of our action against Norway upon world opinion and upon our own reputation must be considered. We have taken up arms in accordance with the principles of the Covenant of the League in order to aid the victims of German aggression. No technical infringement of International Law, so long as it is unaccompanied by inhumanity of any kind, can deprive us of the good wishes of neutral countries. No evil effect will be produced upon the greatest of all neutrals, the United States. We have reason to believe that they will handle

the matter in the way most calculated to help us. And they are very resourceful.[21]

To the Allies as well as to the Germans a decisive factor must have been the extent and character of a possible Norwegian resistance. The British seem to have believed that Norway certainly would protest very energetically to whatever they might do, but finally acquiesce and refrain from armed resistance. The chances for this seemed to be reasonably good, but there were many problems requiring a great deal of discussion concerning the possible use of force. How much would be needed? Could Norway be brought to terms by economic pressure and blockade measures or would some sort of armed intervention be necessary? The British appear not to have taken Germany seriously into account until they were well under way with their own operations.[22]

The Germans were in a much worse position. They were obviously interested in maintaining Scandinavia as the quiet corner of Europe. But on the other hand, if this proved impossible and the Scandinavian peace had to be broken, they preferred to be the ones who broke it. As they did not think they could afford to let the Allies get in ahead of them, they had to keep a close watch all the time, and be prepared to strike at the first sign of an Allied action or in case Norway seemed to change her neutrality policy adversely. The existence and efficacy of Norwegian resistance must have given the German generals many headaches. How much economic pressure could she take? Was her little navy able to prevent her territorial waters from being violated? Were her ground forces sufficiently trained and equipped to protect harbours and strategic points on her long coast? And then the most controversial of all questions: was Norway *determined* to use what little she had in an all out effort to defend her neutrality against both sides?

Military Preparedness.

To understand Norway's astounding lack of military preparedness, a short review of what had happened to her army and navy since 1918 will be necessary. At the beginning of the century, Nor-

---

[21] Winston S. Churchill, *The Second World War*, Vol. I. *The Gathering Storm*, (London 1948) p. 432.

[22] T. K. Derry, *The Campaign in Norway*. (London 1952.)

way had prepared to fight herself free from Sweden. The disunion was however brought about by peaceful means, but due to her quite extensive armaments prior to 1905, Norway was able to put up a relatively strong military defense during World War I. Rear admiral M. W. Consett, British military attaché to Scandinavia during that period, thought Norway's small navy to be «smart, efficient and well disiplined; her army, however, can not be regarded as a reliable instrument of war.»[23]

Shortly after Norway had joined the League of Nations it came to be widely believed that the system of collective security would be sufficient to preserve a general peace, and consequently national armies no longer were needed. Throughout the twenties the compulsory training of the armed forces was systematically neglected. Although the military service in Norway was general, most soldiers did not get more than 48 days of military training out of the 144 they were supposed to have. In 1930 the training period was reduced to 108 days, and the number of officers were cut down from 3700 to 1440 permanently employed and 1100 reserve officers. Even this radical reduction did not satisfy the politicians. In 1931 the Mowinckel government (Liberal) proposed another drastic cut down. According to this only 470 officers were to be permanently employed with 1100 officers in the reserve. The period of military training was now fixed at 84 days. This bill was brought forth by the Liberal and the Farmer's party and became a law in 1933, the very same year that Hitler came to power in Germany.

The military authorities repeatedly and vehemently warned against those new defense measures. They maintained that the forces now at their disposal were absolutely inadequate for an effective defense of the country. But the officers were not prepared to press the issue, and were consequently overruled by the politicians who readily admitted that the force was quite small, but held that trained as an élite corps, it would provide a satisfactory guarantee for the neutrality of the country in case of war. To relieve the military authorities of some of their responsibility, it was expressly stated that the new regulations were dependent upon great foresight on the part of the Foreign Minister and the government's experts on foreign affairs. They were

[23] M. W. W. P. Consett, *The Triumph of Unarmed Forces*. (London 1928) p. 107.

supposed to give timely warnings when and if a new war was approaching and thus make it possible to strengthen the national defense.

The Conservative party was opposed in principle to any reduction of armaments, but did not make any real effort to have the bill defeated. The Labor party, at that time the biggest single party in the Storting, also disliked the new army law, but on entirely different grounds. True to the socialist doctrines of their day, the Labor politicans were very pacifistic and included general disarmament as one of the main planks in their platform. The socialists wanted to do away with both the army and the navy and substitute them with «national guards». This *vaktvern* was not supposed to put up an effective, armed resistance, but should in some rather mysterious way guard the neutrality of the country and keep the belligerents out.

This anti-militaristic attitude was only partly due to the ideologic background. For as most Norwegian officers were recruited from the conservative camp, Labor regarded army and navy as strongholds of their political enemy, the bourgeois, capitalistic class. Pointing to fascism and nazism, the Labor leaders seem to have feared that the armed forces some day might be used as a state police in order to suppress their socialistic movement. The complete abolishment of the national armed forces was apparently felt as sort of a guarantee against such eventualities. If it were impossible to get rid of the forces all together, they ought at least to be kept as small as possible. Labor held on to this view with great consistency and with little or no understanding of the development on the international scene.

The Labor party took over the government in 1935, just as the Italo—Ethiopian war demonstrated to all the world that the League of Nations had failed to build up a system of collective security. The party nevertheless continued to preserve its ideas of disarmament and antimilitarism. The training period in the army was again reduced, this time to 72 days.[24] There is, however, reason to believe that some of the Labor leaders by that time saw the need for a stronger national defense; but they had for years worked up such a powerful anti-militaristic sentiment among their voters that they would need years to break it down, and make to some extent the masses military minded.

[24] *Innstilling fra undersøkelseskommisjonen av 1945.* (Oslo 1946) p. 23.

However, the military authorities now began to press hard for appropriations, and late in 1936, with the Spanish Civil War as a background, the government put an extra grant of 4 millon crowns at the disposal of army and navy. Additional grants were made in 1937—38, but they did not come any where near to the 40 million crowns a year that the General and Admirality Staffs demanded as their minimum requirement. From 1938 on the soldiers were again given 84 days of training. In 1939 considerable amounts of money were appropriated to military expenditures, but by then it was then too late to bring about a real improvement of the national defense. By September 1939 Norway could put only 100.000 men in the field. The navy was as small as ever and most of its ships dated from the nineteenth century. The forces lacked trained men and officers, as well as modern equipment and weapons.

It should be emphasised that even if the Liberals and particulary the Labor party are directly responsible for the inadequate defense measures, *all* the political parties have to take their share of guilt for having consistently neglected national defense in the period between the wars. None of them seems to have had a realistic conception of the international situation. Neither the politicians nor the people were willing to take the economic sacrifices necessary for an adequate armament program. Confused by the high ideals for a general peace, disarmament and collective security, hampered by party strife and mutual suspicion, they clung in despair to a course of neutral opportunism, and closed their eyes to the hard facts of the actual situation.

The Iron Ore.

Information about Norwegian military matters was not difficult to obtain in Norway, and the Allies as well as the Germans must have known the strength and the state of preparedness of Norwegian armed forces during the winter of 1939—40. Their deficiencies were obvious and it goes without saying that they could hardly detain an aggressor or provide a guarantee for the maintenance of neutrality. On the other hand, could the lack of trained soldiers and equipment be compensated if the Norwegian Government and people were ready to bring any sacrifice of life and property that prove necessary to ward the belligerents off? Was such a desparate resistance possible and if so, would it bring other countries into the picture?

The uncertainty on the part of the belligerents as to the existence of Norway's determined, undiscriminating will to self defense and secondly, the question of the plans and intentions of the enemy, are two of the universal keys to an understanding of the breakdown of Norwegian neutrality on April 9, 1940.

The British and French knew well that Norwegian neutrality worked against their interests, and a strict observance of international law would actually benefit the German cause. The Allies had realized this from the very outset, and as early as September 19, 1939. Winston Churchill, then First Lord of the Admirality, drew the attention of the Cabinet to «the importance of stopping the Norwegian transportation of Swedish iron ore from Narvik, which will begin as soon as the ice forms in the Gulf of Bothnia». In his memorandum Churchill went on to tell that «the Cabinet, including the Foreign Secretary, appeared strongly favourable to this action». He therefore thought it necessary to take all steps to prepare for it.

But the operation could not be undertaken right away as Great Britain was hard up for Norwegian tanker tonnage. It was thus necessary to secure a substantial part of Norway's merchant marine before any action against her might take place. Churchill also pointed at the importance of securing American acceptance of the action and of making arrangements with the Swedes for the purchase of their ore. Great Britain had demanded a tonnage agreement from the beginning of the war, and during the last days of September Churchill thought that such an agreement could be reached «in a few days».[25] The negotiations were however delayed, as Norway made a vain attempt to get a trade agreement, based on «normal trade», in return for the 1,5 million tons of tanker tonnage that England wished to charter. However, she was given no guarantee for her trade, and the shipping agreement was signed November 11 and finally ratified on November 20.

The tonnage obstacle was now out of the way and on December 16, 1939 Churchill wrote a third memorandum to the Cabinet, now stating that «the effectual stoppage of the Norwegian ore supplies ranks as a major offensive operation of the war.» He then went on to describe how this could be done and why the Allies had to

---

[25] Memorandum of 20 September 1939, *Churchill I.* 422—423.

do it. The outlines for his action have a direct bearing on the principle of conditional neutrality, and provide an extremely interesting illustration to the relations between a great belligerent and a small neutral state. His memorandum said very little of neutral right and duties. The problem was seen from above, from the viewpoint of a great power. Churchill referred to the cruelty and lawlessness of the German submarine warfare, violations of Norwegian territorial waters and the sinkings without warning. These actions could not be tolerated and necessitated an Allied counterstroke. The British response would be the laying of a minefield in Norwegian territorial waters. This would press the German ore freighters out of the Leads and make them liable to interception by British naval forces.

The action was thus supposed to be justified by the inhumanity of the German warfare, but Churchill was not blind to the possibility that Norway might consider it to be a grave violation of her rights as a neutral and sovereign state. Suggestions had been made that Norway

> by way of protest may cancel the valuable agreement we have made with her for chartering her tankers and other shipping. But then she would lose the extremely profitable bargain she has made with us, and this shipping would become valueless to her in view of our contraband control. Her ships would be idle and her owners impoverished. It would not be in Norwegian interests for her Government to take this step; and interest is a powerful factor. Thirdly, Norway could retaliate by refusing to export to us the aluminium and other war materials which are important to the Air Ministry and the Ministry of Supply. But here again her interests would suffer. Not only would she not receive the valuable gains which this trade brings her, but Great Britain, by denying her bauxite and other indispensible raw materials, could bring the whole industry of Norway, centering upon Oslo and Bergen, to a complete standstill. In short, Norway, by retaliating against us would be involved in economic and industrial ruin.[26]

Churchill apparently was well informed of sentiments in Norway, and he very rightly pointed to the fact that Norwegian sympathies were on the side of the Allies and that the future

[26] *Churchill I*, pp. 430—33.

independence of the country was dependent upon their victory. Therefore, he argued «it is not reasonable to suppose that she will take either of the counter-measures mentioned above (though she may threaten them), unless she is compelled to do so by German brute force.» This Churchill thought, would be applied to her anyway, provided the Germans found it would serve their interests to dominate the Scandinavian peninsula by force of arms. In that case Churchill saw

> no reason why French and British troops should not meet German invaders on Scandinavian soil. At any rate, we can certainly take and hold whatever islands or suitable points on the Scandinavian coast we choose. Our northern blockade of Germany would then become absolute. We could for instance, occupy Narvik and Bergen, and keep them open for our own trade while closing them completely to Germany. It cannot be too strongly emphasised that British control of the Norwegian coast-line is a strategic objective of first-class importance. It is not therefore seen how, even if retaliation by Germany were to run its full course, we should be worse off for the action now proposed. On the contrary, we have more to gain than to lose by a German attack upon Norway and Sweden.[27]

It ought to be expressly stated that Churchill did not write this memorandum as Prime Minister, but as the head of the Admiralty, one of the many ministers in the British Cabinet. But the fact that his plan was seriously considered by the government and at any rate seems to have had its principal approval, gives it a great significance. Churchill did not, at that time, get the authority to go ahead with his mine-laying action. But the decisions that were taken; the plans for landing a force at Narvik, the diplomatic action concerning the German abuse of Norwegian territorial waters, and the considerations about the military consequences of a German occupation of southern Norway, were indeed sufficent to open up grave prospects for the future of Norwegian neutrality.

Watchful Waiting.

About the same time as Churchill wrote his first memorandum about an action against Norway, the German admirals, Carls,

[27] *Ibid.*

Doenitz and above all, Grand Admiral Raeder, had begun working with plans for extending the scope of German naval warfare by obtaining bases in Norway. In his memoranda Raeder had stressed two major points, the dangers that an Allied occupation of the Norwegian coast-line would bear to Germany, as well as the great usefulness of establishing German bases there for attacks on Allied shipping in the Atlantic. Raeder had brought these plans to the Fuehrer's attention but did not then get his approval. On the contrary, Hitler stressed his wish to maintain Scandinavian neutrality as long as possible. However, in the middle of December 1939, almost simultaneously with Churchill's memorandum of December 16, Admiral Raeder secured audiences to Hitler for two Norwegians, Vidkun Quisling and his friend Hagelin. These men told Hitler that the British prepared for an invasion of Norway which might be expected at almost any time. Obviously Hitler long since must have been aware of such a possibility but until then he seems to have been convinced that Norwegian neutrality would be preserved. Quisling's information, together with other reports which he received through his special channels must at any rate have made Hitler question whether this view ought to be revised.

Further developments increased his fears and shortly after Quisling's visit in Berlin, Hitler ordered the first introductory plans to be made for a German attack against Norway and Denmark. Throughout December and January there were certainly no signs that the Allies had cancelled their plans against Norway. On the contrary, a series of events seemed to indicate that the British and particularly the French not only planned, but actually prepared for some sort of action to deny to the Germans the benefits of Norwegian neutrality.

About the middle of December, 1939, the British threatened to stop all Norwegian exports to Germany, and by the end of the month they started a diplomatic offensive against the Norwegian Government. The Foreign Minister, Lord Halifax, maintained in a series of notes and memoranda dating from December 22 to January 6, that as the Norwegians were unable to prevent the Germans from using Norwegian territorial waters for their naval operations, the British would have to step in themselves, with their own naval forces.[28] The threats caused quite a panic in Norwegian governmental circles and led to vigorous protests from both the Norwegian and Swedish Governments. The King found the situation so serious that he in a letter to King George VI asked him to «prevent such steps which inevitably would bring Norway into war and imply the greatest danger for Norway's existence as a Sovereign State.»[29] This diplomatic pressure was shortly afterwards relaxed, and the proposed Allied actions were not carried out at that time.[30]

Interest now centered upon the Russo—Finnish war which opened new prospects for Allied intervention in Norway. Until the end of December 1939 nobody dared to think that the Finns would be able to stand up against the Russian war machine. However, by January 1940, the Finns had not only held their positions, but also inflicted serious defeats on the Red Army of Russia. This gave new actuality to the Allied plans and preparations. There now seemed to be a fair chance of killing two birds with one stone: to sending troops to Finland and at the same time gaining control of Narvik and the Swedish ore fields at Gällivare.

The wide publicity given to this enterprise could hardly escape Hitler's attention, and from the German point of view there now seemed to be a very great possibility of a an Allied action against Scandinavia. Consequently German planning was speeded up. The small staff that had worked on the «Study N.» was now enlarged and comprehensive preparations were made under the code name *Weserübung*.

In the beginning of January 1940 a German pilot made an emergency landing in Belgium and the German plans for the offensive on the west front were exposed. This action was postponed and in the meantime reports kept coming in which seemed to indicate that the Allied preparations for actions against Scandinavia were well under way. It should be noted that what

[28] «German naval forces have made Norwegian waters a theater of war and have in practice deprived them of their neutral character. ... His Majesty's Government are, therefore, taking appropriate dispositions to prevent the use of Norwegian territorial waters by German ships and trade. To achieve this purpose it would be necessary to enter and operate in those waters.» *Förspelet till det tyska angreppet på Danmark och Norge den 9 april 1940.* (Stockholm 1948.) 21—23.

[29] *Innstilling* fra undersøkelseskom. 1945. 234.

[30] *Sveriges Forhaallande till Danmark och Norge under krigsaaren.* (Stockholm 1945), 8—9.

really counted was not so much the actual extent of the British and French preparations, as the information Hitler received and what he *thought* the Allies were about to do. A German major named Deyhle wrote in his war diary that Hitler made the principal decision to invade Norway and Denmark «in the middle of January 1940»,[31] but it is generally supposed that the *Altmark* incident gave Hitler the decisive proof of aggressive Allied intentions. The *Altmark,* a German auxillary ship was boarded by the British cruiser *Cossack,* in a Norwegian fjord in the presence of three Norwegian torpedo boats, which, however, did nothing but protest.

The Race.

The *Altmark* affair made Hitler realise two very important things. First, it seemed to prove that the Allied threats against Norway early in January were based on actual planning and not on bluff. As it will be remembered the British had previously warned the Norwegian Government that if it did not stop the German traffic in the Leads, they would have to extend their naval operations to these waters. That was exactly what had happened when the *Cossac* went into the Jössingfjord. To Hitler the incident confirmed the reports from his *Abwehr* agents. From then on he could not doubt that the British and French did *not* intend to respect Norwegian neutrality.[32] On the contrary, such actions as the *Altmark* affair were likely to be repeated on an ever increasing scale, and consequently the neutral corridor along the coast of Norway would be useless to the Germans.

The *Altmark* episode also revealed to the Germans something about Norway. The demonstration of military weakness did not surprise them; that they had known all the time. But as no resistance was even attempted, the Germans thought it to be a strong indication that the Norwegian Government did not intend to fight for the preservation of her neutrality. They knew that the torpedo boats had not shot at the British in the Jössingfjord, and were not likely to shoot the next time British naval forces appeared in Norwegian waters. So what should then prevent the Allies from

---

[31] Major Deyhle's war diary, *Bilag til Beretning til Folketinget,* Supplement 12, vedrørende Forholdene ved Danmarks Besættelse 9. April 1940, (København 1951) p. 6. Deyhle was First Staff Officer at general Jodl's staff.

[32] Peter de Mendelsohn, *Design for Aggression* (New York 1946) 124—125, Anthony Martienssen, *Hitler and His Admirals,* (New York 1948). 48—49.

taking over control, when Norway took no action to keep them out? The Nygaardsvold government's reaction to the violation must have added greatly to this impression. Of course, the Foreign Minister protested very emphatically, but the government made no attempt to strengthen the national defense of the country. It ordered no mobilization or even a transfer of ground or naval forces into areas on the west coast where similar incidents might be expected.

There were also rumors of a secret understanding between the Norwegian and the British Governments although no evidence was ever brought to prove it. However, the existence or nonexistence of such an agreement could not have been decisive to Hitler. What counted was the fact that the British had demonstrated their readiness to violate Norwegian neutrality, and the Norwegians on their part had shown that they were not going to defend it with armed force. Whether this had reference only to the British, still remained a doubtful question, but temporarily the Germans might at least hope that even they would not be met with armed resistance, provided they came «to defend Norwegian neutrality» — and their own interests.

At any rate, from February 17, 1940 on, the Germans knew that whether they were received as friends or not, they would have to act. If there were to be no radical change of strategy in the Allied headquarters, if the French and the British continued to regard Scandinavia as an object of major strategic importance, Hitler realized that he would have to invade Norway sooner or later in order not to lose the precious Swedish ore together with the strategic and economic advantages that so far had been obtainable through Norwegian neutrality.[33] If the Germans struck too late the Allies might get ahead of them, shut them out from all those articles that they needed so badly;[34] and at the same time threaten their positions in the north of Germany and in the Baltic. On February 21 Hitler placed General Falkenhorst in charge of the planning for the invasion of Norway and Denmark, with expressive orders to have the invasion forces ready as soon as possible. In giving him reasons for this operation Hitler put particular stress

[33] *Förspelet.* Bilaga 6, 310—312, *Brassey's Annual Naval Reports.* H. M. Stationary Office (London 1948). 79.

[34] *Trial of the Major War Criminals* before the International Military Tribunal. (Nuremberg, 1946—49). Vol. XXXIV. 334.

on the Swedish ore and the disasterous consequences of an Allied occupation of the Norwegian port Narvik. «We can under no circumstances afford to lose the Swedish ore. If we do, we will soon have to wage the war with wooden sticks.»[35]

From then on the preparations on both sides went on with steadily increasing speed and actually developed into a virtual race between the two belligerents; each of them working independently, trying to get ready as fast as possible.

It should be emphasized that the Russo—Finnish armistice, March 13, 1940 was of no decisive importance for the carrying out of either plan. It meant some delay to the Allies who had originally hoped to start their operations by the end of March.[36] It deprived them of their pretext; they could no longer pretend to be carrying out a League of Nation's action against an aggressor state. But on the other hand, and this was particularly important to the British, they no longer ran the risk of getting into a conflict with Soviet Russia. The French had all the time been pressing hard for the final decision to launch the attack, and on March 28, the Supreme War Council decided that the operations were to start with the mine-laying action that Churchill had been advocating since September 1939. This «small and innocent» operation was no doubt intended to provoke Germany into exposing her naval forces and sending troops to Sweden and the south of Norway. An effective provocation might in turn lead to the opening up of a new theater of war in Scandinavia, which might relieve the pressure on France. Whatever was to be the final result, it was supposed to give the Allies a full control of Norwegian territorial waters with a subsequent occupation of strategic points on the western and northern coasts of Norway.

The Germans, however, needed no direct provocation. The termination of the war in Finland had also put them in need of a

---

[35] «Das Schwedenerz ist für uns absolut unentbehrlich. Fällt es aus müssen wir bald den Krieg mit Holzknütteln führen. Da der südliche Ausfuhrhafen Luleå in den Wintermonaten zugefroren ist, erreicht uns das Erz in der Hauptsache über den norwegischen Hafen Narvik. Setzt sich der Feind hier oder irgendwo an der norwegischen Küste fest, so ist dieser Seeweg und damit die Erzlieferung selbst ohne unmittelbaren Zugriff auf das schwedishe Erzgebiet abgeschnitten.» B. von Lossberg, *Im Wehrmachtführungstab* (Hamburg 1950) p. 57.

[36] T. K. Derry, *The Campaign in Norway*, p. 12.

pretext, but it had by no means changed their plans.[37] They had hoped to be ready to strike by March 20, but as the ice did not break in the Danish Belts and in the Baltic as soon as expected, they had to postpone the action until April. As there was no proof, no reliable report to indicate that there had been a significant change in the Allied conception of the importance of the Swedish ore and of Norwegian neutrality, — and as Norway still floated on as ownerless property and was unprepared and seemingly unwilling to defend heartedly her neutrality, Hitler on April 2 decided to strike a week later.

The Allied action was first scheduled to take place on April 5, but as the French objected to a projected mining of the Rhine,[38] it was held off for three days. The British force which had been held ready for operations in Norway had been dispersed after the end of the Russo—Finnish war, but a smaller British expeditionary force, mostly consisting of untrained troops, embarked for Norway on the seventh but were temporarily disembarked. The initial operations started on April 8 with the laying of mines in Norwegian territorial waters. By that time most of the German forces had left their ports of embarkation and were on their way to Norway. Thus the two belligerents had started their actions almost simultaneously; and the final stage of the race for Norway was on.[39]

«Lop-sided» Neutrality.

The sad story of the belligerent's race for Norway in April 1940, involves vital problems for all small countries. Why was Norway invaded; why could she not go on staying neutral? Could she have prevented it or will the belligerents have to take all the blame for the action?

A question of war guilt will always be very extremely hard to settle and in the case of Norway one can not hope to reach a

---

[37] Cif. Jodl's diary, March 1940. *Nuremberg Trials.* Vol. XXVIII, 400 ff.
[38] Operation Royal Marine.
[39] For those who are interested in more details of this race and the campaign in Norway, the following secondary sources may be of some help.
Jacques Mordal, *La Campagne de Norvège* (Paris 1949). Paul Reynaud, *La France a sauvé l'Europe* (Paris 1947). T. K. Derry, *The Campaign in Norway* (London 1952). Kurt Assmann, *Deutsche Schicksaalsjahre* (Wiesbaden 1950). Walther Hubatsch, *Die deutsche Besetzung von Dänemark und Norwegen 1940* (Göttingen 1952).

universally satisfactory answer. It was an interplay of a great many of factors, and the three main actors in the tragedy will have to share the responsibility among themselves.

Great Britain and France did plan an invasion of Norway that would put her territorial waters, some strategic points on the west coast, and possibly Narvik and the Swedish ore fields under their control. They hoped this could be done with the tacit approval of the Norwegian Government and people; and without having to interfere with the internal affairs of the country. Their preparations were quite advanced by the end of January, and on February 5 the Supreme War Council took the decision to put the plans into effect.

The German staffs knew that something was brewing, and the indications that the plans eventually would be carried out were too strong for the Germans to neglect them. Germany obviously preferred the preservation of strict neutrality on the Scandinavian peninsula. Her navy was too small to make full use of bases in Norway and what little she might gain from such, could hardly compensate the cost of an occupation and the many advantages Norwegian neutrality had secured her. Germany could not afford to lose all these, and when she discovered that the Allies would not limit themselves to purely economic measures against Scandinavia, but actually intended to come over and take the west and north part of the peninsula under their direct control, Germany had no doubt as to which course to take. She had to beat or be beaten, so she decided to strike hard, fast — and first.

Naturally, this does not excuse what else the Germans have done before and after the occupation of Norway. There was no sentimentality, no general respect for international law on the German side. Their main object was to win the war and if Norwegian neutrality from the outset had been more advantageous to the Allies than to them, the Germans would have destroyed it with no hesitation. As things were, they would rather not. In the case of Norway the first days of April 1940, Germany principally did exactly what her democratic enemies had long planned to do themselves. The cynical disregard for international law was quite substantial on the Allied side as well. In short, it was a matter of power politics, and history has repeatedly demonstrated that when vital issues are at stake in a general war between great powers, legal and even human arguments carry little weight.

The French general Weygand has once said that «the case of Norway is a confirmation of the fact that neutrality is not a safe position. It can not be defended by armed forces unless the two opponents are equally interested in preserving it».[40] As already mentioned, this may to some extent explain why Norwegian neutrality survived the first great war, but not the second.

General Weygand's statement raises a very important question. Is it impossible to defend neutrality, when the scales are uneven, when it works to the benefit of only one belligerent and not the other? If this holds true, Norway might as well have put up no armed defense at all, and consequently Sweden and particularly Switzerland must have wasted the money they spent on armaments for national defense. Obviously, Weygand's comment can not be given a general application. There will always be certain proportions between investment and gains. Different objects may be of a varying strategic and economic importance, and even a great power will have to make careful estimates of the calculated risks in relation to what it may gain — or lose. There is evidence to show that Churchill did not think there was much to lose by an Allied action in Norway. On the other side, Hitler believed that the Swedish ore was *kriegsentscheidend,* that is of decisive importance to the outcome of the war, and that the Allies under no circumstances should be allowed to gain control of Scandinavia. The French and the British seem to have taken the risks and the consequences very lightly, whereas the Germans were fully aware of the fact that they risked the total loss of most of their navy. Still they did not hesitate to venture it.

Then, would the belligerents have been discouraged and frightened had Norway been defended by an efficient, well-trained and equipped navy backed up by a fully mobilized army which the Norwegian government was firmly determined to use against any one who tried to violate her neutrality? — Had such a desparate, suicidal effort proved sufficient to keep the Allies away and make the Germans feel confident that no Allied offensive operations would be carried out against Norway? It may seem futile to ask such hypothetical questions, and of course no certain answer can be found to them, but nevertheless it is sometimes

---

[40] Mordal, *La Campagne de la Norvège,* p. 10.

helpful to the understanding of an event to see what was, in the light of what might have been.

Norway lacked trained soldiers as well as implements of war. Her rudimentary army was not mobilized, and there is every reason to believe that the government was not disposed to fight those who were on «the right side». Dr. Koht, the Foreign Minister, has repeatedly said, both before and afterwards, that if neutrality no longer could be preserved, Norway had to make sure not to get into the war on the wrong side.

> We never had neutrality of thought in Norway and I never wanted it. ...I did not mean that we should give the violations of neutrality an equal treatment regardless of which side. If we did not succeed in keeping up our neutrality we had to see that we in no case were drawn into the war on the German side.[41]

Koht also emphasized that he wanted to do and did what he could to keep his neutrality as close to the letter of the law as possible, but it obviously was a handicap from the very start that the decision as to an eventual participation already was taken. In plain words, if the Allies for some reason had happened to get there first, the government is most likely to have offered no resistance at all.

To some extent it may be said that the Labor government was in the same position as the Wilson administration found itself during the first years of World War I. They both tried to carry out a neutral policy, but only to a certain limit. They could not risk incidents that might lead to shooting and warlike actions against the British. Ideologically and economically Norway belonged in the Allied camp. Socialists and Conservatives alike disapproved most heartily of Hitler and his Nazi system. The Norwegians firmly believed in the thc high ideals of democracy, individual freedom and international justice — and they were not at all blind to their country's dependency of the western economic system. Their hearts and hopes were with the Allies and their cause, though some of they certainly realized that the war was also a deadly struggle between two great powers for economic and political domination of

---

[41] Koht, *Utanrikspolitikk*, 16—17, see also Koht, *Norway, Neutral and Invaded*, 17.

Europe. According to the Foreign Minister, such a *Machtpolitik* was of no concern to Norway, who preferred to step aside in the truly neutral way, and let the belligerents settle their quarrels between themselves.[42] But how could this be possible in a world where the ideologies had penetrated down to the smallest of the small citizens? How could they close their eyes and remain indifferent?

Necessity versus Legality.

The Allies knew that the small countries of Europe were their potential friends. The northern neutrals had also seen how the big, German wolf had devoured one small country after the other, and they did not want to keep them company. This was clearly realized by both the French and the British who consciously used this argument in pleading the justice of their cause. The Allied point of view found an eloquent expression in Churchill's address broadcast Januar 20, 1940. The lot of the unfortunate neutrals was the central theme of the speech and he left them with no illusions as to what might happen to them if they did not line up with the Allies.

> Whether on sea or land, they are the victims upon whom Hitler's hate and spite descend. ...Every one of them is wondering which will be the next victim on whom the criminal adventurers of Berlin will cast their rending stroke...
> But what would happen if all these neutral nations I have mentioned — and some others I have not mentioned — were with one spontaneous impulse to do their duty in accordance with the Covenant of the League, and were to stand together with the British and French Empires against aggression and wrong? At present their plight is lamentable; and it will become much worse. They bow humbly and in fear to German threats of violence, comforting themselves meanwhile with the thought that the Allies will win, that Britain and France will strictly observe the laws and conventions, and that breaches of these laws are only to be expected from the German side. Each one hopes that if he feeds the crocodile enough, the crocodile will eat him last. All of them hope that the storm

---

[42] Koht in the Students Union in Trondheim, February 17, 1940.

will pass before their turn comes to be devoured. ... There is no chance of a speedy end except through united action; and if at any time Britain and France, wearying of the struggle, were to make a shameful peace, nothing would remain for the smaller States of Europe, with their shipping and their possessions, but to be divided between the opposite, though similar, aims of Nazidom and Bolshevism.[43]

Churchill's speech caused great anxiety in the neutral countries. Dr. Koht stated February 17, 1940 that the position of the neutrals was much more difficult this time, because men of great influence, as Churchill and Leon Blum, maintained that the Allies fought for the cause of the neutrals and held it to be their duty to help them in the struggle. But with due respect for their idealism, said the Foreign Minister, one had to realize that after all it was a fight for power and in such a war, neutrality was a matter of course for the small states.[44]

The Foreign Minister of Sweden, Chr. Günther, commented on Churchill's speech in an address given in Stockholm February 8, 1940. Taking a realistic view, he warned against putting too much confidence in neutrality legislation. A declaration of neutrality could not make neutral territory sacred and inviolable. A military defense was necessary to make it valid. If, for instance, Swedish territory was violated by Germany, Sweden would no longer be regarded as neutral in her relations to Great Britain. From a British point of view, the important thing was not Germany's attack on Sweden, but the fact that Sweden lacked the means and the will to resist violations of her neutrality.[45] Koht, however, maintained that according to the League Covenant, Norway had no duty to help the Allies. Nor did he think that violations from one side gave the other any right to reprisals.[46]

March 30, two days after the Allied Supreme War Council had taken the fateful decision to start their operations against Scandinavia, Churchill in another radio speech heaped more blame on the neutrals. The war might have been very short, he said; in fact there might not even have been a war if all the neutral states who

---

[43] Address broadcast, 20 January 1940, Winston S. Churchill, War speeches, *Into Battle*. (London 1941) p. 160.
[44] Koht's speech in Trondheim 17/2—40.
[45] Günther's speech 8/2—40, *Aftenposten* 9/2—40.

believed in the same fundamental matters as the Allies did, and who openly or secretly sympathized with them, had joined their ranks.

> We have the greatest sympathy for these forlorn countries, and we understand their dangers and their point of view; but it would not be right, or in the general interest, that their weakness should feed the aggressor's strength and fill to overflowing the cup of human woe. There can be no justice if in a mortal struggle the aggressor tramples down every sentiment of humanity and if those who resist him remain entangled in the tatters of legal conventions.

Churchill again stressed the difficult position of the neutrals, «but when we are asked to take as a matter of course interpretations of neutrality which give all the advantages to the aggressor and inflict all the disadvantages upon the defenders of freedom, I recall a saying of the late Lord Balfour: This is a singularly ill-contrived world, but not so ill-contrived as that.»[47]

In most quarters this was felt as a threat against Norway, and in a newspaper interview on April 2, Koht warned Churchill not go too far. For the sake of their independence and national honour, the small nations might be obliged to take up arms, if they were driven beyond a certain limit.[48] The fact that Chamberlain spoke the same day without saying anything that could weaken Churchill's speech March 30, added to the impression that the situation was really serious. British newspapers interpreted it to mean that from now on anything might be expected at any time.

From what has been said above, it appears that the neutrality of Norway could not be maintained because it rested on an artificial basis. The government tried earnestly to keep the neutrality as close as possible to the letter of international law, but as long as it was not backed up by a strong and undiscriminating military force, it was all in vain. The more so since the government as well as the people lacked the impartiality of mind, the ideological indifference which is the cornerstone, the basic requirement of a true neutrality.

[46] Koht, 17/2—40.
[47] Churchill, 30 March, 1940. *Into Battle*, 181—182.
[48] *Innstilling, 1945.* Bilag I., p. 164.

From the time of Woodrow Wilson, the idea of one belligerent fighting for the right, the other for the wrong cause, had steadily been gaining ground. The aggressor theory had become generally accepted and was well rooted in peoples' minds, and Hitler's and Mussolini's annexations of small countries had made it quite easy to single out the aggressive nations in Europe. Even if most statesmen clearly saw the basic issues, the struggle for economic and political power, the moral arguments retained their popular force and became of decisive importance in forming a world public opinion. Both belligerents knew this well, but the Germans never were in a position to use these moral arguements very effectively; their ideology had little appeal outside of Germany. The Allies, however, applied theirs with vigour and conviction — and with considerable success. The British propaganda had been among the strongest single factors in making the American people line up with the Allies in World War I. In the Second War the same arguements created in the minds of neutral peoples a sort of guilty consience, which to an ever increasing degree worked to the benefit of the Allies. In justifying his proposed action in the memorandum of December 16, 1939, Churchill wrote that no technical violation of international law could deprive the British of the good wishes of all neutral countries, «so long as it is unaccompanied by inhumanity of any kind.»[49] The last part of his memorandum is particularly interesting and should be quoted in full:

> The final tribunal is our own conscience. We are fighting to re-establish the reign of law and to protect the liberties of small countries. Our defeat would mean an age of barbaric violence, and would be fatal not only to ourselves, but to the independent life of every small country in Europe. Acting in the name of the Covenant, and as virtual mandatories of the League and all it stands for, we have a right, and indeed are bound in duty, to abrogate for a space some of the conventions of the very laws we seek to consolidate and reaffirm. Small nations must not tie our hands when we are fighting for their rights and freedom. The letter of the law must not in supreme emergency obstruct those who are charged with its protection and enforcement. It would not be right or rational that the Aggressor Power should gain one set of advantages by tearing

---

[49] *Churchill I*, p. 432.

up all laws, and another set by sheltering behind the innate respect for law of its opponents. Humanity, rather than legality, must be our guide.[50]

No further explanation should be needed to indicate that in the 20th century world, where the moral conceptions are given so much weight, and legality so little, neutrality is not feasible. In this our world, where wars between states are pictured as crusades, as battles between the good and the evil forces, the true impartial neutrality based on law will find no place and will be denied any future existence.

---

[50] *Ibid.*

3. Neutrality and the United Nations

The United Nations has been established as an attempt to create an international organization which can regulate the relations between peoples and countries in a peaceful way, and thus eliminate the danger of war. It is based on the same principles as the League of Nations, but has tried to avoid some of the traits which weakened the League and decreased its efficiency. The stress is, to a much greater extent, on actual force rather than on ideologies and moral pressure. The recognition of the dominant influence of the great powers is an indication of this new attitude.

The United Nations, as well as the League, means a limitation of the sovereignty of the member states. It consequently precludes neutrality, at least in theory, even if as yet no official declaration has been issued to that effect. Neither is there any reason why such a statement should be necessary. Neutrality, in its accepted and legalised version never regained its respectability after the First World War, and may be said to have been almost completely liquidated by the recent struggle. Thus, since 1945, few references have been made to the concept of neutrality, and when it occasionally has appeared in discussions, it has not fared well.

The writers on international law who have recently commented on neutrality do not seem to think that it has much chance in the postwar world. E. A. Koravin said in 1946, that under the existing conditions neither weak countries nor great powers could stay out of a general war,

> In the future a member of the United Nations will be able to remain neutral only in the exceptional event that a war breaks out between two non-members, and if the United Nations itself does not deem it necessary to stop this war ... with aggression an international crime, neutrality becomes a connivance in this crime.[1]

[1] E. A. Koravin, «The Second World War and International Law,» in *American Journal of International Law*, 40 : 753 (October, 1946).

Neutrality, as such, was not on the agenda at the Dumbarton Oaks Conference, but the question was taken up at the San Francisco Conference in the spring of 1945. The French Government played quite an active part in the discussions of the Charter, and brought forth several amendments to it. One of the most interesting was the proposal that «participation in the organization implies obligations which are incompatible with the status of neutrality.» That is, in order to become a member of the United Nations, the applicants had to give up formally any adherance to the theory of neutrality. If accepted, this proposal would have meant a formal and absolute abolition of legal neutrality, much stronger than the corresponding denunciation which the League effected in 1920, as it now would be a requirement for acceptance. No immediate decision was made on the French amendments, but in commenting on the proposals, the Equador Government brought up some related points of great importance.[2]

In Chapter III of the proposals, it was proposed that the organization should be open to «all peace-loving states». The Equador Delegation took the position that this classification as a condition for acquiring membership in the organization was «merely pursuant to a circumstantial, historical, and therefore, relative criterion which should characterize the new international structure.» Thus, if the organization should aspire to change the present order of sovereign states into a juridical community, «all of them, without exception must have the original capacity to belong to their concert.»[3] The Equador Delegation, therefore, suggested that only those states should become members who subscribed to the Charter without any reservations. The Delegation further proposed that no member of the organization could be expelled or be allowed to withdraw voluntarily from it.

This last provision was intended to prevent the appearance of a situation which had proved so embarrassing to the League of Nations. The League had been greatly weakened and impaired by the diminution of the number of its members, which caused an increasing lack of universality. Such a situation might arise «when members, losing their condition as such, may fall outside the

[2] *Documents of the United Nations Conference on International Organization, San Francisco, 1945*, III : 383 (New York, 1945).
[3] *Ibid.*

system of rights and duties of which a universal juridical community presupposed.»[4]

During subsequent discussions the same point of view was advocated by other delegations, particularly that of Uruguay. The Uruguayans argued very insistently that it was vitally necessary to be faithful to the principle of universality in the organization. Consequently, all communities should be members and their participation should be obligatory. In the days of the League of Nations it had been a voluntary matter depending on whether a state wanted to join the organization or not. Now it should no longer be left to the choice of any nation whether to become a member or to withdraw its membership. Thus the question of expulsion could not be raised. According to the original text, any «peace-loving» state could be a member. This certainly left room for many interpretations and it was a general agreement that this phrase had no juridical connotations. Even so, the formulation was retained, but defined to mean that it was not sufficient for a state to declare itself peace-loving. The applying nation had to prove that it was ready and able to accept and fulfill the obligations of the Charter. No denunciation of neutrality was required.

Withdrawal and Expulsion.

The related questions of withdrawal and expulsion naturally became matters of heated discussion. The question was put this way: «Can a member state cease to be a member either on its own initiative or as a result of measures taken against it by the organization?»[5] The sad experience of the League had shown that the acceptance of a withdrawal clause had a weakening influence on that organization because it was contrary to the principle of universality. It was now stressed that complete universality was hard to achieve. Even under the present conditions it did not exist as in reality. It must, therefore, be regarded as an aim, an ideal towards which one should constantly strive. A withdrawal clause would give recalcitrant members the possibility of securing concessions from the organization by threatening to leave it, and further,

---

[4] *Ibid.*, 401.
[5] *Documents of the United Nations Conference on International Organization, San Francisco, 1945,* III 290.

withdrawal would be a means of escape for states unwilling to fulfill their obligations and who might evade them by leaving the organization. Some of the delegates would, however, permit withdrawal on certain conditions, for example, when the rights and obligations of a member are altered by amendments which it was not in a position to accept. The supporters of this theory, therefore, wanted a clause permitting withdrawal in general or with certain specifications.

As a result of the discussions, the Committee declared itself against a withdrawal clause. The question was thus officially left floating, but it was further admitted in the report that if a member, because of exceptional circumstances, felt constrained to withdraw, the organization could not feel justified to compel that member to continue its cooperation with the organization. Likewise, if the organization, «deceiving the hopes of humanity, was revealed to be unable to maintain peace,» then withdrawals from it would be inevitable.[6] The question of universality naturally reappeared in the Committee's discussions concerning expulsion from the organization.

The Dumbarton Oaks proposals had favored expulsion in certain cases, and recommended that upon recommendation of the Security Council the General Assembly should be empowered to suspend or expel from the organization «any member which persistently violates the principles contained in the Charter.» When this issue was taken up in San Francisco, there were strong arguments both for and against the inclusion of such a clause in the Charter. Those opposed to expulsion advocated that this would be more of a disadvantage for the organization itself than for the expelled state. Namely, the latter was expected to create a center of opposition for all discontented states. On the other hand, delegates in favor of expulsion argued that the primary purpose of the organization was peace and security, not universality, and that in certain cases expulsion would be necessary.[7]

At a meeting of the Committee on May 25, 1945, a proposal was made for the adoption of an expulsion clause. It was approved by a simple majority, but did not win the two-thirds support of the delegates. Evidently the Committee on Chapter III must have been

[6] *Doc. 1074*, 292.
[7] *Doc. 1160*, 312.

sharply divided on this issue. The decision was then referred back to the Steering Committee. In the new discussion which ensued it was strongly pointed out that if a guilty government were allowed repeatedly to violate the Charter, it would involve the justification of the government by its entire people. A nation led to form such convictions would obviously no longer be qualified as peace-loving and would, therefore, lack the essential quality for participation in the organization. This new argument seemed to carry much weight, and when the final vote was taken a large majority voted in favor of the insertion of an expulsion clause stating: «The organization may expel from the organization any member which persistently violates the principles contained in the Charter.» The right to suspend a member from the organization for a longer or shorter period had met practically no opposition and had no difficulties in getting the necessary majority.[8]

As pointed out above, the question of universality must be considered vital to the future of neutrality and to the United Nations as well. As long as a state is able to keep aloof, unbound by obligations, it may have a theoretical, legal basis for declaring its neutrality or more correctly its non-belligerency, even if the pursuance of such a policy probably will bring meager results and is likely to be a shortlived affair during a general world war.

Neutrality under the Charter.

The relations between the United Nations and neutrality were given a more specific treatment at the forty-first conference of the International Law Association, meeting in Cambridge, England, in August, 1946. The British international lawyer, C. S. Dehn, took up this problem on a broad basis to find whether neutrality might still have a chance under the United Nations Charter.

In spite of the fact that the Charter had filled in many gaps that the Covenant of the League of Nations had left open, there still seemed to be points so vaguely defined that some kind of neutrality or non-belligerency still might be possible. But on the whole, the Charter has greatly limited the chances. The Security Council now has not only the right, but the duty to determine when the peace

[8] *Doc. 1160*, 313.

is threatened and by whom, and *all* members will be bound by its findings.

In Mr. Dehn's opinion the member states had given the Security Council the right to go to war. The obligations towards the belligerents which neutrality involved, and the rights which it conceded to them, he said, «are wholly inconsistent with the positive obligations assembled by members under provisions of the Charter.»[9] According to Article 41, the Security Council may call upon them to sever diplomatic relations and completely interrupt economic relations and all means of communication by land, sea, and air. By Article 42, the member states are further bound by any decision of the Security Council to take action with land, sea or air forces as may be necessary to restore the peace. Article 42 gives the right of passage and makes territory of all member states available to the Security Council forces. Article 45 provides that the Security Council may undertake to hold national air force contingents immediately available for combined international action.[10] The members are further compelled to refrain from giving assistance to any state against which the United Nations is taking action.

From these provisions of the Charter, it seems clear that «when an authorized and therefore lawful force is being used against an aggressor state, the performance of neutral duties to that state would be a violation of the positive obligations assumed by members under the Charter.»[11]

Mr. Dehn concluded: «Neutrality involving as it does, obligations to both belligerents, is no longer a permissible status.» He also stated that neutrality was not even permissible in the period between the attack and the United Nations armed intervention.[12] Mr. Dehn thought that in such a case the members would be entitled to come with armed forces to the aid of the state attacked.[13] In his opinion, the only safe course, as long as aggression was not determined, would be to

> adopt a status of strict non-intervention withholding aid of every kind from each belligerent until the aggressor state has

[9] *Doc. 1160,* 42.
[10] For the text of the provisions see, *United Nations Charter,* (San Francisco 1945).
[11] Leland M. Goodrich, *Charter of the United Nations* (Boston, 1946).
[12] C. S. Dehn, *Report of Cambridge Conference,* 43.
[13] *Ibid.,* 43.

been identified. Such a temporary status, wholly distinct from that of neutrality, with its rights and duties toward both belligerents, would not offend any provisions of the Charter.[14]

Thus, if neutrality, once and forever is ruled out of international law, there still exists an actual legal possibility for a *non-belligerent* status which in certain cases will permit a state or a group of states to stay out of a war which is waged between two other nations or groups of states.

Another weak point is the question of non-member states, although the Charter has a provision for such an eventuality. According to Article 2 (6)

> it is the duty of the organization to ensure that states which are not members shall act in accordance with its principles in the maintenance of international peace and security. The preclusion of neutrality is a principle derived from the Charter and applicable in the maintenance of international peace and security.[15]

It would, therefore, in Mr. Dehn's opinion, be the duty of the United Nations to see that the principle was applied also to non-member states.

The implications of the Kellogg Pact, the thesis that war is unlawful, seems to be an accepted fact among the post-war international lawyers. At the International Law Association's conference in 1946, it was generally thought that the loopholes left open by the Covenant had been closed by the Kellogg Pact. However, it was stressed that the Pact was silent as to whether a state violating its provisions could claim belligerent rights and require the performance of neutral duties by the states it had not attacked. Mr. Dehn maintained that in case the Pact were violated, there could be no neutrality. Consequently, if a state cannot have the right to be a belligerent, it can neither have belligerent rights, and every belligerent act committed by an aggressor must be unlawful. The laws and rules of the Hague Conventions which are based upon the legality of war, are thus no longer applicable and cannot be maintained in their present form. A revolution in international law

---

[14] *Ibid.*, 44.
[15] *Ibid.*, 44.

has taken place and international law must now concern itself with the consequences of that revolution.[16]

Most of the international lawyers at the Conference seem to have shared this view. The Scottish lawyer, Mr. Murray, held that in view of Articles 41, 43, and 45, it would be impossible to maintain the status of neutrality. «It can no longer be recognized under international law.»[17] Professor F. C. Witenberg of the United States stated that «it is today very hard to say which rules of international laws are still valid.»[18] Dr. Vladimir Vochoc of Czechoslovakia put it: «The status of neutrality is, in principle, incompatible with the obligations taken by the members of the United Nations under the San Francisco Charter.»[19]

Dr. Loewenfeld, England, quoted Paul Boncour as having emphasized on May 9, 1945, «that neutrality be incompatible with the prescriptions of the draft charter.» In spite of the fact that the meetings of the Security Council did not reveal any express dealings with neutrality,[20] Loewenfeld added that even if special conditions in the future would require special arrangements, for instance, with regard to passage, «the character of the abolition of neutrality will not be touched thereby from a legal point of view.»[21] Several others spoke to the same effect, that «neutrality is no longer a legitimate status.»[22]

It would, however, have been too much to expect complete unanimity as to the abolition of such an important part of international law. The provisions of the Charter put the great powers in a dominating position, and the limitations of state sovereignty were naturally most painfully felt by the small states which had the least to lose. Mr. von Baumhauer, Holland, thought that it was all well and good if the great powers actually had sufficient force to serve as a world police, but if this were not the case, there is the more reason for us to try to maintain neutrality. Von Baumhauer did not think that the revolution in international law, which had invalidated so many of the old rules, should be recognized. He

[16] Dehn, *Report of Cambridge Conference*, 45.
[17] Ibid., 52. C. de Bois Murray.
[18] Ibid., 54. J. C. Witenberg.
[19] Ibid., 54.
[20] Ibid., 55.
[21] Dehn, *Report of the Cambridge Conference*, 56.
[22] Ibid., 57. Mark Vilenkin, England.

rather preferred that international law be developed and protected as it stood.[23] The Dutchman was, however, about the only one who took that point of view, and his arguments were clearly characterized by his reluctance to acknowledge that the influence of the separate small nations was about to come down to its right proportions.

There was one small state, however, which once again, with admirable persistence, tried to secure for itself a privileged place in the society of states. That country was Switzerland. The French proposal for abolition of neutrality, presented at the San Francisco Conference, made no distinction between different kinds of neutrality. On the contrary, during the discussions it was clearly understood that the status of permanent neutrality was incompatible with the principles declared in paragraphs 5 and 6 of the second chapter.[24] No state could evade its obligations under the Charter by availing itself of the status of permanent neutrality. Nevertheless, Guggenheim, the spokesman of the Swiss group at the conference, tried to get recognition for the special kind of Swiss perpetual neutrality. He was unwilling to exclude the possibility of all sorts of neutrality in the future. He realized, however, that the traditional neutrality as it had existed in the period of international anarchy could not be preserved. Nor was he inclined to recognize its twentieth century substitute, the nonbelligerent status, which he thought lacked a basis in international law. His main point was that «a coté des statuts de neutralité traditionelle et de nonbelligérance, il existe le statut de la neutralité permanente.»[25] So even if traditional neutrality had been abolished and discredited, the permanent neutrality of Switzerland still existed. His arguments were the same as the ones which the Swiss so successfully applied in 1920, but in addition to the recognition in 1815, and the First World War, they could now add the triumph of having survived also a second world war. To prove the justification of this «situation unique,» the Swiss group prepared a memorandum where they listed, besides their traditional legal claims, the great advantages that the permanent neutrality of Switzerland already had brought the world and would

[23] *Ibid.*, 55—56.
[24] *San Francisco Documents*, VI : 313—315, Doc. 423.
[25] *Ibid.*, 51.

bring it in the future, provided the Swiss were granted a general recognition of their status.[26] This, however, has not been given so far.

In spite of the rough treatment that the principle of neutrality received at this conference in 1946, the last word about neutrality in relation to international organizations has not yet been said. The question reappeared in April, 1949, this time on the agenda of the International Law Commission's first session at Lake Success, New York. On this occasion a list of topics was to be selected for codification from a survey of international law. At the sixth meeting of the Commission on April 20, the topics were discussed and decisions made as to what parts of international law were in a most urgent need of codification.[27] The last items on the agenda were the laws of war and neutrality. During the discussion concerning the law of war, it soon came out that there was no general agreement on this point. The great majority advocated that since the Charter imposed on the United Nations' members the obligation to settle their disputes by peaceful means, the Commission could not well draw up regulations governing the conduct of war. If it took up the question of the law of war, it might be interpreted as a lack of confidence in the United Nations and its work for peace. Such an act would have a deplorable psychological effect.

A small minority thought, however, that one should not completely overlook the fact that wars still might occur, at least punitive wars might be waged by the international police against war criminals. They thought it important to give this possibility some consideration before such an issue became controversial. The majority was, nevertheless, reluctant to discuss any kind of war, and it was finally decided that the law of war was not to be put up for codifiaction.

After this decision was made, there could be no more discussion as to the codification of neutrality, since that concept was inseparably connected with war. Consequently, the Chairman of the Committee ruled that neither the law of war nor that of neutrality should be regarded as topics for codification.[28] This discussion did not exclude the possibility that the question of neutrality in relation to the United Nations might reappear.

[26] *San Francisco Documents*, VI : 60—63, Doc. 423.
[27] United Nations General Assembly, *Doc. A/CN.4/S.R.6*, 15—18.

Northern Neutrality in the Post War World.

It must be fully realized that the question of neutrality as well as most other concepts will always bring forth a difference between theory and practice. In theory, from a legal point of view, it seems that a status of neutrality is impossible for a member of the United Nations. But we must remember that the international lawyers in the 1920's said the same thing about the League of Nations and neutrality, and yet this concept experienced a revival of great dimensions in the years immediately preceding the Second World War. It must be admitted that this neutrality was of a later date and essentially different from the pre-1914 conception, but its basic principle was still to keep out of war, to be the indifferent third party making opportunistic cruises between the two combatants. In spite of the lesson those small countries received during this last world war, attempts are still being made in some areas to breathe a new life into the decaying doctrines of neutrality.

In the spring of 1949, at the same time as the International Law Commission refused to discuss neutrality, Sweden in her refusal to join the North Atlantic Pact, in fact returned to her age old foreign policy of neutrality. It had, admittedly, served her well, even if the ways and means by which her neutrality had been preserved, not always conformed to international law. This new situation was an immediate result of the cold war, the increasing friction between the East and the West. As this actually is a growing conflict between the two greatest powers in the world, Soviet Russia and the United States, the smaller European states have found themselves between the devil and the deep blue sea. Whether they move in one direction or the other they will risk considerable limitations of their sovereignty.

The war made all small states bitterly aware of their dependency on the greater states, and at the San Francisco Conference, their fear of the veto power and their distrust of the great powers became one of the main points. Though they were aware of the fact that their equality of sovereignty with the great powers had been a fiction for some decades, the reluctance to have this formally acknowledged is rather remarkable. Finn Moe, the Norwegian delegate to the United Nations, gave some consideration to this point, when he said that «the small states' insistence on full sovereignty» did not rest on a sound basis. They had not used it in times of distress to influence positive action, as for instance when Hitler rose to power. Instead they used their sovereign status to set themselves outside, to get away from their responsibility as members of the international society. They declared their indifference by staying neutral, and if they now had full sovereign rights to determine their actions, they were likely to do it again. But the great powers would eventually decide, and it would be futile to deny the fact. «There does not exist a natural basis,» he continued, «for cooperation between the smaller states directed against the great powers.»[29] Neutrality once gave them such a basis, but since the war, when this concept had proved itself outmoded and futile, their regional position must instead provide the basis for cooperation for all of the countries in that region, regardless of their size.

The Scandinavian countries, as well as the other small states, were obviously very suspicious of the great powers, and were anxious for their future sovereignty. These factors were influential in the somewhat reserved attitude which those northern countries adopted after the war. They tried to preserve the balance with the Soviet Union as carefully as they had tended their relations with Germany before the war.[30] Their period of balancekeeping and watchful waiting was greatly disturbed by the *coup d'état* in Czechoslovakia and the increasing communist pressure on Finland. The Scandinavian states had already realized that each of them alone would prove to be too small if a new crisis should come, and consequently, they looked for cooperation with their nearest neighbors. It seemed natural for the three Scandinavian countries to unite in a defensive alliance, and this was no doubt what they all wanted, but to put that plan into effect proved to be more difficult than any of them had anticipated. The Swedes had, from the very beginning, insisted that they could not join a defense pact if this did not include adequate guarantees against association with states outside the Northern Pact. The Scandinavian countries should not be tangled up in any western alliance, either as a bloc or individually. Sweden was willing to abandon her isolation as far as

[28] United Nations General Assembly, *Doc. A/CN.4/S.R.6*, 18.
[29] Finn Moe, *Norge i den nye verden* (Oslo, 1946), 58—59.
[30] Wilfred Ryder, «The End of Nordic Neutrality» in *Soundings* (March, 1949), 16.

Scandinavia was concerned, but she persistently refused to give up her traditional neutrality between the East and the West.[31]

At this time, from 1948 on, the discussions began to center around some organization for defense of the Atlantic area, and the governments both of Norway and Denmark felt that a Scandinavian neutrality was neither possible nor desirable. The Norwegian Foreign Minister, Halvard Lange, stated that «we paid a high price to learn that isolation offers no solution. The democracies must stand together to maintain the peace.» The Prime Minister in a speech to the Storting, recalled the emptiness of Norway's former neutrality policy, and of the belief that she could remain outside any eventual conflict. «We must realize,» he said, «that Norway's peace and Europe's peace are part and parcel of the whole world's peace.»[32] The same position has been taken by most of the leading statesmen in Denmark.

Apart from this principal difference in attitude, there were also practical obstacles which alone might have wrecked attempts to establish a Scandinavian defense pact. In the first place, neither Norway nor Sweden was willing to defend Denmark if she were attacked from the continent; and second, the financial situation in Norway and Denmark made Sweden somewhat doubtful as to who was going to pay for extensive rearmaments. It was realized that the two countries which had had their financial resources depleted during the war, would scarcely be able to keep a balanced budget for many years to come, even under peace-time conditions.

On January 5—6, 1949, the Prime-, Defense- and Foreign Ministers of Denmark, Norway, and Sweden met in Karlstad, Sweden, to attempt a compromise for common defense. This resulted in the so-called Karlstad Plan. This defense scheme was dependent upon the presumption that the three Scandinavian countries would obtain limited American resources and military guarantees without accepting any of the obligations of joint defense.[33] They were informed soon afterwards, however, by the American embassies in Oslo, Stockholm, and Copenhagen, that states not being members of the North Atlantic Pact would have to pay for whatever they might get.

---

[31] Sweden's position in this, as well as in earlier cases, makes an interesting comparison to the isolationist policy of the United States.
[32] *News of Norway*, March 5. and 12, 1949.
[33] Ryder, *The End of Nordic Neutrality*, 21.

The Karlstad Plan was further discussed and revised at a meeting in Copenhagen on January 22, and in Oslo on January 29. It was eventually rejected because of Sweden's persistent refusal to join any western defense system. Norway's ambassador in Washington, W. Morgenstierne, put it this way: «As the Charter of the United Nations was found incapable of providing security, Norway wanted a regional Scandinavian defense pact under the Charter of the United Nations and in some way affiliated with the western democracies.» This possible solution was abandoned when Sweden's offer of a pact, based on neutrality but with no «solidarity with a larger democratic defense group, fell short of Norway's security needs.»[34]

Whatever may be said about the Swedish position, it must be admitted that Sweden was consistent in her policy. As early as October 22, 1945, while the world still believed in the United Nations, and the cold war had not yet quite started, the Swedish Government issued the following official statement:

> We are willing to join a collective organization for security, and in case of a future conflict abstain from neutrality to the extent that the organization may want us. However, if there should appear within this organization, a tendency among the great powers toward a partition into two groups, then it must be our policy not to be driven into such group-making or formation of blocs.[35]

This is almost exactly the same position as Sweden and the less fortunate Oslo States took in the late thirties. They would undertake their obligations toward the League of Nations as long as this was nearly universal, but when the great powers in and outside the League tended to congregate in two hostile camps, they reserved the right to maintain freedom of action and a policy of neutrality. The question of the United Nations is not quite parallel as the two chief opponents still are members of the organization. This, however, does not seem to make much difference as to the seriousness of the conflict. The United Nations has, at any rate temporarily, lost much of its importance. The greater part of its

[34] *News of Norway,* April 16, 1949.
[35] Undén, *Sveriges Utrikes-Politik,* 24. See also *New York Times,* July 15, 1946, p. 5, for similar statements.

influence and some of its functions have been transferred to the eastern and western concentrations of great powers.

When the formation of blocs took place in the 1930's, the League obligations were the only ties that bound the member states. Those who wanted to keep out of the approaching conflict, could do so by withdrawing from the League or repudiating their obligations, as the northern states did in 1938. This time such an eventuality has apparently been foreseen by the great powers who have taken appropriate measures to meet it. The eastern bloc is not going to be cracked by UN resolutions, and on the western side defense organizations are established outside the United Nations, binding the members in an independent alliance system. Whether the small ex-neutrals withdraw from the UN or refuse to take on the obligations, is a matter of minor importance as long as they stay in the pacts they have signed with the great powers. In the case of the North Atlantic Pact these states are assured against a Scandinavian return to neutrality, while Norway and Denmark have obtained guarantees for the protection of their territories.

Sweden has preferred to place herself between these two huge constellations of hostile powers. But nearly all other nations have realized that their own might and resources probably will prove insufficient to keep them outside another conflict, and they consequently must find their place while there is still time and some kind of option. The Swedish Foreign Minister, Undén, realizing the difficulties in this connection, said,

> whether the policy of neutrality in this hypothetical situation (of war) is possible or not, does not depend entirely on ourselves, and it is hard to judge the chances in advance. But we do not want to be bound by a treaty and thereby deprive ourselves of the right and ability to stay outside another war.[36]

There is no point in concealing the fact that membership in the pact implies a considerable limitation of national sovereignty. This has been clearly realized by Norway. The Foreign Minister, at the establishment of the Council of Europe on May 5, 1949, made the statement that Norway would lose sovereignty only to the extent which it alone will determine. «But we must be willing,» he went on, «to relax our sovereignty to some extent if we wish to achieve

---

[36] Undén, *Sveriges Utrikes-Politik*, 29.

positive results.» He further showed his understanding of the situation by saying, «Modern civilization with its new means of communication, and the new technological basis of our entire life, is rapidly rendering obsolete our present system of national sovereignties.» [37]

Everybody knows that the world is becoming small. Planes, trains and ships travel faster, take more passengers and give the average man greater opportunity for travelling than he has ever had before. There is an economic interdependency that leaves no country untouched. The complexity of modern life, capital investments and the enormous productive capacity of some countries have created a network of economic interrelation. All states depend more or less on others for their imports and exports, and what happens to one affects the others. It is impossible for one nation to follow its independent course and completely disregard all the rest. Its actions will very soon be limited by its economic, political and cultural dependency on other states. A full national sovereignty is thus unattainable even for the greatest state as long as it has not subdued all the others and forced them into its particular system. The smaller the state, the greater its dependency on great powers and the more fictional is its national sovereignty. In the world of today, a small state can not stand alone. For the sake of its future existence and prosperity, it cannot avoid being influenced by the greater states.

In spite of this, Sweden seems to cling desperately to the nineteenth century definitions of full national sovereignty and freedom of action. What are her motives? Why did she not join Norway and Denmark?

One reason, naturally, is that she has not felt the strain of war and occupation. She does not know from her own experience what it means to be too small, to have inadequate strength to resist attacks. With her two recent neutral victories, the temptation must be very great to try the profitable experiment a third time. On the other hand she no doubt realizes that the strategic situation is entirely different this time. In the two previous wars the «lines of action» went from Germany to Britain, France, Italy, and Russia. Thus Norway, with her long coastline was in the strategic danger zone, while the Swedish sector and the Baltic sea never reached the same

[37] *News of Norway,* May 14, 1949.

importance. But in the event of a conflict with Russia as the eastern, continental opponent of the western powers, the lines of belligerent action will cross Sweden, and her Baltic coast will become of major importance. Besides, the Swedish military defense might be many times stronger than it was in 1940 and still be hopelessly inadequate when exposed to an attack on a larger scale, even unsupported by atomic weapons. This has been pointed out by General Helge Jung, former Chief of the Swedish Armed Forces. «We will not be able to keep our stand, however well prepared we may be, if we are exposed to aggression from one of the world powers.»[38] When Norway joined the North Atlantic Pact, the military situation became impossible.

If we then realize the violent hatred and fear of Russia which has been predominant in Sweden for centuries, the almost total absence of communistic elements, the clever Swedish «corps diplomatique,» and its great traditions and experience in the field of foreign policy, only one explanation for the Swedish neutrality seems possible. The Swedish Government does not believe that war between the East and West is imminent. It seems to hope for a period of peace during which Sweden can take all possible advantages of an independent position by bargaining and trading freely with both sides. It also knows that if Sweden joined a Western pact the tension between the two sides would be greatly increased and the position of Finland endangered. And acting on the presumption that the war still is far off, she seems to do a better service to the peace, and to herself by staying neutral. Besides, she probably realizes that, under no circumstances, the western powers can afford to let her down in case of an attack from Russia. As there is no doubt that Sweden, ideologically as well as economically belongs in the Western camp, her present neutrality can hardly be explained on other grounds than being construed for peace, not for war.

While Sweden seems to have gambled on a long period of peace, Norway plainly feared that the war might break out any day and that consequently maximum preparations had to be made at top speed. This has particular relation to the North Atlantic Pact, which no doubt is the most important event in Scandinavia since the German occupation of Norway and Denmark. While there was

[38] *Morgenbladet,* November 26, 1949, 1.

little reaction at the time when the Pact was signed, it has by and by grown to become a touchy point in Norwegian politics. Norway's adherence to the Pact is now being criticized from various quarters on the grounds that the people were not given time to express their opinions. Thus the result might have been different if the government had not pressed so hard to have it accepted at once.

It is very interesting to note that the severest criticism comes from the extreme left and the extreme right. The Communists are, of course, strongly opposed to Norway's participation in the NATO system because it forms a definite obstacle to a closer understanding of and collaboration with Soviet-Russia, and will place Norway in the opposite camp in case of war. The left-wing Socialists may still have their sympathies with Russia, but they usually keep her out of the picture in their criticism of NATO and Norway's participation in it. Instead they point at the many dangers that are connected with a close tie-up with the United States. Their scepticism of American leadership is shared by a mixed group of pacifists and idealists of various denominations, who at times even argue that the best solution is no defense at all.

Most remarkable, however, is the strong conservative opposition to the A-pact. Those people stand up for liberalism and private enterprise and hate socialism almost as much as communism. They represent the true isolationist element and their argumentation is primarily based on nationalism and narrow patriotic grounds. They point back to the time when Norway was granted her full independence and argue that the national sovereignty won on that occasion is too precious to be risked in an alliance pact with great powers. They all agree that Norway in most respects belongs naturally in the western group, and though they admire American ideals and some traits of the American way of life, they fear American materialism and think that in the determination of the steps taken by the USA, Norwegian interests will carry little weight. In their opinion Norway should not make entangling alliances with any country except Sweden, but together with that country step aside and leave the arena to the great powers.

Regardless of the differing motives of the various anti-A-pact groups the alternative plan which they all aduce, seems to be some sort of keeping aloof, staying out, that is reminiscent of the neutrality agitation in the late thirties. Though Norway is in the pact already, it is felt that if the northern powers keep out of both groups, the Scandinavian peninsula may be spared when the East and the West clash on the continent. But there *is* a difference. This time there is no talk of Hague Conventions, international law, impartiality or neutrality in its formal sense. There just exists a hope that if the great powers somehow can be kept away from Scandinavia, the flood of war may pass by and the Scandinavian states live in peace to see what might be done next.

The anti-A-pacters have had a hard time defending their theory on ideologic and economic grounds, but their greatest dilemma has been the question of national defense. The government, in giving the reasons for the signing of the pact, based this almost entirely on the experience from April 9, 1940, when Norway was occupied by Germany. On these grounds it has also been accepted by most of the people. In our 20th century world, a sovereign state simply can not exist without a sufficient amount of force to back it up. The debatable question is whether the necessary power could be provided by Norway alone; in cooperation with Sweden, or only with the support of a great power or a great-power group.

The belligerent's race for Norway 1940 seemed to indicate that a power vacuum will be occupied by one or the other of the warring powers, provided it has some strategic and economic importance. If it will be defended, interference or non-interference becomes a matter of precise calculation. If the cost of the enterprise appears to be greater than the possible gains which could be won by an occupation, the small state has a reasonably good chance of being let alone. But it is hardly doubtful that the Scandinavian peninsula would be of no less importance in an eventual World War III, than it was in World War II; the national defense, that proved so pitifully inadequate in 1940, must necessarily be many, many times stronger this time if the belligerents are to keep their hands off. The crucial problem is, where to acquire the necessary strength?

It is hardly necessary to point out that modern warfare is becoming more and more wasteful and expensive all the time. Even small states could afford the swords, muskets, cannon and the like that were the decisive weapons a hundred years ago. But which of the small ex-neutrals have the economic resources to manufacture or to buy jet planes, tanks, radar equipment, and atomic bombs? Unless they possess ultra-modern weapons, their defense is worthless. The Swedes have proved that they are able to produce some of these new implements of war, but the question is, are they strong enough to repel an attack from one of the great powers?

Suppose that Norway and Sweden, somehow or other, by straining their economy to the breaking point, managed to create armies and navies with trained soldiers and modern equipment in sizable numbers. But how will they be used? If the two countries wanted to attain and maintain an intermediate position between the two great-power blocs, they would have to use them indiscriminantly against the first who tried to break in. Will they shoot as readily at Western ships as on planes and soldiers from the East? This requires the solid conviction that one side is in principle just as «bad» as the other, and is such an impartiality of mind and judgement possible in Scandinavia today? Whether the status is called neutrality or non-belligerency makes little difference as to the real issues. A state which has not proved its determination to shoot at the first intruder regardless of identity, must either be regarded as a potential friend or a potential enemy. Belligerents will always watch each other's steps very closely, and one party will naturally try to take or destroy what may be of use to the other. Thus it may be of interest to apply the same «questionnaire» that had reference to the belligerents in 1939—40. Which of the two opposing groups today would benefit most by Scandinavian non-participation in World War III, and whose interests will suffer? Can a non-belligerent status be defended by the country's armed forces? If one belligerent party thinks the other is about to prepare an action to improve his position, will he not do his best to forestall it? If so, will the world see another race for Scandinavia?

The Norwegian dilemma of 1939—40 is in reality quite similar to the problem the Scandinavian countries face today. Now as then their first aim is security. They want to secure their national sovereignty, fully or in part: their right to self-determination, their national economy and their way of life. At first they hoped to find this security in the United Nations. But while it took them 15 years to find out that the League was no safequard, they needed only a few years to realize that the UN was also not capable of guaranteeing them the security they so urgently needed. After a vain attempt to establish a Scandinavian defense pact, Sweden returned to some sort of vaguely defined neutrality or non-belligerency, while Norway and Denmark joined the North Atlantic Pact. Both alternatives involve considerable risks and no one can say today which choice was the wisest. Norway is likely to be better off if an unprovoked Russian attack is inevitable and will come within few years, while Sweden will profit from a long period of peace. In this connection the future rôle of an independent, united and possibly non-belligerent Germany will be of the greatest importance.

The Scandinavian dilemma is not insolvable, but regardless of the ways these countries choose to go, whether each of them wants to perish alone or the three or four of them unite in a Scandinavian superstate, or whether they prefer to link their fate to a combination of great powers, they will have to submit to radical limitations of their national sovereignty, a necessary requirement for a true neutrality policy.

V. Conclusion

From what has been said in the preceding chapters, neutrality seems to have gone a long way in the last forty years. In that relatively short period, 1909—1949, it developed from an honored political principle of major importance to become something «not desirable and not feasible» in political life. Neutrality in its original sense is no longer a debatable question. The antiquity and impracticality of traditional, impartial neutrality are today regarded as accepted facts.

How could this happen? How could such a fundamental change come about in so short a time? The decline of neutrality is obviously not due to one single factor but to a great complexity of causes that directly and indirectly have made such a status impossible. It will not be possible to review all of these in detail, but in conclusion an analysis of the most important trends will be attempted.

It has commonly been said that neutrality is no longer feasible because conditions have changed. The world became different. This is undoubtedly true, but it also brings out the question, when and under what conditions was neutrality ever actually possible? Neutrality meant keeping aloof from other peoples' wars. The neutral state drew a circle around its territory and said to the belligerents, «Do what you please, but stay out of this area and leave my business alone.» In order to carry out this policy the state had to be absolutely sovereign and absolutely independent of other states in all matters. When did a nation enjoy that status? In the period of feudalism all the states were technically as self-sufficient as they could possibly be, but they did not fill the second requirement since the rulers as well as the people were members of the papal and imperial systems and thus did not enjoy a sovereign status. The feudal states were economically free and unrestrained but bound by spiritual dependence, which prevented a neutrality policy.

The period between the Renaissance and the French revolution was the time when neutrality came nearest to being a working principle. Foreign and ocean trade was slowly developing but had not yet reached the complexity which creates inter-dependence. Most of the European countries were practically self-sufficient. Very few were entirely dependent on import- and export trade. The mercantile system, with its stress on the favorable balance of trade and maximum self-sufficiency, was naturally well adapted to a neutral policy. The spiritual dependence of the medieval period was gone. The universal church and the Holy Roman Empire had broken down. Instead Europe had fallen into complete international anarchy. Small and great rulers everywhere had unlimited power; their sovereignty was theoretically absolute and without flaws No ties of obligation bound them together or restricted them. They were sovereigns par excellence. They could go to war or stay neutral, just as they pleased and their neutrality could be partial or impartial, as they thought would best serve their interests.

Apart from self-sufficiency and sovereignty, a third and very necessary pillar of neutrality was available in this period; a reasonably general decency and stability in international relations. In other words, it was an accepted principle that treaties should be respected. Thus, if the states were bound by treaty to remain strictly neutral or to give all help short of war, that fact was respected and recognized by all. Besides, the wars were then gallant and polite affairs which did not greatly disturb the country and the people as such. The armies and navies were small, their arms were cheap and comparatively non-destructive. There were codes of war and honor in victory as well as in defeat. The conception of just wars was fading, but was still of some importance.

At the end of the eighteenth century conditions changed radically. In the economic sphere, mercantilism was rejected and succeeded by liberalism and free trade, which accentuated inter-dependence and made self-sufficiency look ridiculous and futile. In the political field, the kings' divine right to rule was challenged. The absolute sovereigns had themselves greatly contributed to the disrepute into which royalty was rapidly falling. With the divinity of personal rulers went also some of the respect for treaties, which was a prerequisite of neutrality. New men, unbound by obligations to traditions and the society of noblemen, were ready to sell their souls, if necessary, and use all means to gain their ends. The small states had already played their parts, and Britain assumed the rôle as balance keeper while Napoleon started his race for world domination.

All of the major states lost their neutral status during the Napoleonic wars, regardless of their intentions to maintain it. In spite of this obvious failure, neutrality was almost immediately restored and appeared to gain in importance all through the nineteenth century, until it reached its peak with the London Declaration in 1909. How can this be explained? The natural conditions for a working neutrality were gone. There was no longer a general self-sufficiency among the states, only a few countries like the United States and Russia came anywhere near to being self-sufficient. Most states were growing more and more dependent upon imports and exports. There was no longer a society of divine-right rulers. In most countries the responsibility was shared by many, and often by men who felt obligated only to themselves and their country. Napoleon had demonstrated how easily and effectively treaties could be broken by a self-made ruler. Very few states could claim an absolute sovereign status, and still neutrality became of major importance in international relations.

This development was only possible because neutrality in this period was never put to a real test. It was an artificial neutrality of peace, and it prospered because there were no wars. This is not the place for an analysis of nineteenth century developments, but to note a few traits may shed more light on neutrality.

In the first place, during the nineteenth century the principle of neutrality was adopted by the small states which realized that their sovereignty was no longer real, and as a general war would necessarily expose this sad fact to the world, some device had to be found which could give them an acceptable reason for staying out of wars. When the United States, by introducing its municipal neutrality legislation, provided a legal basis for a state to mind its own business, regardless of what happened all around it, this new principle was eagerly accepted and adopted by most of the states, great and small as well. One of the smallest even went so far as to get recognition for permanent neutrality. Neutrality, now seemed to fit right into the ideologies of the century. The catch words were liberalism, individualism, and unrestricted freedom of action. These ideas were applied to states as well as to individuals. According to the ideas of the French Revolution, all men were equals and the states also considered themselves to be equally sovereign, regardless of size and population. So they did in spite of the fact that the wars at the beginning of the century had demonstrated that this was far from being true. But as the period saw no general wars, the falsity and instability of these artificial structures were not revealed.

The previous wars had been wars for expansion, for national recognition and economic gains. After the struggle had ended, England was found on top, and her navy ruled the seas unchallenged. She was completely in control of the situation and was not interested in wars. She had attained what she wanted and now she was much more interested in a period of peace which would give her time to develop the enormous possibilities which the new science and industry had opened up. She could keep the political equilibrium by use of her seapower and concentrate on her new position as the «workshop of the world». Her example was followed by other countries. Aided by English money and industrial skill, small and great started on a campaign for industrialization within their own borders. For a time the eternal quarrels for strips of land were forgotten. There was such a wide field for development *within* the countries themselves that there was no need to expand territorially. The possibilities appeared to be unlimited, and a general optimism spread throughout the world. Individuals and states had the right to live their own lives and to deal peacefully with each other. So treaties and international agreements, as the Declaration of Paris, were signed to that effect. If quarrels arose between some states, the others should be allowed to carry on their normal life.

By the end of the century this optimism tended to fade away. Expansion within the states had reached the saturation point and they began to look for gains *outside* their own borders. The world was big and great areas were still unclaimed. So the states again started a race for colonies, which had begun at the time of mercantilism; however, now for a different purpose. In a couple of decades the best lands had been taken and the race ended with a common realization that the world was not limitless after all. There was no more good free land. To use Turner's phrase, the last frontier had disappeared, and slowly the conviction dawned upon them that from then on the only possibility for expansion was to take what someone else already had.

By this time British supremacy, which had guarded peace and general order for nearly a century, began to give way. Britain was no longer the only workshop of the world. She had to compete with the new triumphant Germany, with the United States, and later on with Japan. Where there had previously been domination, there was now keen competition. Not only was Britain's industrial leadership challenged, but her naval supremacy as well. No longer were there opportunities for all. What one gained another would have to lose, and they all wanted to gain, or at least keep what they already had. So the nations, more or less unwillingly, entered the road of war preparations which led to World War I.

It is hard to explain the last minute legislation which attempted to save neutrality and regulate wars. How could those who made these provisions hope to have them respected? There seems to have been a genuine optimism which disregarded all considerations as to the time in which they lived. Both the Hague conventions and the Declaration of London were helpless in controlling the great forces of the twentieth century world. Perhaps the effort represented a desperate attempt to stop the wheel, to do something, however futile it might appear to be.

The First World War killed impartial, legal neutrality as effectively as the Napoleonic wars had done away with the neutrality of the earlier centuries. The second stage of neutrality then came to an end. The old truth was again revealed in all its clarity. «If you lack the force to back up your legal claims, the law cannot help you. You will have to submit.» The European neutrals were too weak, even combined, and as the only great neutral, the United States, refused to collaborate to help them provide the force necessary to check the belligerents, and make them respect the law, they had to yield and take the terms they were given. But though the United States helped to destroy the status of neutrality, it can hardly be blamed for having done so. It can be accused, in both world wars, of having neglected its responsibility as a world power by putting on a false cloak of neutrality until the war was actually a fact, but there was no reason why it should help the small neutral states to try to preserve the appearance of full sovereignty which they lacked. Their status as sovereign states was utterly unrealistic in the twentieth century world and it seemed only right that they should be reduced to their proper proportions. But, on the other hand, the United States also lost its chance of creating a strong, forceful neutral league. That might have proved exceedingly helpful to the balance and the organization of a stable world society.

The small states, however, refused to admit their weakness, as they had refused to acknowledge it in the nineteenth century. Since their policy of neutrality had failed, they were now eagerly looking for some other means to obtain security without giving up the illusion of sovereignty. They enthusiastically joined the League of Nations, but were reluctant to take on any obligations that might expose their lack of force. Thus they were, from the beginning, opposed to participation in military sanctions.

The League claimed to have abolished neutrality, but as it became evident that it was unable to provide the collective security which was proclaimed as the new world order, the small states soon showed a tendency to return to some kind of neutrality. The bilateral non-aggression or neutrality treaties are typical expressions of this trend. The Kellogg Pact contained no direct reference to neutrality, but by outlawing war, it had indirect implications for that concept. It was now commonly recognized that if neutrality were to have a chance in the future, it would have to be remodelled. Different theories were introduced to bring the principle back to respectability, but they all had one trait in common. The principles of impartiality and passivity, the cornerstones of pre-war neutrality had to be given up. Instead a new active, and partial neutrality was advocated.

The failure of the League became manifest after the Italo—Ethiopian fiasco and the Sino—Japanese wars. There were great aggressive groups outside the League, and as those were sharply opposed to the original League powers, England and France, the small European powers deserted the League to avoid being drawn into the war which they felt would come. They officially returned to the old traditional neutrality, not because they believed in it, but because no other means of security seemed available. They did not even hope to carry through an impartial passivity, but aimed at copying their feats of the First World War. By skillful cruising and due deference to both sides, they hoped to stay out of the shooting war. What they attempted was non-belligerency, not neutrality.

The first world war had stripped neutrality of its legal mask.

The second demonstrated that if not helped by very special strategic and economic factors, in addition to a great portion of good luck, it was impossible to maintain even a policy of nonbelligerency.

The history of neutrality thus falls into three main stages. First, the period of partial neutrality, which was terminated by the Napoleonic wars. Second, the impartial neutrality, built on law, which flourished in the nineteenth century, and was killed by World War I and the theory of collective security. The final stage was the confused period of nonbelligerency before and during the Second World War. The neutrality of the national states thrived in peace and could survive a minor war, but failed miserably when the balance was upset and the issue of world domination became important. Even reduced and modified to mean only abstinence from direct participation in war, regardless of price and means, neutrality has proved itself to be insufficient for its purpose.

It has been stated before that a status of strict neutrality can only be maintained during a general conflict if a state is fully sovereign and independent, self-sufficient, and protected by a general respect for treaties and agreements. None of these conditions can be fulfilled today. It requires very little documentation to prove that the world of today is so inextricably interrelated and interdependent that self-sufficiency is unattainable even for the greater states, not to speak of the smaller ones. Because of the development of communications, production for a world market, and great dependence on raw materials for their innumerable manufactures, the countries have been completely interwoven economically, in peace as well as in war. To pretend indifference, impartiality and passivity under such conditions would be hopeless.

A related point is the different character of the modern wars, which makes the Jeffersonian distinction between a state and its citizens artificial and out-dated. Wars are no longer waged by armies alone; the whole people participate in one way or another. Wars have become total, a fact which has made a term like contraband obsolete and meaningless. The new weapons on land, sea, and in the air have done the same to blockade. Conditions like these have deprived neutrality of its feasibility in practice.

Besides, international relations are no longer regulated by treaties and agreements. Bernard Baruch once said that «international agreements are almost worth nothing. Since Belgium was invaded in violation of a scrap of paper, the nations have regarded treaties as a matter of expediency ... We can rely on the strength of our own might and very little else ...»[1] C. S. Potts summed up all the treaties made and repudiated since the First World War and said that this experience showed «that treaties are ropes of sand, when vital national interests are at stake.»[2] The stress is on force, not on legal rights. To claim equal sovereign rights for all nations meant a serious disregard of facts. This was observed by Robert Lansing, among others. As early as 1906 Lansing wrote,

> The equality they speak of is not an equality of power and influence, but of legal rights ... rights unsupported by actual power are only moral precepts, which may possess influence, but never positive force. An equality among sovereigns to be real must be an equality of might, otherwise it is artificial ...[3]

Lansing was fully aware of the fact that most of the small states claimed a sovereignty which was entirely artificial. Twentieth century politics was a question of facts, of physical might to compel obedience, not of theoretical legal rights. If sovereignty rested in law only, it was artificial and impracticable in its application.[4] As neutrality is dependent upon the extent of sovereignty the country enjoys, the neutrality of the small states was doomed in advance. Wright said of the previous periods, «It was a system of security for the militarily strong, and of insecurity for the militarily weak. Law governed the unimportant transactions; force, the important ones.»[5] The period since the First World War has been called a period of international anarchy, in which force has taken the place of law and treaties are hardly worth the paper on which they are written.[6] Wright characterized it as follows. «The League of Nations was meant to succeed the British dominance, but as it failed to do so the world fell into anarchy in a strife between

---

[1] Bernhard Baruch, «Neutrality,» in *Current History*, June, 1936, 44 : 44.

[2] C. S. Potts, «World Chaos Once More,» *Southwestern Social Science Quarterly*, September, 1938, 16 : 6—10; Undén, *Neutralitet och Folkrätt*, 31.

[3] R. Lansing, *Notes on Sovereignty*, 11.

[4] Ibid., 94.

[5] Q. Wright, «National Sovereignty and Collective Security,» *Annals of American Academy*, July, 1936, 186 : 100.

[6] Politis, *Neutralité*, 8.

several states to become the dominant power.»⁷ This brings in an important aspect of the present situation.

The world has become interrelated and interdependent not only in an economic sense, but politically and ideologically as well. It was once theoretically possible for a state to stay neutral in a war between the other states, whether it was waged for expansion or fought as a trade war. If this war should spread it might involve technical difficulties for neutral trade, but the neutral state was justified in being indifferent as to the cause of the war. Its neutrality was based on the presumption that each of the belligerents was fighting for the right cause.

The twentieth century saw a reversal from this principle to the Grotian theory of the just war. This new situation was expressed by the Spanish Minister of Foreign Affairs, senor Alvarez del Vayo, who said in the League Assembly in September 1936,

> The era of national wars, the classic form of war by the attack of one state upon the other, is steadily vanishing. The war in the future... will in fact be a conflict, a clash in the drama of history between two ideologies, two neutralities, two different conceptions of life... The world of today is divided by two political ideals, democracy and aggression.⁸

Halvdan Koht has spoken to the same effect and stated, «in such a war, neutrality in the old sense is impossible.»⁹ In this century the political ideologies have been more strongly stressed than at any other time since the «holy» religious wars of the 16th and 17th centuries. The wars were not only wars between states, they were wars between different «isms». The First World War was a war for democracy against «Kaiserism» and autocracy. The last war was waged against Nazism and Fascism, and if there is ever a third world war, it is quite safe to assume that the fight for one ideology against some or other «ism» will play a predominant part in the agitation on both sides; and the ideological motives will provide the justification for the war. This theory of the just cause has been further strengthened by the new stress on war guilt and the proceedings of the Nürnberg trials, which have given reality to

---

[7] Wright, «The Present State of Neutrality,» *American Journal of International Law*, July, 1940, 34 : 415.

[8] League of Nations, *Official Journal*, Special Supplement, 155 : 47—50.

[9] H. Koht, «Neutrality and Peace,» *Foreign Affairs*, January, 1937, 15 : 283.

the principle of collective security and illegality of war brought forth in the Kellogg Pact, the League of Nations, and the United Nations.

It goes without saying that under such conditions a genuine neutrality is not possible, Where the struggle exists for world domination by one system or the other, neutrality will not be tolerated. Who is not for, is against, and even if a state may think that neither of the systems is any good, it will nevertheless be compelled to choose. The destinies of Norway and Denmark, Holland and Belgium during the last world war are illustrative examples of weak states that chose too late, and instead had the belligerents choose for them.

The world of today is getting smaller all the time. Thanks to the new means of communication any point on the globe can be reached from anywhere within a matter of hours. As distances are diminishing peoples are brought closer together. With trade, industry, communications, and ideologies woven tightly together, the problem becomes basically the same all over the world. No nation is a world by itself; all are smaller or greater parts of the same whole. Thus, no state can truthfully declare that the problems of other states are none of its concern. Such a declaration would be an outright denial of facts. Any state, regardless of how small and insignificant it may appear to be, is nevertheless a part of the whole world system, and as a member of the world community it has a duty to take make up its mind as to the solution of the problems that will determine the future of the world. In the realistic, interrelated world of today, a true, impartial and legal *neutrality* is impossible.

The concept of neutrality was formulated on the theory that there existed a society of equally sovereign nations. That society obviously does not exist, and today it is hardly possible to maintain even the illusions of equality. In our time there is a tendency that points away from the existing national states toward greater units. We have come to recognize the vital role played by *regions*, of groups of states in certain areas bound together by economic, cultural and ideological ties. Whether they will develop into superstates as a preliminary stage in the development toward a world organization is hard to tell. We can only note that *nations* no longer seem to be able to follow independent policies, and neutrality will no longer correspond to their needs.

We must, however, make a clear distinction between neutrality and *non-belligerency*. It is not likely that all the countries of the world will be shooting at each other as soon as a third world war starts. Obviously some states, as for instance, India, Egypt or some of the Latin American countries will try to maintain a policy of non-participation. But it would be most remarkable if they claimed to be protected by the Hague Conventions and the codes of international law. Let us say, a Swedish declaration of neutrality, claiming neutral rights and guaranteeing impartial dealings with all belligerents would hardly be taken seriously by anyone. The duration of a non-belligerent status would not be a question of international law, but would be completely dependent upon the *military strength*, the *economic force* and the *strategic position* of the non-belligerent state. It is very doubtful whether any single national state can fill these requirements today. Even giants as China and India, with their enormous resources of man power are too weak in an economic and military sense to act independently of the rest of the world. On the other hand, each of the European states is too small to steer an independent course. The United States and Norway have provided examples of states being too big and too small to remain neutral. Great powers as the United States and Russia may theoretically be strong enough to stand alone. But they can not and dare not, because they are afraid to lose their influence on world affairs. The small states, however, have no claims to world domination and would, because of their economic and military weakness, prefer to hide until it was all over; but they will not be allowed to do so.

It seems as if certain regions are in the best position to maintain a status of non-belligerency. If the great states in the Far East or rather all the Latin American countries joined forces and declared their determination to use all possible means to keep their region out of the shooting war, they might succeed, at least for a while. But even they could not truthfully say that a general war between the East and the West was none of their concern. With the strong stress on political ideologies, closely tied up with different economic systems, it is not likely that modern warfare would leave even such regions untouched for a longer period. Therefore, on basis of the present situation it seems that even non-belligerency will have a small chance of surviving a future world war.

VI. Appendix:

NON-ALIGNMENT AND NEUTRALITY SINCE 1952

Neutrality and Non-belligerency

In 1949–1952 when the preceding chapters of this book were written, the concept of neutrality had three recognised versions:

1. Permanent neutrality, often called neutralization
2. Traditional—meaning legal—impartial neutrality, as codified in the Hague conventions of 1899 and 1907
3. Non-belligerency, codified nowhere, but recognised as a fact of international politics

Of these three versions, permanent neutrality, as roughly synonymous with *neutralization*, hardly justified being called a category. Its basic requirement, a neutral policy imposed and upheld by an international treaty, was then met only by one country—Switzerland.[1] There were even those who questioned Switzerland's status as a truly neutralized state: First, because its 1815 treaty only provided guarantees for territorial integrity, not necessarily or explicitly for Swiss neutrality. Secondly, because the remarkable permanence of Switzerland's neutral policies might just as well be a result of its favourable strategic position and its own strong military defences rather than of the beneficial effects of the treaty. Thus, with even Switzerland as a special case, neutralization was more of a theoretical possibility than an established fact of international relations.

The first edition of my book focused mainly on the second category—*traditional, impartial neutrality* based on international law. Traditional neutrality presupposes armed conflict between sovereign states. The Hague conventions were based on the assumption that until a state of war had been declared and the shooting had begun it would not be known who was on either side. Thus neutrality was regarded as a means of avoiding involvement in an armed conflict between identified participants. This, of course, did not prevent states from preparing for neutral policies before the opening of hostilities. Major wars seldom come as bolts from the blue. Prior to both world wars, the basic patterns of conflict and the two potential camps of belligerents were to a large extent predictable years before the actual outbreak of shooting war. As a consequence, a number of countries, such as the United States and some smaller European states, signalled their intent to stay neutral as much as four or five years in advance. When the war finally began, they issued formal declarations of neutrality.

Thus, in the twentieth century customary traditional neutrality as it was practiced, prior to 1939, there were two necessary initial steps. The first—a *signal of intent*—was taken when the likelihood of a major conflict became apparent. Most of the then-traditional neutrals reached that point in the late thirties. The second step—a formal *declaration of policy*—was taken after the shooting had started. When the belligerents on their side acknowledged this policy—as they usually did—the respective legal statuses had been duly recognised and the rules of war and neutrality were deemed to be in force.

The last world war was a major point of departure. A great number of small and large nations issued declarations of neutral (impartial) behaviour in September, 1939. As far as the two initial steps go—signal of intent and declaration of policy—most of the neutral nations seemed to have used the same formula for their declarations. With the notable exception of the greatest neutral, the United States,[2] there was no reason to believe that they were not sincere in their intentions to conform to accepted neutral behaviour. However, by noting their geographical location and by comparing their capabilities one could easily distinguish some which would seem more or less likely than others to carry out their publicly announced intentions.

A declaration of intent was certainly not enough in itself to secure success. There were always additional conditions whose fulfilment, in part or in full, would determine whether a prospective neutral actually would be allowed to reap the fruits of neutrality or not. In their acknowledgements of Norwegian neutrality, the British as well as the German government made their recognition explicitly conditional upon strict observance of the principle of impartiality. The conditions for impartial neutrality are discussed at length in the preceding chapters of this book, but they may be summarized and recapitulated here. They require:

1. General respect and observance of the relevant rules of international law.

2. Remoteness from the area of armed conflict, in terms of geographical distance as well as in terms of strategic importance.
3. Geographically-limited wars, or local or regional conflicts; absence of large wars involving several great powers.
4. Wars fought for rational, concrete and limited objectives, where ideological differences are not seriously at issue.
5. A loosely organized international system, with few military, economic, social or other binding obligations that might prevent or hinder the execution of impartial dealings with both sides.
6. A reasonable degree of economic and military self-sufficiency to avoid involvement through blackmail and blockade. The neutral state would need an economic potential of vital necessities for its population and for its productive capacity as well as a level of technology sufficient to develop and maintain a weapons system for military defense strong enough to prevent the use of neutral territory by any belligerent.
7. A stable domestic political system to make it credible that the neutral policies would be continued consistently and capabilities used according to declared intentions.

It was possible to fulfil most of these conditions in the nineteenth century, the heyday of impartial neutrality. Can they also be met in the middle twentieth century?

As far as meeting the first condition, the answer was a clear and unqualified no. The First World War had undermined and partly destroyed vital elements of the neutrality and war legislation. The second global conflict finished off most of what was left. The very few nations that had avoided direct involvement in the last great war did so for reasons other than legal ones. Reviewing the status of international law in the early 1950's, there was no visible prospect of reviving the legal protection for neutrality that had once proved effective. Nothing that had happened since 1945 substantiated hopes for strict observance of neutral rights.

As to the second and third conditions, there had already been several armed conflicts in the relevant period. But the way they had been conducted gave no reason to believe that they would engulf unwilling nations in other parts of the world. As long as they enjoyed the conditions of geographical limitation and remoteness then non-involvement was no problem to those nations that preferred to stay out.

As for the fourth condition, there were strong ideological elements in the Korean war, a direct confrontation between Eastern communism and

Western capitalism. There was also a clear realization that if the Korean war should escalate into a major East-West showdown few had illusions that any country would be spared from involvement through a policy of impartial neutrality. But, as the immediate goals centred on objectives in North and South Korea with a military concentration on the 38th parallel, there seemed to be no need to announce or even prepare for a policy of neutrality. Then as in earlier times, non-involvement in local limited conflicts presented few problems for states outside that particular area.

The proliferation of international organizations that took place from 1948 on clearly made it harder to fulfil the fifth condition of the loosely-organized international system. The creation of so many new organizations, universal or regional in membership, seemed to indicate that within a few years small and large nations would be tied together in a cobweb of intertwining obligations. As most traditional neutrals participated in these international organizations, it seemed unlikely that they would be able to withdraw *de facto* from a war situation and all of a sudden adopt such independent policies that would allow for their neutrality in a major war.

Formal arrangements did not solve the core problem of credibility. A declaration of traditional, legal neutrality would hardly be credible when a state's economic and perhaps also military capabilities depended upon continued massive exchange and co-operation with the states that would be involved in a major conflict. Even if the legal obligations of membership were suspended in such situations, the ties of organized interaction could not be undone overnight.

The organizational aspects were very closely tied up with the fifth condition of economic and military self-sufficiency. The isolationist motivations, which perhaps form the deepest core of neutral policies, would seem extremely hard to apply in the kinds of large-scale armed conflict that could be visualized in the early fifties. The two world wars had shown that a few larger nations, and most notably the United States, though able to fulfil the requirements of self-sufficiency nevertheless were too big to avoid involvement, while the smaller states were too weak and too dependent on the external environment to practice neutrality successfully. Most of the small neutrals were unable to meet the military imperatives for safeguarding their territorial integrity and dealing impartially with the warring nations in matters of trade and economy. Even so, a few small neutrals—Ireland, Spain, Turkey—did nevertheless maintain their neutrality successfully throughout World War II. Over a longer period, however, those that were most exposed could be forced to partiality by economic pressure. And, even if they were willing to accept the sacrifices of subsistence living, for demographic and technological reasons they were unable to put up the military defense that could demonstrate convincingly their determination and capacity to deny the use of neutral territory to belligerents on either side.

The final condition—domestic stability—bears directly on the obligations to deal impartially with both sides. Already in the early post-war period the difficulty of maintaining an "ideological neutrality" was long recognized. If the national policy of impartial dealings with both belligerents was not supported by most of the populace of the neutral nation, then the legal obligations of traditional neutrality no longer were credible. Though a declaratory policy expressing the firm intention to conduct an impartial neutral policy was, and is, always possible for some states in the absence of large-scale wars, it seemed, and seems, highly unlikely that these seven most important conditions would, or will, be met satisfactorily in a major conflict involving the great powers.

It cannot be stressed too strongly that the intricate refinements of traditional, legal neutrality were devised in order to stay out of such shooting wars where the greater powers were the main actors. Only the great powers had the widespread interests and the physical capacity for curtailing or destroying the sovereignty of smaller states. Maintaining sovereign status as a neutral with reasonable freedom of action *in times of peace* was a different and much easier task. It could usually be done purely on a declaratory basis. Also, keeping out of small, local struggles presented few problems to states that were not physically attacked or in other ways directly involved. In such contingencies non-involvement could be ensured without referring to a formal neutral status. The real problem was non-involvement in the great global wars, and in the early fifties this could not be solved on the basis of traditional neutrality.

Non-belligerency—meaning: not officially participating in a shooting war, must find its place between neutralization, which requires a formal treaty with explicit guarantees for each individual case, and traditional, impartial neutrality which relies on general legal principles sanctioned by the power elite in the international community. In fact, very often there was not a wide gap between the two legal versions of either neutralization or traditional neutrality, and on the other hand, the pragmatic policies of non-belligerency. A traditional neutral which, prior to a pending armed conflict, took the initial step of announcing its neutral intention could place no reliance on international law until the shooting had started. In this respect it was really not much different from a potential non-belligerent that preferred to say nothing and keep others guessing whether it would be in or out of a future war.

Thus, in the years preceding the Second World War there seemed to be three major groups of states each with varying relations to any future war which would involve the great powers. There were the potential belligerents, who by their national interests, their ideological leanings, and/or their geographical location seemed bound to become participants in a major war. There were the traditional neutrals, who for the most part identified themselves by announcing their neutral intentions in the late thirties. Finally, there were the "non-belligerents", a remaining group of states who either were to be counted as potential belligerents or were merely temporarily undecided, depending on their past and present behaviour, the special issues at stake for them, and on the other specifics of their situation. In terms of international stability, this third group of "X-nations" whose future course could not be predicted at all confidently. For some people these ambiguous "non-belligerents" seem dangerous, because they heighten uncertainty, especially in times of increasing tension.

Each of these three pre-World War II categories have some—but limited—relevance in the present day world. Only Austria and Laos are neutralized in the technical sense of having their status as permanent neutrals defined and recognised in international agreements: Laos by the Geneva agreement of 1962, though subsequent experience has shown that her neutralization is more of form than of substance; and Austria by domestic enactment, the Austrian State Treaty, and by Austro/Soviet memoranda.[3] The fact that several constitutional and international lawyers subsequently have debated whether this properly constitutes neutralization in international law serves as a reminder of how specific and idiosyncratic the precise details of any neutralization agreement inevitably must be. Non-belligerency certainly survives in fact and apparently, somewhat tenuously, in international laws. Whenever there is limited war there are always some non-belligerents.[4] Thus current—and often very volatile—variations of an ancient theme have appeared and may be expected to appear as long as wars occur and are less than universal. Hence the occasional appearance of sections in contemporary international law texts on "non-belligerency".[5]

Non-Alignment and Neutralism

The last fifteen years have seen the growth of a new version of uncommitted policies which has been termed "neutralism" and/or "non-alignment" by various authors and politicians. This vaguely defined concept might be listed as the fourth version of the old neutral theme—non-participation in other nations' wars. The complicating factor is that the same period has seen no major wars. And without a major war, there could be neither non-belligerency nor neutrality. The two bitter conflicts in Korea and Vietnam, in spite of their considerable intensity and American involvement, must still be listed as limited local wars. Thus, the points of reference are conflicts, not wars. Non-alignment must be viewed in a somewhat different context than the three previous categories, which were all directly related to large-scale armed conflicts involving several great powers. On the other hand, it seems unlikely that this fourth version, which was developed in the nineteen-fifties and sixties, should be a political mutation completely divorced from its predecessors. It is, however, difficult to make any assessment of its past, present, and future potentialities without a closer look at some relevant conceptual usage and terminology.

The group of distinguished authors which so far (1968) have dealt in a scholarly way with the concept of non-alignment have been remarkably inconsistent in their use of the term. Peter Lyon, who has given a most comprehensive treatment of the issue, called his book *Neutralism*, and just that. Others, like John W. Burton and the participants in the symposium directed by Cecil V. Crabb, for the Annals of the American Academy of Political Science, have used the term "non-alignment". Laurence W. Martin, who headed one of the first large-scale attempts to deal with the same problems, demonstrated a truly impartial attitude by naming his book *Neutralism and Non-Alignment*.[6] The native speakers and writers from countries that apply such policies have hardly been more consistent. Some leaders, such as Jawaharlal Nehru, had a clear distaste for the word "neutralism" while others, and from 1951 onwards Nehru himself, had a distinct liking for the label "non-alignment".[7] Consequently, with all these conflicting usages, terminology becomes a matter of personal preference.

Most people seem to agree that the term "neutralism" was first used in the late forties to describe factional attitudes in France.[8] That is, factional attitudes were first observed and described there, but they were by no means limited to France. In the early fifties similar groupings and expressions were noted in Germany, Britain, the Netherlands, and in the Scandinavian countries as well.[9] There can be no doubt that the sentiments voiced by these factions were closely connected with the Cold War and the tensions and frustrations that followed in its wake. But they did not express opinions of governments. On the contrary, the neutralist movements in Western Europe were on the whole anti-government. To some extent they may even be called anti-oppositional. This was particularly true in Britain and Scandinavia where they did not represent the major parties but were rather factions within them. In Western Europe the neutralists behaved as domestic interest groups, which by various means tried to press the national governments to alter their foreign policy orientations.

Thus, it is fair to say that "neutralism" is a movement rather than a policy.[10] The way it has been observed and described gives it a closer identification to groups and individuals within certain nations than to the policies of national governments. According to Denis Healey, "neutralism differs from neutrality since it is primarily an attitude of individuals rather than a policy of states".[11] Since non-alignment in peacetime (by which I mean the absence of large-scale war) aspires to fill the role which neutrality plays in war, it seems justified to apply the same reasoning to non-alignment. Therefore, in this study *neutralism will refer to attitudes of groups and individuals within a nation, while non-alignment will refer to policies of states.*

It is neutralism when factions and groups within a state strive to have non-alignment adopted as a national policy. The movement may be domestic or linked to groups and governments outside the country. If they are successful in either taking over the national government or influencing it, neutralist leaders may then direct non-alignment policies. The goal of neutralism is non-alignment. Usage of the two terms depends on whether the actors are national states or groups and individuals working within the national framework of a particular country.

I am aware of the fact that other writers who distinguish between neutralism and non-alignment give other definitions. Some talk of "militant neutralism".[12] Others vary between terms such as active, positive, dynamic, and even "messianic" neutralism. Very often it remains unclear whether the term refers to foreign policies, or movements within countries. There are also those who define non-alignment as a mainly static concept: "absence of alliance with either of the major groups in a cold war context". Neutralism is seen as a further extension of non-alignment: "a further commitment to participate in cold war issues, to play leading roles in neutralist conferences, to offer advice to the great powers, especially the West, to exert influence ... and to display ... a positive attitude toward bloc conflict".[13]

No state can in all respects be either permanently active or consistently passive. If activity is the yardstick, then states constantly shift from one category to another, depending upon the momentary degree of "extended activity". With a large number of non-aligned states, this makes systematic categorization almost impossible.

The definition which I have chosen, with the actors as the main determinant, may be hard to apply in cases where governments as well as interest groups participate in neutralist movements. But we need definite terms for both, and with non-alignment linked to policies of sovereign national states that term becomes at any rate more manageable. Depending on our approach, there will be many sub-categories of non-alignment, but they will all be dealt with as policies of states.

At varying times and in certain connections one may find—non-alignment, neutralism, and neutrality—used as rough synonyms. To some extent this is due to a general lack of precision. Nevertheless each of them does have definite nuances which distinguish one from the other and may produce different effects. In a given situation, one term applied to a particular group would produce a reaction entirely different from the same word applied to another group. It seems likely, for example, that the suffix "ism" in neutralism would imply a stronger ideological touch, relating neutralism to other "isms". It thus associates with values, beliefs, emotions, and creates an image of a movement, a crusade. It is hardly accidental that the word "neutralism" seems to have had a much broader usage in the early post 1945 period when the ideological connotations of neutralism were more accentuated.

Non-alignment is a cooler and more detached term. The emphasis is on the *functional* aspects rather than the emotional, normative ones, as is appropriate to the policy of states. As nations, once referred to as neutralists, gradually become more established, they will tend to adopt a more consistent use of the non-alignment label for official policy.

Why should some non-aligned nations insist on being referred to as neutrals and consistently characterize their own status as neutrality rather than non-alignment; while, on the other hand, there are non-aligned states that meticulously refrain from using that word at all? Of the three terms, neutrality has by far the oldest and longest tradition. The government of Finland, which has since 1955 consistently referred to its country's "neutrality", might see some advantage in stressing the fact that it is an old state (independence since 1917) and in many respects ought to be looked upon and categorized within the same group as its traditional neighbour, Sweden. Until someone sits down and sorts out in a systematic way the varying usages of the three terms, we shall continue to speculate over the psychological effects of such nuances.

While neutralism was a driving force from the late forties on, non-alignment as a state policy did not achieve prominence until well into the fifties. The turning point came with the recognition of the Cold War in 1947 and with the emergence of the great alliances and economic organizations about 1950–1953. These events reintroduced involvement versus non-involvement as a problem. At that time traditional neutrals like Sweden, Ireland and, of course, Switzerland had already announced their intentions not to become involved in the alliances and conflicts of the great powers. So had Yugoslavia, which broke away from the Soviet orbit of Communist nations in 1948. When India, Indonesia and some Middle Eastern states emerged as independent nation-states they also announced their non-alignment in relation to the great powers and their conflicts.

The general principle of non-alignment is certainly not an innovation of the late fifties. There have always been some states which try to stay out of conflicts. Over the centuries there have been a number of "schools" for neutral behaviour. We have had benevolent partial neutrality and legal impartial neutrality, neo-neutrality and non-belligerency. Where should we place non-alignment? Is it based on new principles, new theories, or is it just a modified, dressed-up version of the old and well-known concept of non-commitment or non-participation which existed at the close of the Second World War? What makes non-alignment different?

Taking the Bandung conference in 1955 as a starting point, the era of non-alignment so far has only lasted a little more than a decade. For a political concept this is a very short period. However, it is desirable to view it in a larger perspective in order to see not only how it developed, but also how it relates to past patterns of international behaviour as well as to the demands of the present and future situations.

In retrospect, one can see that the Korean war must have made a considerable impact on the new nations, partly for the way it was initiated and partly for what it did not achieve. The speeches in these years of pioneering leaders such as Nehru and Sukarno gave numerous indications of a more consolidating trend among the new nations.[14] However, it was not until the non-committed nations met in Bandung in April, 1955, that non-alignment became known as a distinct group-concept in international relations. Less than half of the states that took part in the Bandung conference could claim a non-aligned status. Among the "odd numbers" were Turkey, Japan, Pakistan and two Communist states, China and North Vietnam.

In the middle and late 1950s Jawaharlal Nehru, Gamal Abdel Nasser, and Kwame Nkrumah manifested their positions as leaders of the non-aligned group. The number of non-aligned nations greatly increased as many more new Afro-Asian nations achieved statehood in the late fifties. In the United Nations their voting power added greatly to non-aligned influence. But there was still considerable vagueness as to what criteria were needed in order to qualify for non-alignment. Most of them were new and underdeveloped nations. These were important characteristics, but they were clearly not sufficient. Lack of development was not synonymous with non-alignment. The choice of Belgrade as the site for their first non-aligned conference was to a large extent an attempt to emphasize the more general aspects of non-alignment.[15]

Although definitions of non-alignment and the enunciation of common goals had been one of the main reasons for calling that conference, in fact the proceedings brought little clarification. The non-aligned nations could not agree between themselves what non-alignment actually was or what it aimed to become. These quite important questions remained unanswered even after the conference of non-aligned states held in Cairo in October 1964. However, there is no lack of individual definitions. Most of the non-aligned governments have from time to time given public statements of their policy; their leaders have described and discussed what they mean by non-alignment, and a host of writers and scholars have tried to analyze what a policy of non-alignment actually involves.

Most writers seem to agree that the basic earmarks of non-alignment are:

1. *Dissociation from the Cold War.*[16] This has been further elaborated to mean: "a deliberate and calculated refusal to enter into any military or political commitment with great powers or to permit foreign military bases on one's territory".[17] John Burton's version is: "[not to enter] into the strategic planning of any major power and not to allow any foreign power the use of non-aligned territory".[18]
2. *Absence of ideological commitment* to either the Western or the Eastern ideologies.[19] This requirement is actually implicit in the first.
3. *Economic independence*—equally as important as military or political independence. "A policy of non-alignment cannot be effective, enduring or genuine unless the economic basis is sufficiently diversified as between the two blocs."[20]
4. Public commitment to the principles of *peaceful co-existence* (Panch Sheel).[21]

Non-alignment is also connected with some other points which are more like general characteristics or goals than actual criteria or conditions.

5. One of these goals is the non-aligned demand to act as a *"third force"* in international politics.[22] The non-aligned countries are themselves not in full agreement on how and whether such a force should exist, how much coordination would be needed, or whether this is, in fact, another form of "positive non-alignment".
6. The idea of a "third force", in whatever form, is closely related to the *peace-making activities* which have been an implicit goal of most non-aligned leaders. The idea is that their non-commitment policies will make them acceptable as mediators, go-betweens, in international conflicts where the larger powers are involved in vital issues.
7. There has also been great concern about *anti-colonialism*, which has been a very important and immediate issue to most of the non-aligned states who have a colonial past.[23] It is accentuated somewhat differently in Asian and African countries, and sometimes formulated as a struggle against imperialism or neo-colonialism.[24]

These seven conditions listed above seem to be the most prominent in the policies of states that characterize themselves as non-aligned. In order to get some ideas as to the prospects of non-alignment and the extent to which it corresponds to other versions of non-commitment, such as neutrality, a reasonable approach would be to view the problem through each of these conditions and discuss them in past, present and future connotations.

Non-alignment and the Cold War

We have already noted the inconsistent and often confusing terminological use of neutralism and non-alignment. The situation is hardly any better when we come to neutrality versus non-alignment. As non-alignment and neutrality are both policies of state, it would be useful to agree on some definition that could set one apart from the other. "By neutrality is meant non-involvement in war, while by neutralism [= non-alignment] is meant non-involvement in *the* Cold War."[25] Neutrality in its legal and traditional sense exists only in a "hot" war, that is, a conflict dominated by large-scale military operations; while non-alignment refers to a situation, like the present one, where there may be conflicts but either no war at all or just localized and limited ones. In most scholarly writings the Cold War appears as the touchstone, the basic characteristic that makes non-alignment so fundamentally different from other forms of non-commitment policies.

The uniqueness of non-alignment is derived from the uniqueness of the Cold War. The conflict between the two large blocs, the Soviet and the American, is so serious that it "normally" would have led to a hot, shooting war. As it remains cold, there can be no traditional legal neutrality in relation to it and thus no pledges of impartial treatment. But as the conflict is very intense with a constant risk of hot war between the two blocs, the non-aligned cannot be indifferent but must have an active and positive policy where they criticize or support the two sides, depending on the issues in each case.

These assumptions which have been called a "theory of non-alignment"[26] raise several questions. The first refers to the chronological discrepancy between non-alignment and the Cold War. How can there be such a close interrelation when the Cold War notoriously dates from 1947 and non-alignment did not become internationally recognized as an international concept until 1954–1955? Why, then, were not the seven basic principles of non-alignment developed in the late forties rather than in the middle fifties?

The chronological discrepancy seems to support my hypothesis that instead of non-alignment being a line of action which all uncommitted nations pursue in periods of high tension, non-aligned activities are relatively low when there is no immediate probability of general war. The first five to six years of the Cold War were the "coldest" ones. From the initial major confrontation in the spring of 1947, there was a series of grave situations—the Czech coup in 1948, the Berlin blockade, the Korean war and the testing of the first thermo-nuclear bombs. Until the death of Stalin the continued test of wills between the United States and the Soviet Union made the "war" really freezing cold.

In this period there would seem to be an obvious need for the inputs which the non-aligned later claimed as their major contribution to peace and international understanding. Nevertheless, they refrained from intermediary actions based on an independent judgment of each separate case, which has been said to be the core of non-alignment. One would assume that they were no less interested then in offering such services as they became later. Why did they hold back?

There is, of course, no single answer to this question. But one explanation is that they considered the level of international tension too high for such experiments. In the late forties and early fifties there was assumed to be an overwhelming superiority in the Western side. It was bi-polarity in the sense that two powers were distinctly ahead of the others. But the two poles were not yet considered to be equally strong. The might of the United States had been demonstrated amply during the Second World War, and although the relative power and influence of the two second powers in the Western camp, Britain and France, was diminished, they still hung on to their rank as great powers in a world perspective. Under these circumstances it must have seemed unwise for the non-aligned to engage in the kinds of strong criticism of the western powers which became a routine practice in the late fifties.

There was also in the late 1940s and early 1950s a much greater feeling that general war might come at short notice. The Soviet consolidation of its power in Eastern Europe, the Communist takeover in China, and the drive toward further expansion, which many felt was the real cause of the Korean war, as well as the pressure on Berlin, seemed to indicate to some new states that the protection of the West might be needed very urgently, particularly for those new states within reach of either China or the Soviet Union. To adopt attitudes of outspoken criticism about one's political protectors was just too risky to be attempted.

What, then, brought about the change? Which were the events that made non-alignment emerge as a major factor in international politics? There were many reasons, the most important ones being: Firstly, the sobering effect on the two bloc powers of the thermo-nuclear explosions, which brought home to them with unquestionable authority the enormously destructive potential of thermo-nuclear warfare. Secondly, the introduction of the five principles of peaceful co-existence, which appeared for the first time in the preamble to the Chinese-Indian treaty of April, 1954. This was a major turning point. A year later, in the spring of 1955, the Soviet Union followed China's earlier course. While introducing the first "thaw" in East-West relations, the Russians also adopted a course of selective approval for neutralism, meaning non-alignment, as an important part of their foreign policy. To some extent this was expressed in their policy of making available cheap loans and aid to some non-aligned countries.[27] With the two leading Communist nations committed to a policy whose professed foundation was the recognition of national independence and a programme of non-interference with the sovereignty and independence of other nations, there could be, it seemed, no immediate danger of war—and consequently, no urgent need for protection.

Thirdly, there was the changing strategic balance. The spectacular advances which the Soviet Union made, first in the nuclear and then in the space field, strengthened the growing impression that the two blocs were fairly well balanced. With the mutual potential for retaliation and assured destruction, they could hardly be expected to engage in conflicts that might bring about nuclear war. Every brush-fire incident was viewed in terms of escalation. It is important here to remember the all-or-nothing approach to war that prevailed through the later part of the fifties. In Western Europe it brought about some almost hysterical anti-nuclear campaigns. There was popularly assumed to be only two possible alternatives, either general peace or general war. And if war came it was imagined that it must become a catastrophe of such giant dimensions that normal considerations of national security and problems of independence and integrity would be irrelevant.

Fourthly, the non-aligned were clearly reassured by the decline in power and influence of their two former colonial masters, France and Great Britain. The stunning defeat of France by the Vietnamese Communists at Dien Bien Phu in 1954 left a deep impression of French impotence and national decay, which seemed to be confirmed by the domestic political chaos and the lack of progress in North Africa. The 1956 Suez crisis, together with increasing problems in Africa and elsewhere, indicated similar trends for Britain. Furthermore, the interference of the United States in the Suez affair showed a lack of cohesion among the Western allies which weakened the fears new states might have had as to a recurrence of Western colonialism by means of alliance activities and of possible renewed attempts of interference.

Finally, the non-aligned were greatly encouraged by their sense of success as independent nations. "Success" varied of course from country to country. Compared to national liberation processes of earlier periods, their sovereign status had come about more as a result of decaying empires than because of their own strength and persistence. But the immediate results were gratifying nevertheless, and it was undeniable that there were many more newly independent non-aligned countries. The voting power they gained when they became members of the United Nations—as they almost automatically did after 1955—also gave them some bargaining power in important roll calls in the General Assembly. This also boosted their self-esteem and prestige.

From this summary of relevant trends, it seems that the more the Cold War thawed (which meant less likelihood of an armed confrontation between the two blocs) the more open and widespread were demonstrations of non-alignment. Thus, the development of policies and theories introduced by the non-aligned from the Bandung conference appear as functions of "thaws" rather than as Cold War tensions.

The Cold War has always been identified with bi-polarity. Many saw the Soviet-American confrontation of the forties and fifties as *the* Cold War—which again produced non-alignment. If we should follow this line of reasoning we might conclude that if there were no cold war, non-alignment would lose its justification to the same extent that traditional, impartial neutrality becomes a meaningless term without the existence of a hot war. Has that already happened, or is there now still a cold war situation in the late sixties?

There will be those who say this *is* a cold war situation, and others who say it is not. However, many would agree that political bi-polarity was gone before the 1960's began. Some date its departure from the first signs of Soviet-China rift, others from the Congo crisis. There have been attempts to distinguish between political and military bi-polarity. In strictly nuclear terms this might be justified. But we are rapidly moving into a period of multi-polarity. In fact, we have been there for some time already, in a military as well as in a political sense. This means that it has now become almost impossible to talk of the non-aligned as a "third force" or third party as one did a decade ago. The tighter the "bloc-members" hang together the easier it is to define the non-aligned. And, correspondingly, the looser and less cohesive alliances and blocs become, the more diffuse becomes the concept of non-alignment. Without tight alignments, non-alignment becomes a meaningless term.

This is what happened during the sixties. The alliances have become more diffuse, less cohesive, and this has affected non-alignment. Whether the yardstick is voting behaviour in the General Assembly of the United Nations or any other forms of international behaviour, it has become increasingly harder to draw clear distinctions between aligned and non-aligned countries.[28] Instead of alliance systems with the stress on rights and duties, we tend to think more in terms of "spheres of influence", that is, areas—including non-aligned as well as aligned countries—that are dominated and to a large extent controlled by one large state. The Soviet Union has recently announced its doctrine of influence within the sphere of socialist countries in Eastern Europe—with no specific reference to the Warsaw Pact countries. Some would include non-aligned states such as Finland and Yugoslavia in that sphere as naturally as they would list Sweden and Switzerland in the Western sphere. If one approaches the problem from the point of alignment, one finds a corresponding diffusion. Countries such as Norway and Denmark and certainly France, which all have made a point of partial participation, might be called "semi-aligned" or perhaps potential semi-neutrals.

Non-alignment and international violence

Non-alignment has not been a truly international movement; nor has neutralism. The non-aligned have been unable to agree on common goals and courses of joint action. Non-alignment consists of various sets of national policies, practised by countries who have certain traits and problems in common, but widely different solutions. In terms of principles, the major goal for each of them was the safeguarding of their national sovereignty and integrity. Operating from a basis of varying degrees of weakness, they know that a number of larger states, either alone or in alignment with others, have the power to deprive them of their national status or can enforce dependence. If such states interfere, they have lost out as fully independent nations and will have to accept continued existence with a reduced independence. Therefore, what the non-aligned want and strive for is *non-interference*.

If non-interference could be obtained and maintained without any fixed price, as for instance alignment, it would of course be preferable. This was in fact what happened to the non-aligned during the bi-polar period. In this system of "loose" bi-polarity and assumed strategic balance, there was a certain competition for the favours of non-aligned states. Under such conditions non-alignment seemed the most natural course. Their energies and efforts could be devoted to essentially domestic pursuits, such as industrialization, aid and development in various sectors of national activity. Non-alignment had no high cost, as long as the basically bi-polar competitive system prevailed. The crucial question is what is the price of non-alignment when these favourable conditions changed and the loose bi-polar system no longer could be maintained?

Until quite recently, there have been various opinions as to whether this has happened or whether the international system still remains basically unchanged from what it was in the middle fifties. At this time, now in the late sixties, the matter is hardly in doubt. There have been a number of quite important changes.

The first of these indications of a new situation is the increased rate of *armed interference* by major states. Non-alignment was to a large extent made possible and popular by the Chinese and Soviet acceptance of the principles of non-interference with sovereign nations. In 1962, China invaded India. The invasion had apparently limited aims, but the example was set and there was nothing to indicate that it would not be repeated.

The Soviet Union had through most of the 1960's helped a number of non-aligned states to build what must have seemed to them as bulwarks against interference by military force. National liberation, sovereign rights and no meddling with the internal affairs of other states had been the common cry of the Soviet Union and their favoured non-aligned friends for more than a decade. Then suddenly in August 1968 came the Russian invasion of Czechoslovakia, assisted by some Warsaw pact allies. The Soviet explanations of such measures can hardly have carried much weight with keen observers in non-aligned countries. The fact of the situation was that all of the three major nations in the world—the United States, China and the Soviet Union—*had now practised violent interference at the expense of smaller nations*. As far as the larger Western states go, most of them were already in that category. The American engagement in Vietnam has been strongly criticized by the non-aligned and condemned as interference.

The second indication of substantial change in the contemporary international system is the *intensification of the arms race*. Since the early sixties two more members, China and France, have entered the nuclear club. Even without engaging in any open hostilities, the expenses for defense have risen very steeply for virtually all major military powers. The increase is not limited to nuclears and missiles. There has been an intensified arms race in naval, air and ground arms and equipment. Much the same is true for the Warsaw pact countries. The Western alliance shows a more uneven development, but generally the same trend. The Vietnam war has brought the U.S. defence budget from about fifty million a few years ago toward the present eighty million mark.[29]

The tendency to pay much more attention to military capabilities than to military procurements is also a predominant trait in most non-aligned countries. With very few exceptions they have set about acquiring stronger military forces. In many cases these ambitions seem out of proportion with other sectors of their national activities. The motivations behind these military policies vary. In some cases they may be prompted mainly as matters of prestige. Armed force is a symbol of sovereignty. As the majority of non-aligned nations practice some sort of dictatorship, their forces might be designed primarily for domestic use. The important fact is, however, that military forces are available in most non-aligned countries. Whether they will be used inside or outside the national borders will depend on particular situations.

A third factor, and a very disturbing one, is the conspicuous *lack of success in concluding international agreements* for stopping or checking the arms race and the incidence of violence. Non-alignment was to some extent connected with the great hopes of the fifties for sweeping and comprehensive arms control and disarmament arrangements. Most of these hopes have come to nothing. The partial nuclear test ban treaty did not prevent more states from acquiring nuclear capabilities. The watered-down non-proliferation treaty is unlikely to become more effective.

Consideration of these three important variables leads to the conclusion that there has been a definite rise in international tensions and in the rate of organized interstate violence during the last decade. The stress on force and violence in international relations is probably heavier now than it has been since the Second World War. If this trend continues, how and by what means can the non-aligned hope to avoid involvement?

Immunity from military violence is dependent upon the observance of what one could call a set of ground rules for international behaviour. This assumes that unless restrained in some way or other a stronger state will use force when it wishes to impose its will on weaker states. The whole philosophy (if we may use such a pretentious word) of non-alignment is that this is no longer possible. The ground rules of non-interference must be observed. This contention may well be true. Nothing has happened so far to completely disprove the proposition. But the trends dealt with above have raised serious doubt whether it is valid.

The relevant factors are very complex indeed. But it seems that the following variables were the main ones which were instrumental in maintaining some general observance of non-interference rules in the late fifties:

1. The basically bi-polar struggle of mutual retaliation and destruction, keeping both superpowers in check.
2. The assumption that even limited brush-fire wars would escalate into general war. In order to avoid that, the two blocs would in their own interest either refrain from interference themselves or prevent middle powers from doing so (1956 Suez crisis).
3. The United Nations—where the non-aligned had an increasing share of the vote—might stop an interference by military means, if necessary through the use of international peace forces.

All three factors amounted to some sort of exercise in international police power, either by individual superpowers, or by both blocs in concert, acting within or outside the framework of the United Nations. In other words, the intent, combined with sufficient actual power in the hands of both to control the situation, which in fact meant backing the ground rules of non-interference.

If we check these basic conditions of the fifties with the present situation, one could of course argue both ways. There is still some kind of a nuclear balance, although with more participants, but the assumption that limited wars will inevitably lead to major war does not hold any longer. The nuclear ceiling permits a much higher level of conventional violence than was ever thought possible ten years ago. Neither is there much left of hopes for the peace-keeping efforts of the United Nations. It may be important for reconciliation[30] but it has no answer to interference by military force—if reconciliation fails.

Limited war* is becoming increasingly frequent, and as demonstrated by the six-day Middle East war of 1967, it may run its course without being decisively affected by the major powers. But, whenever there is limited war without general war there must always be neutrals and non-belligerents. Today, bi-polar and multi-polar systems coexist and interact. The rate of interstate violence is increasing. This situation is clearly different from that of a decade ago, when non-alignment was flourishing. How are the non-aligned going to meet the challenge of change? What can they do?

Non-alignment and the levels of conflict

In the last instance each individual nation will naturally have to work out its own problems in its own way, depending on the special circumstances. But if generalizations are permissible at all, there would seem to be three major courses of action for the non-aligned:

1. Continue as now with non-alignment policies of the fifties, hoping that "the changes will go away" and the present trends will be reversed.
2. Adopt traditional neutrality as a guideline, preparing for impartial neutrality in war (Swedish model).
3. Prepare for a policy of diplomacy and bargaining, where any means, neutrality, semi-alignment or even regional alignment, might be considered in order to prevent military interference. Such unprincipled bargaining in a no-war situation might be compared to non-belligerency in war. Any means that works to achieve the goal is good and justifiable.

There are indications that the non-aligned may consider returning to some sort of undeclared neutral intent; some seem even ready to adopt the principle of impartial behaviour which until recently most non-aligned theorists condemned very strongly.[31] Some have gone as far as to point at impartial neutrality as the likely policy for the non-aligned states in war. "In the event of open warfare between the main power blocs, non-aligned countries would be obliged, as all countries are, to declare themselves either neutral or at war. Those who chose neutrality would immediately be subject to restraints of, and have their rights and duties associated with, neutrality. These would override rights claimed by non-alignment."[32] If this should have any claim to credibility, it would have to be prepared a long time in advance, which in fact would be the acceptance of the Swedish model of traditional neutrality; "allians-frihet" aiming for neutrality in war.

As indicated by the rate of abstentions in the United Nations assembly, the smaller and weaker non-aligned countries would be most likely to adopt impartial attitudes. One might even find a positive correlation between states with very limited bargaining powers and those that adopt impartial attitudes. This pattern is well-known from the inter-war period.

The larger states would be expected to maintain the facade of non-alignment to the extent of their actual bargaining power. Their greatest problem would be to balance off conflicts on various levels. These are basically three:

1. *Global:* At least two of the nuclear powers are involved. All-out nuclear war is considered an imminent possibility (e.g. Cuba missile crisis).
2. *Regional:* None or only one of the nuclear powers is involved. Military operations reach a high degree of scope and intensity (e.g. China-India war 1962, Middle East crisis 1967).
3. *Local:* Armed conflicts within a region involving two or more neighbouring countries in border fights, civil war, infiltration, or open invasion of neighbours.

Of course to represent these three levels schematically is not to deny their mutual interaction.

One might well get situations when states were non-aligned or pledged to impartial behaviour to conflicts on the *global* level, non-aligned or semi-aligned on the *regional* level, and actually participatingly aligned on the *local* level. At the moment one can clearly see distinctions between an upper and a lower level of international conflict. It does not seem far-fetched to visualize some characteristics of the local levels as well, although there would always be some overlapping between regional and local conflicts.

There might also be room, and there is certainly need, for a recognition of another form of non-alignment: *semi-alignment* (in war = semi-neutrality) or partial participation. Here we would place states that are formally aligned but which have made certain explicit reservations as to the degree of involvement in the alliance. The position which Norway and Denmark take within the North Atlantic alliance could qualify for this category. Both countries are full members of the alliance system, and it would be impossible for them to claim non-aligned status. At the same time, they have made reservations regarding military bases and certain kinds of weapons which restrict the operations of the alliance in peacetime.

There seems to be no reason why the principle of partial participation should not find other forms as well where contributions from aligned states are made available only on certain conditions specified in formal treaties prior to the crisis. The eighteenth century patterns of "partial neutrality" offer many models that might be applicable to semi-aligned policies under present conditions.[38] Neutrality referring to an internationally recognized codex such as the Hague Convention of 1907 cannot be expected to reappear.

The number of possible combinations could probably be multiplied many times over on the local level of conflict. Again, we would have states that were impeccably non-aligned and pledging impartial intent on the global and regional levels but deeply immersed in conflicts on the local level. The positions taken by some of the countries in South East Asia during the Vietnam war might serve as an illustration. With the wide spectrum of participation and non-participation which could be expected in such cases it seems very hard to apply strictly even the flexible terms we have introduced so far.

Non-alignment is a meaningless word without its counterpart: alignment. One can make a table of the corresponding variations in alignments at the three levels of conflict. Many of the questions posed with great practical urgency in the fifties, concerning alignment or non-alignment—with us or against us—have become close to irrelevant in the late 1960s. Instead of an "either-or" there is now often likely to be a "both-and" situation. There is no longer a sharp distinction between alignment and non-alignment. The so-called aligned and non-aligned move and intermingle on a continuum which has full alliance membership at one extreme and neutralization at the other. It is already difficult and it will become increasingly more so to place a small or medium-sized state for a long period at any fixed point on that line. At best we might locate it right or left of the centre, and even then we need to specify the relevant time period.

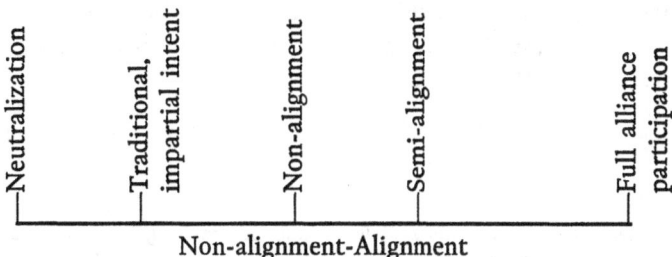

Non-alignment-Alignment

Whatever position a state may choose as its international orientation, either right or left or centre, it will have to apply a wide range of bargaining techniques to attain a dual purpose: *to stave off interference and at the same time to have a reasonable degree of the fulfilment of national objectives.*[34]

If we assume that the present trends will continue, it is hard to believe that all the states which now claim non-alignment will survive and maintain their present sovereign status. On the global level none of the major states seems inclined to give up its influence. They must be expected to extend rather than surrender their present spheres of influence. Newcomers like China and potential leaders of regions in, for instance, North, West and East Africa will probably be trying to establish their own spheres of influence at what I have characterized as the regional level. At the local level one might expect unions and disunions in a variety of combinations. New localised patterns might spring up in other parts of the world where the major powers have not already secured their control.

An analysis trying to deal with the general problems of non-alignment rather than with the problems of separate, identified states can hardly produce many definite conclusions. If anything at all conclusive can be said, it is that problems of non-alignment in a tight, no-general-war situation are quite similar to those of neutrals in a hot war. Whether and how long a state will be able to survive as a non-aligned, independent operator on the international scene depends not on international law, nor on any non-aligned third force, nor on any ground rules of peaceful coexistence and non-intervention, but on *military* resistance, *economic* strength and potential, and on its strategic geographical position.[35]

With the recent changes in the international situation it seems that the assumptions which provided the basis for non-alignment when it was developed a decade ago, can no longer be maintained. Non-alignment in a no-war situation is a rough equivalent of non-belligerency in a hot war situation. Both are really pragmatic tools, with no profound principles or doctrines. Each aims to achieve a particular purpose: non-alignment to bargain for non-interference in times of peace, non-belligerency to prevent involvement in a hot war.

NOTES

1 The two other classic cases, Belgium and Luxembourg, had lost their status as neutralized states earlier.
2 See page 196.
3 Cyril E. Black, Richard A. Falk, Klaus Knorr, Oron R. Young, *Neutralization and World Politics* (Princeton University Press, New Jersey, 1968).
4 Robert R. Wilson, "Non-belligerency in relation to the terminology of neutrality" in the *American Journal of International Law*, January 1941.
5 J. L. Kunz, *The Changing Law of Nations* (Ohio State University Press, 1968), 892–904.
6 Peter Lyon, *Neutralism* (Leicester University Press, 1963); John W. Burton, *International Relations: A General Theory* (Cambridge University Press, 1965); Cecil V. Crabb (ed.), *Non-Alignment in Foreign Policy* (*American Annals of Political and Social Science*, November, 1965); Lawrence W. Martin (ed.), *Neutralism and Non-Alignment* (New York, 1962); see also Paul F. Power, *Neutralism and Disengagement* (Scribner Research Anthologies, 1964).
7 Lyon, 15ff.
8 John T. Marcus, *Neutralism and Nationalism in France* (New York, 1958), 13ff.; Dorothy Pickles, *French Politics* (London, 1953) 185ff.; Peter Lyon, "Neutrality and the Emergence of the Concept of Neutralism", *Review of Politics* (1960), 255–268.
9 Marina Salvin, *Neutralism in France and Germany* (New York, 1951); Aneurin Bevan, *In Place of Fear* (London, 1952); Leon Epstein, *Britain, Uneasy Ally* (Chicago, 1954); William Zartman, "Neutralism and Neutrality in Scandinavia", *Western Political Quarterly* (1954), 125–160.
10 Cecil V. Crabb, *op. cit.*, 6; Crabb, *The Elephants and the Grass* (New York, 1965), 23–25).
11 Denis Healey, *Neutralism* (London, 1955), 11.
12 "Non-alignment can be adopted on the basis of rational estimates of the conditions required for national security and domestic stability; but a policy of militant neutralism, on the other hand, is likely to be strongly affected by non-rational ideological preoccupations and by an almost too pragmatic quest for aid and status internationally." George Liska, in Martin, *Neutralism and Non-Alignment*, 83.
13 Theodore L. Shay, "Non-Alignment Si, Neutralism No", *Review of Politics* (April,

1968), 228. Shay draws here on Michael Bresher, *The New States of Asia, A Political Analysis* (New York, 1966).
14 The 1954 meeting in Colombo was of a more preparatory nature and did not really deal with the issues. See G. H. Jansen, *Afro-Asia and Nonalignment* (Faber, 1966).
15 In fact, it was very far from general. Yugoslavia and Cyprus were the only European states present, and less than half of the independent African states appeared in Belgrade. Cf. Lyon, *Neutralism*, Chapter VI.
16 Lyon, *Neutralism*, 16 60–63; Crabb and K. J. Babaa, "Non-Alignment as a Diplomatic and Ideological Credo", *Annals* (November, 1965), 8.
17 M. S. Rajan, "The Future of Non-Alignment", *Annals* (November, 1965), 122.
18 Burton, *op. cit.*, 224. "The most common form of non-alignment today is found among those states which on their own initiative and without the guarantee of other states refuse to commit themselves militarily to the goals and objectives of other states." K. J. Holsti, *International Politics* (New Jersey, 1967), 104.
19 Rajan, *op. cit.*
20 *Ibid.* Rajan includes also "freedom of opinion". In order to speak freely a state cannot be associated with either bloc.
21 Holsti, *op. cit.*; Crabb and Babaa, *op. cit.*; Lyon, *Neutralism*, 66; Burton, *op. cit.*, 203; "Panch Sheel" (Pancha Shila) refers to the Chinese-Indian treaty of April 29th, 1954.
22 Lyon, *op. cit.*, 64.
23 Lyon, *op. cit.*, 76ff.
24 Michael Kremnyev, "The Non-Aligned Countries and World Politics", in Paul Power, *Neutralism and Disengagement*, 94–98.
25 Lyon, *Neutralism*, 20.
26 Burton, *International Relations* (Cambridge University Press 1965), 228ff.
27 Heinz Fiedler, *Der sowjetische Neutralitätsbegriff in Theorie und Praxis* (Verlag für Politik und Wissenschaft, Köln, 1959).
28 Cf. by the present writer, "NATO, NAFTA and the Smaller Allies", *Orbis* (1968).
29 *The Military Balance* (Institute of Strategic Studies, London). Annual publication all through the 'sixties.
30 Ernst B. Haas, *Collective Security and the Future International System* (University of Denver Monograph Series, 1968).
  *There is now a very considerable literature about limited war in the nuclear age. See especially Morton Halpein, *Limited War in the Nuclear Age* (Yale University Press, 1961), which has an excellent bibliography.
31 Theodore L. Shay, "Non-Alignment Si, Neutralism No", *Review of Politics* (April, 1968), 230–231.
32 John W. Burton, *International Relations*, 220.
33 See 11–17.
34 See page 278. See also Robert L. Rothstein, *Alliances and Small Powers* (Columbia University Press, New York, 1968), 213; David Vital, *The Inequality of States* (Oxford 1967), 118–119.
35 ". . . non-alignment by itself carries no assurances of the limitation of exclusion of external intervention . . .", Robert E. Osgood, *Alliances and American Foreign Policy* (John Hopkins Press, Baltimore 1968), 10–11.

Bibliography

		Side
Section I	Official Documents	306
	Collections of Documents	307
Section II	Books and Pamphlets	308
Section III	Periodicals	310
	Newspapers	313

Bibliography

Section I
OFFICIAL DOCUMENTS

American State Papers. 1789—1794. 2d ed. Boston, 1817.
Bilag til Beretning til Folketinget, Supplement XII, vedrørende Forholdene ved Danmarks Besættelse, 9. april, 1940. København, 1951.
Brasseys Annual Naval Reports. London, 1948.
Förspelet till det tyska angreppet på Danmark och Norge den 9 april 1940. Handlingar vedrörande Sveriges politik under andra världskriget. Stockholm, 1948.
Frågor i samband med norska regjeringens vistelse utanfor Norge. 1940—1943. Handlingar vedrörande Sveriges politik under andra världskriget. Stockholm 1949.
Innstilling fra Undersøkelseskommisjonen av 1945 med bilag. Oslo 1946.
Innstilling fra Undersøkelseskomiteen av 1945, vol. VI. Regjeringen Nygaardsvolds virksomhet fra 7. juni 1940 til 25. juni 1945. Oslo, 1947.

League of Nations Documents:
    Only the most important documents are listed below.
    Constitution. Special number. Vol. II. Boston, 1919.
    Official Journal. 1920. Assembly Plenary Session. London, 1920.
    Official Journal.
        Assembly. *Records of the Tenth Ordinary Session of the Assembly Minutes of the First Committee.* Geneva, 1929.
        Assembly. *Report of the Committee for the Amendment of the Covenant in Order to Bring it into Harmony with the Pact of Paris.* Doc. A. 8, 1930 V. Geneva, 1930.
        Assembly. *Reports and Resolutions on the Subject of Article 16 of the Covenant.* Doc. A. 14, 1927 V. Geneva, 1927.
        Special Supplements. No. 147, 1935; no. 154, 1936; no. 155, 1936, and no. 180, 1938. Geneva, 1935, 1936, 1938.
        Treaty Series. Vol. XXXVIII, no. 702. Geneva, 1924.
Norges forhold til Sverige under krigen, 1940—1945. Aktstykker utgitt av det Kgl. Utenriksdepartement. Oslo, 1947.
Norway and the War. Documents on International Affairs. London, 1941.
The Signing of the North Atlantic Treaty, Proceedings. Washington, 1949.
Sveriges Förhållande till Danmark och Norge under krigsåren. Redogjörelser avgivna till den svenska utrikesnämnden av ministern för utrikes ärenda. 1941—1945. Stockholm, 1945.

Transiteringsfrågon och dermed sammanhängande spörsmål. April—Juni, 1940. Handlingar vedrörande Sveriges politik under andra världskriget. Stockholm, 1947.
Transiteringsfrågan. Juni—December, 1940. Handlingar vedrörande Sveriges politik under andra världskriget. Stockholm, 1947.
Treaties and Conventions. 1776—1887. Washington, 1889.
Trial of the Major War Criminals before the International Military Tribunal, Nuremberg, 1946—1949.

United Nations Documents.
　Only the most important documents are listed below.
　Documents of the United Nations Conference on International Organization. San Francisco 1945, vols. III, IV, VI and VII. New York, 1945.
　The International Law Commission Documents. (ILC)
　　Document ILC. A/925.
　　«　　«　A/CN.4/1.
　　«　　«　A/CN.4/SR.6.
　　«　　«　A/C.6/SR.158—164. Lake Success, New York, 1949.
　United Nations. *Survey of International Law* in relation to the work of codification of the International Law Commission. New York, 1948.
The United States Department of State.
　Nazi-Soviet Relations. 1939—1941. Washington, 1948.
　Papers Relating to the Foreign Relations of the United States. Supplements for the years 1914—1919. Washington, 1928.
　Press Releases. Washington, 1935, 1937 and 1939.
United States, *Statutes at Large.* Vol. 1. Boston, 1848.

COLLECTIONS OF DOCUMENTS

Baker, Ray S. and William Dodd. *The Public Papers of Woodrow Wilson,* vols. II—IV. New York, 1925.
Bourquin, Maurice, ed. *Collective Security.* A Record of the Seventh and Eighth Studies Conferences, Paris, 1934, London, 1935. Paris, 1936.
Churchill, Winston, S. *Into Battle,* war speeches. London, 1942.
International Conciliation. Documents 1928. Worchester, 1928.
International Law Association, *Reports of the 41st Conference.* Cambridge, 1943.
Pfankuchen, Llewellyn. *A Documentary Textbook in International Law.* New York, 1940.
Richardson, James D. *Messages and Papers of the Presidents. 1789—1897.* Vol. I. Washington, 1896.
Rosemann, Samuel I., ed. *The Public Papers and Addresses of Franklin D. Roosevelt,* vols. 1932—1940. New York.
Scharffenberg, Johan. *Norske Aktstykker til okkupasjonens forhistorie.* Oslo, 1951.
Scott, James B. *The Declaration of London,* February 26, 1909. A Collection of Official Papers and Documents... New York, 1919.
— *The Hague Conventions and Declarations 1899 and 1907.* Baltimore, 1909.
Stearns, Raymond Phineas. *Pageant of Europe,* Sources and Selections... New York, 1947.

Section II
BOOKS AND PAMPHLETS

Alemann, Peter. *Die Sweitz und die Verletzung der belgischen Neutralität im Weltkrieg 1914*. Buenos Ayres, 1940.
Angell, Norman. *The Worlds Highway*. New York, 1915.
Assmann, Kurt. *Deutsche Schicksaalsjahre*, Wiesbaden, 1950.
Bailey, Thomas. *A Diplomatic History of the American People*. New York, 1946.
Baker, Ray Stannard. *Woodrow Wilson, Life and Letters*, vol. V, *Neutrality, 1914—1915*. New York, 1935. Vol. VII, *War-leader, 1917—1918*. New York, 1939.
Beard, Charles A. *American Foreign Policy in the Making, 1932—1940*. New Haven, 1946.
— *President Roosevelt and the Coming of the War, 1941*. New Haven, 1948.
— and Mary R. *The Rise of American Civilization*. New York, 1946.
Benns, F. Lee. *Europe Since 1914 in its World Setting*. New York, 1945.
Borchard, Edwin and W. P. Lage. *Neutrality of the United States*. New Haven, 1940.
Boye, Thorvald. *De væbnede neutralitetsforbund*. Kristiania, 1912.
Bowles, Thomas Gibson. *The Declaration of Paris of 1856*. London, 1900.
Bradley, Phillips. *Can We Stay Out of War*. New York, 1936.
Brierly, J. L. *Staternes Neutralitet*. København, 1936.
— *The Outlook for International Law*. Oxford, 1945.
Buckley, Christopher, *Norway, The Commandos, Dieppe*. London, 1945.
Carr, Edward Hallett. *Nationalism and After*. New York, 1945.
Castberg, Frede. *Folkerett*. Oslo, 1937.
Churchill, Winston S. *The Second World War*, vol. I, *The Gathering Storm*. Cambridge, 1948.
Cohn, Georg. *Neo-neutrality*. Translated from Danish. New York, 1939.
Consett, M. W. W. P. *The Triumph of Unarmed Forces*. London, 1923.
Derry, T. K. *The Campaign in Norway*. London, 1952.
Dulles, Allen W. and Hamilton Fish Armstrong. *Can We be Neutral?* New York, 1936.
Easum, C. V. *Half-Century of Conflict*. Unpublished manuscript. University of Wisconsin, 1950.
Fenwick, Charles G. *American Neutrality, Trial and Failure*. New York, 1940.
— *The Neutrality Laws of the United States*. Washington, D. C., 1913.
Gihl, Torsten. *International Legislation*. New York. 1937.
— *Neutralitetsproblem*. Stockholm, 1938.
— *Den svenska utrikespolitikens historia*, Vol. IV, 1914—1919. Stockholm, 1951.
Gordon, David and Royden Dangerfield. *The Hidden Weapon, The Story of Economic Warfare*. New York, 1947.
Grey, sir Edward. (First Viscount of Falloden.) *Twenty-Five Years 1892—1916*, vol. II. New York, 1925.
Grotius, Hugo. *De Jure Belli ac Pacis*. Liber Tres. English translation from the 1648 edition. London, 1925.
Hall, W. E. *A Treatise on International Law*. Oxford, 1924.

Hambro, C. J. *Historisk Supplement*. Oslo, 1947.
Heckscher, Eli. *Sweden, Norway, Denmark and Iceland in the World War*. New Haven, 1930.
Hogan, Willard. *International Violence and Third States since the World War*. Chicago, 1941.
Holstein, Lage Stael von. *Norden inför världsbrannen*. Stockholm, 1940.
Hubatsch, Walther. *Die Deutsche Besetzung von Dänemark und Norwegen*. Göttingen, 1952.
Hyneman, Charles G. *The First American Neutrality*. Urbana, 1934.
Jessup, Phillip S. and Francis Deak. *The Origins*, vol. I, *Neutrality, its History, Economics and Law*. New York, 1935.
— *Today and Tomorrow*, vol. IV, *Neutrality, its History, Economics and Law*. New York, 1936.
Jones, Shepherd S. *The Scandinavian States and the League of Nations*. New York, 1939.
Kenney, Rowland. *The Northern Tangle, Scandinavia and the Post War Period*. London, 1946.
Keilhau, Wilhelm. *Vaar egen tid*, vol. XI, *Det norske folks liv og historie*. Oslo, 1938.
— *Tidsrummet fra omkring 1875 til omkring 1920*, vol. X, *Det norske folks liv og historie*. Oslo, 1938.
— *Norge og Verdenskrigen*. Oslo, 1927.
— *Sweden, Norway, Denmark and Iceland in the World War*. New Haven, 1930.
Koht, Halvdan. *Norway, Neutral and Invaded*. New York, 1941.
— *Norsk Utanrikspolitikk fram til 9. april 1940*. Oslo, 1947.
— *Frå skanse til skanse*. Oslo, 1947.
La Cour, Wilhelm. *Paa Vey mod Katastrofen*, vol. III, *Som Saeden, saa hoesten*. Koebenhavn, 1949.
Lansing, Robert. *War Memoirs of Robert Lansing*. New York, 1935.
— *Notes on Sovereignty, from the Standpoint of the State and the World*. Washington, 1921.
Linder, Erik. *Sveriges Neutralitetspolitik*. Stockholm, 1943.
Lippmann, Walter. *U. S. Foreign Policy*. New York, 1943.
Lossberg, Bernhard v. *Im Wehrmachtführungsstab*. Hamburg, 1950.
Mendelssohn, Peter de. *Designs for Aggression*. New York, 1946.
Millis, Walter. *Road to War, America, 1914—1917*. New York, 1935.
— *This is Pearl! The United States and Japan 1941*. New York, 1947.
Moe, Finn. *Norge i den nye verden*. Oslo, 1946.
Mohn, Paul. *Sverige i utrikespolitisk perspektiv*. Stockholm, 1938.
Mordal, Jacques. *La Campagne de Norvège*. Paris, 1949.
Morrissey, Alice M. *The American Defense of Neutral Rights 1914—1917*. Cambridge (Mass), 1939.
Nevins, Allen and H. S. Commager. *A Short History of the United States*. New York, 1944.
Neumann, Erwin. *Die Neutralität der Vereinigten Staaten*. Berlin, 1939.
Notter, Harley. *The Origins of the Foreign Policy of Woodrow Wilson*. Baltimore, 1937.
Örvik, Nils. *Norsk Militær i Sverige, 1943—1945*. Oslo, 1951.

Perkins, Dexter. *America and Two Wars.* Boston, 1944.
Phillips, Allison and Arthur Reede. *The Napoleonic Period,* vol. II, *Neutrality, its History, Economics and Law.* New York, 1935.
Politis, Nicolaus S. *La Neutralité et la paix.* Paris, 1935.
Reuterswärd, Pontus. *Bör Sverige i framtiden frångå neutralitetspolitiken?* Stockholm, 1945.
Reynaud, Paul. *La France a sauvé l'Europe.* Paris, 1947.
Rhee, Syngman. *Neutrality as Influenced by the United States.* Princeton, 1912.
Sandler, Richard. *Strömväxlingar och lärdommar.* Stockholm, 1939.
— *Utrikespolitisk kringblick.* Stockholm, 1937.
Schempp, Otto. *Der neutrale Westen.* Leipzig, 1939.
Seymour, Charles. *American Diplomacy During the World War.* Baltimore, 1942.
— *American Neutrality, 1914—1917.* New Haven, 1935.
— *The Intimate Papers of Colonel House.* 2 vols. New York, 1926.
Sherwood, Robert E. *Roosevelt and Hopkins.* New York, 1948.
Shotwell, James T. *The Pact of Paris.* Worchester, 1928.
Tansill, Charles Callan. *America Goes to War.* Boston, 1938.
Thomas, Charles M. *American Neutrality in 1793.* New York, 1931.
Thulstrup, Aake. *När Demokratin bröt igjenom.* Stockholm, 1937.
Tingsten, Herbert. *Svensk utrikesdebatt mellan världskrigen.* Stockholm, 1944.
Tumulty, Joseph P. *Woodrow Wilson as I Know Him.* New York, 1921.
Turlington, Edgar. *The World War Period,* vol. III, *Neutrality, its History, Economics and Law.* New York, 1935.
Undén, Oesten B. *Neutralitet och folkrätt.* Stockholm, 1939.
— *Svensk utrikespolitik.* Stockholm, 1941.
— *Sveriges utrikespolitik.* Stockholm, 1948.
Utrikespolitik och försvar. Dagens Nyheters Skriftserie. Stockholm, 1948.
Valentin, Veit. *Entente und Neutralität.* Leipzig, 1917.
Vigness, Paul. *The Neutrality of Norway During the First World War.* London, 1932.
Ward, Paul. *Sovereignty.* London, 1928.
Whitten, John G. *La Neutralité et la Société des Nations.* The Hague, Academy of International Law. *Receul des cours de l'Academie des Droits International,* 1927. Paris, 1928.
Wright, Quincey. *A Study of War.* Chicago, 1942.
Wright, Quincy, ed. *Neutrality and Collective Security.* Chicago, 1936.
— *The Future of Neutrality.* Worchester, 1928.
— *The United States and Neutrality.* Chicago, 1935.

Section III.

PERIODICALS

Arbaiza, G. «The Monroe Doctrine, 1937 edition.» *Current History,* 46:55—60. June, 1937.
Baker, Newton D. «Why We Went to War.» *Foreign Affairs,* 15:26. October, 1936.
Baruch, Bernard M. «Neutrality.» *Current History,* 44:43. June, 1936.

Bishop, D. G. «International Organization, A Necessity and Not a Luxury.» *World Affairs*, 107—162. September, 1944.
Borchard, Edwin. «Dragging America into War.» *Current History*, 40:392—401. July, 1935.
— «War, Neutrality and Non-belligerency.» *American Journal of International Law*, 35:620. October, 1941.
— «Was Norway Delinquent in the Case of Altmark.» *American Journal of International Law*, 34:289—294. April, 1940.
Bradley, Phillips. «Neutral Policy for America.» *The Reference Shelf* 10, no. 7, pp. 145—152. May, 1935.
Brown, Philip M. «Imperialism.» *American Journal of International Law*, 39:84. January, 1945.
— «Neutrality.» *American Journal of International Law*, 33:727. October, 1939.
— «World Horizons.» *World Affairs*, 109:140—144. June, 1946.
Buell, Raymond L. «The New American Neutrality.» *Foreign Policy Reports*, 11:281—292. January, 1936.
Carr, E. H. «Security and the Small Power.» *Christian Science Monitor*, 1—2. December 2, 1936.
Coudert, Frederic R. «Are Neutral Rights Consistent with International Cooperation?» *Academy of Political Science, Proceedings*, 16:170—174. January, 1935.
Coulter, John Lee. «Economic Aspects of the United States' Foreign Trade.» *Annals of American Academy*, 186:169—177.
Eagleton, Clyde. «The Needs of International Law.» *American Journal of International Law*, 34:701. October, 1939.
Editorials:
  «Again Neutrals are Warned.» *Great Britain and the East*, 54:399. May, 1940.
  «Belgium Returns to Neutrality.» *New Republic*, 88:340. October, 1936.
  «The Greatest Neutral.» *Spectator*, 164:616. May, 1940.
  «The Long Arm of Sea-Power.» *Great Britain and the East*, 54:276. April, 1940.
  «Neutrality, An Impossibility.» *Great Britain and the East*, 54:391. June, 1940.
  «Neutrals and Safety.» *Great Britain and the East*, 54:274. April, 1940.
Elbe, J. von der. «The Evolution of the Concept of Just War in International Law.» *American Journal of International Law*, 33:665. October, 1939.
Fenwick, Charles G. «The American Neutrality Committee.» *American Journal of International Law*, 35:12—40. January, 1941.
— «International Law and Lawless Nations.» *American Journal of International Law*, 33:745. October, 1939.
— «Neutrality and International Organization.» *American Journal of International Law*, 28:334—339. April, 1934.
— «Neutrality on the Defensive.» *American Journal of International Law*, 34:697—699. October, 1940.
Foot, Dingle. «Sweden's Dilemma.» *Spectator*, 179:489. October, 1947.
Hopper, Bruce. «Sweden, A Case Study in Neutrality.» *Foreign Affairs*, 23:435—449. April, 1945.

Hudson, Manley. «International Law of the Future.» *American Society of International Law, Proceedings,* 1944, p. 10.
Hull, Cordell. «Our Foreign Policy with Respect to Neutrality.» *Press Releases,* vol. XXXIII, 368—370. November, 1935.
Jessup, Phillip C. «Historical Development of the Law of Neutrality.» *The Reference Shelf* 10, no. 7, p. 77. 1936. A Digest of Phillip C. Jessup, «American Neutrality and International Police.» *World Peace Foundation Pamphlets,* 11:355—522. 1928.
— «The Neutrality Act of 1939.» *American Journal of International Law,* 34:96. January, 1940.
Joesten, Joachim. «Phases in Swedish Neutrality.» *Foreign Affairs,* 23:324—329. January, 1945.
— «Storm Over Northern Europe.» *Contemporary Review,* 151:454—460. April, 1937.
Koht, Halvdan, «Neutrality and Peace, The View of a Small Power.» *Foreign Affairs,* 15:280—289. January 1937.
Koravin, E. A. «The Second World War and International Law.» *American Journal of International Law,* 40:746. October, 1946.
Kunz, Joseph L. «The Covenant of the League of Nations and Neutrality.» *American Society of International Law, Proceedings,* 1935, pp. 36—42.
Lansing, Robert. «Difficulties of a Neutral.» *Saturday Evening Post,* 203:102—106. April, 1931.
Martin, Charles E. «The Legal Position of War and Neutrality During the Last Twenty-Five Years.» *American Society of International Law, Proceedings,* 1931, pp. 161—164.
— «Regionalism and Neutrality on the Basis of Peace in the Americas.» *American Society of International Law, Proceedings,* 1940, p. 18.
Mathisen, Trygve. «Nøytralitetstanken i norsk politikk fra 1890-årene og til Norge gikk med i Folkeforbundet.» *Norsk Historisk Tidskrift,* Vol. 36, May 1952.
Miller, D. H. «Sovereignty and Neutrality.» *International Conciliation,* 1926. pp. 280—286.
Moore, John Bassett. «Appeal to Reason.» *Foreign Affairs,* 11:558—563. July, 1933.
Patterson, Ernst Minor. «Economics of Neutrality.» *Annals of American Academy,* 186:161. July, 1936.
Potts, C. S. «World Chaos Once More.» *Southwestern Social Science Quarterly,* 16:6—10. September, 1935.
Reeves, Emery. «National Sovereignty, The Road to the Next War.» *World Affairs,* 109:109—116. June, 1946.
Ryder, Wilfred, «The End of Nordic Neutrality.» *Soundings,* March, 1949, pp. 16—18.
Shotwell, James T. «Neutrality and National Policy.» *Outlook,* 151:620. April, 1929.
Smith, H. A. «The Future of Neutrality.» *Contemporary Review,* 143:314—318. March, 1933.
Soule, Georg. «Price of Neutrality.» *New Republic,* 84:38—41. August, 1935.
Spitzer, H. M. «Small Nations and the Economic and Social Council.» *World Affairs,* 109:133—139. June, 1946.

Stimson, Henry L. «Neutrality and War Prevention.» *American Society of International Law, Proceedings,* 1935, pp. 123—126.
Stoddard, L. «Europe's Balance of Neutrals.» *Christian Science Monitor,* April 14, 1937, p. 3.
Thomas, E. «Theory of Neutrality.» *Annals of American Academy,* 186:163—168. July, 1936.
Warren, Charles. «Contraband and Neutral Trade.» *Academy of Political Science, Proceedings,* 16:189—194. January, 1935.
— «Prepare for Neutrality.» *Yale Review,* 24:467—478. March, 1935.
— «Safeguards to Neutrality.» *Foreign Affairs,* 14:198—215. January, 1936.
— «Troubles of a Neutral.» *Foreign Affairs,* 12:377—394. March, 1935.
Whittinger, Richard. «Belgium Emphasizes Security.» *Contemporary Review,* 151:23—37. January, 1937.
Whitton, John B. «The Changed Attitude of the Powers Toward Neutrality Laws.» *Current History,* 30:454—461. June, 1929.
Wilson, G. G. «War and Neutrality.» *American Journal of International Law,* 27:724. October, 1933.
Wilson, Robert R. «Some Current Questions Relating to Neutrality.» *American Journal of International Law,* 37:652. October, 1943.
— «The Neutrality of Eire.» *American Journal of International Law.* 34:126. January, 1940.
— «Questions Relating to Irish Neutrality.» *American Journal of International Law,* 36:288. April, 1942.
Wright, Quincy. «A British View of International Law.» *American Journal of International Law,* 36:451. June, 1942.
— «International Law and the Balance of Power.» *American Journal of International Law,* 37:98. June, 1943.
— «League and Neutrality.» *Congressional Digest,* 15:9. January, 1936.
— «National Sovereignty and Collective Security.» *Annals of American Academy,* 186:100. July, 1936.
— «Neutrality and Neutral Rights Following the Pact of Paris.» *American Society of International Law, Proceedings,* 1930, pp. 81—87.
— «The Present Status of Neutrality.» *American Journal of International Law,* 34:391—409. July, 1940.
— «The Proposal of the Neutrality Act.» *American Journal of International Law,* 36:14. January, 1942.
— «The Transfer of Destroyers to Great Britain.» *American Journal of International Law,* 34:680—689. October, 1940.

NEWSPAPERS

Aftenposten. 1939, 1950.
Arbeideren. 1939.
Morgenbladet. 1949.
News of Norway. 1949.
News of Sweden. 1949.
New York Herald Tribune. 1935.
New York Times. 1935, 1937, 1939—1941, 1945—1948.
Verdens Gang. 1949—1950.

Index

Admiralty, British, 63.
Alabama, The, 32.
Alexander, Czar of Russia, 32.
Allies, The, 39, 41—51, 53, 55—58, 64, 65, 67, 78, 80, 82, 84, 86—7, 89, 105, 106, 113, 115, 191, 203, 208, 213, 216 222—6, 231, 233, 235, 237, 239, 241—5.
Altmark, The, 235.
America, see United States.
American Civil War, 31, 32, 38, 116.
American Society of International Law, 138.
Angel, Norman, 90.
Arabic, The, 60.
Argentina, 108, 109, 111, 134, 150.
Argentine Anti-War Pact 1933, 149, 152, 154, 155.
Atlantic Conference, 209, Charter, 209.

Bailey, Thomas, 136, 108.
Baker, Newton, D., 119.
Baker, R. S., 75, 77, 78, 88.
Balfour, Lord A. J., 64, 244.
Balkan, 38, 42.
Baltic Sea, 236, 238, 262, 263.
Barcelona Conference 1921, 133.
Baruch, B. M., 170, 263.
Baumhauer, E. N. von, 254.
Belgium, 25, 28, 48, 83, 87, 142, 147, 148, 183, 184, 234, 274, 277.
Bernstorff, Count J. German Ambassador to USA, 65, 80.
Bloom bill, The, 199.
Blum, Leon, French politician, 243.
Bolivia, 134, 161.
Boncour, Paul, 254.
Borah resolution, The, 159, 160.

Borchard, Edwin, 63, 69, 70, 76, 90, 104, 123, 141, 155, 205.
Bowles, Gibson, T., 31.
Brazil, 111, 132, 134.
Briand, A., French Foreign Minister, 137.
British Guiana, 205.
Briggs, H. W., 206.
Brown, P. M., 119.
Brouckère, M. de, Belgian delegate, League of Nations, 124, 130—3.
Brussels Conference 1873, 32.
Bryn, Harald, Norwegian Minister, USA, 106.
Bryan, W., Secretary of State, USA, 47, 67, 68, 80, 84, 88, 90—3, 95, 96, 108, 109.
Buenos Ayres Conference 1936, 155.
Budapest Conference 1934, 142.
Buckley, Christopher, 223.

Canning, George, British Foreign Secretary, 68.
Canada, 29, 206.
Carls, Otto, German admiral, 232.
Catillo, Salvatore, A., 169.
Cecil, Lord Robert, British Minister of Blockade, 58.
Central America, 29.
Central Powers, 83.
Chaco War, The, 1933, 134, 161.
Chamberlain, Austin, British politician, 78.
Chamberlain, Neville, British Prime Minister, 193, 244.
Chechoslovakia, 258.
Chile, 109, 111, 134.

China, 133, 167, 197, 198.
Churchill, Winston, S., 63, 201, 202, 205, 207, 209, 225, 231, 232, 233, 237, 240, 242—5.
Clarendon, Lord. British politician, 30.
Cohn, Georg, 15, 141, 149—153.
Congress, USA, 22, 24, 29, 67, 79, 107, 110, 141, 162, 197, 202, 209, 210.
Consett, M. W. W. P., 227.
Consolato del Mare, 13, 133.
Copper Agreement, Norway, 56, 57.
Cossack, The, 235.
Council of Europe, 261.
Council of League of Nations, 123—131, 173—5, 182.
Covenant of League of Nations, 107, 119, 121, 122, 125, 128, 130, 131, 136, 138, 141, 143, 146, 173, 175, 177, 178, 179, 180, 182, 184, 189, 243, 245, 251, 253.
Cranborne, Lord., 179, 181.
Crimean War, 30, 38.
Cushing, The, 69.

Danish Treatise, 1924, 141, 152.
Dehn, C. S., 251, 252.
Denmark, 26, 43, 49, 51, 55, 58, 92, 95, 96, 100, 101, 107, 117, 124, 142, 174, 177, 178, 187, 203, 204, 210, 217, 218, 219, 233, 259, 261, 262, 266, 277.
Destroyer deal, 205, 208.
Deyhle, major, 235.
Ditten, Thor von, Norwegian Minister to Germany, 54.
Doenitz, Karl, German admiral, 233.
Dormer, Sir Cecil, British Minister to Norway, 219.
Dulles, Allen W., 75, 169.
Dumbarton Oaks Conference, 248, 250.
Dunkirk, 206.
Dyke, van, American Minister to Holland, 90, 91, 96, 97, 100, 101.

Easum, Chester V., 10, 64.
Eden-Hellner government, Sweden, 51.
Egypt, 278.
Eliot, G. W., 84.

England, see Great-Britain.
Equador, 248.
Estonia, 186.

Falkenhorst, N. von, German general, 236.
Fenwick, Charles S., 74, 119, 141, 155, 192.
Finland, 128, 129, 175, 177, 178, 185, 201, 217, 234, 237, 238, 258.
Fish Agreement, Norway, 53—5.
France, 16, 19, 22, 30, 42, 55, 59, 92, 100, 105, 133, 135, 137, 138, 166, 184, 193, 198, 201, 202, 215, 236, 237, 239, 242, 262, 273.

Gazette de Hollande, 91.
Genferblatt, 147.
Geneva Protocol, 175.
Gerard, James, American Ambassador to Germany, 66.
Germany, 41—50, 52—70, 78, 79, 80, 82, 84—7, 89, 95, 105, 107, 111, 114—16, 121, 132, 133, 135, 166, 177, 183, 187, 203—06, 208, 210, 211, 213, 214, 216, 218—227, 229, 231—245, 258, 262, 265, 267, 272.
Gore-McLemore resolutions, 67, 88.
Great Britain, 15, 16, 20, 23, 24, 25, 29, 30, 31, 33, 38, 40—52, 54—69, 75—80, 83, 85, 86, 88, 92—102, 105, 106, 108, 116, 133, 134, 140, 142, 166, 175, 184, 189, 193, 194, 198, 200, 201—214, 218—225, 230—239, 243—5, 262, 271—273.
Greco-Turkish War, 1921, 133.
Greece, 99, 210.
Greer, The, 218.
Grey, Sir Edward, British Foreign Secretary, 33, 41, 85, 89, 115.
Grotius, Hugo, 11, 39, 85, 120, 143, 226.
Guggenheim, Paul, 255.
Gulflight, The, 69.
Günther, Chr., Swedish Foreign Minister, 243.

Hagelin, William, 233.
Hague Conventions, 9, 30, 32—5, 37, 99, 119, 133, 134, 142, 145, 206, 253, 265, 272, 278.

Hague Postal Convention, 48.
Halifax, Lord, British Foreign Secretary, 233.
Hambro, C. J., Norwegian politician, 218.

Hamilton, Alexander, Secretary of the Treasury, USA, 51.
Hammarskjöld government, Sweden, 51.
Harrington, Fred H., 10.
Havana, Act of, 204.
Havana Convention 1928, 135.
Hitler, Adolf, 183, 198, 203, 209, 210, 218, 222—4, 227, 233, 236, 238, 240, 241, 245, 258.
Holland, 25, 42, 48—9, 59, 90—1, 96, 98, 100, 101, 104, 141, 148, 177, 204, 277.
House, Colonel Edward M., 77, 78, 80, 82, 85, 102, 116.
House Committee of Foreign Affairs, USA, 160, 169.
House of Commons, 40, 193.
Hull, Cordell, Secretary of State, USA, 163, 167, 196, 199, 200, 208, 210.
Hyde, Charles C., 160.
Hyneman, Charles S., 21.
Haakon VII, King of Norway, 219, 234.

Ihlen, Nils, Norwegian Foreign Minister, 46, 57, 93.
India, 278.
International Air Navigation Convention 1919, 133.
— Blockade Committee, 125, 127, 129.
— Law Association, 142—3, 151, 153.
— Law Commission, 1949, 256—7.
— Prize Court, 36.
— Studies Conference 1934, 146.
— Waterways Convention 1921, 133.
Interparliamentary Union, The, 90.
Ireland, 43, 216, 217.
Italo—Ethiopian War 1935, 159, 161, 172, 177, 183, 193, 197, 227, 272.
Italy, 96, 163, 164, 166, 262.

Jagow, von, German Foreign Minister, 86.
Jackson, R. A. Attorney General, USA, 205.
Japan, 121, 132—3, 167, 197, 201, 208, 272.
Jefferson, Thomas, President, USA., 19—22, 40, 74—5, 83, 85, 159, 274.
Jessup, Philip C., 15, 89, 141, 149, 153, 154, 168.
Jones, Shepherd S., 173.
Jung, Helge, Swedish general, 263.
Jøssingfjord, 235.

Karlstad Plan The 1949, 259, 260.
Kearney, The, 211.
Kellogg, Frank, Secretary of State, USA., 138, 140, 141.
Kellogg Pact, see Pact of Paris.
Koht, Halvdan, Norwegian Foreign Minister, 186, 190, 191, 218, 220, 221, 222, 241, 243, 244, 276.
Kogrundsrennan, 51.
Knox, Franklin, Secretary of the Navy, USA., 210.

Lange, Chr., Norwegian politician, 146.
Lange, Halvard, Norwegian Foreign Minister, 259, 261.
Lansing, Robert, Secretary of State, USA., 42, 44, 63—6, 69, 77—82, 88, 97—104, 108, 111, 114, 116, 275.
Latin-America, 108, 109, 111, 114, 135, 157, 204, 278.
Latvia, 185.
Lausanne, Treaty of, 133.
Lauterpacht, L., 146.
League of Nations, 119, 121—132, 134, 137—143, 145, 150—1, 154, 157, 164, 172—183, 186—193, 217, 227, 228, 237, 245, 247—9, 257, 260—1, 266, 273, 277.
Leopold III, King of Belgium, 184—5.
Lend-Lease Act, 208, 210.
Litvinov, Maxim, Russian Foreign Minister, 190—1.
Lloyd George, D., 57, 78, 105.
Loevenfeld, Erwin, 254.

London Conference 1935, 147, 154, 155.
London, Declaration of 1909, 35—7, 39—41, 52, 99, 100, 181, 217, 270, 272.
Lusitania, The, 43, 62, 66, 68, 79, 80.
Luxembourg, 28, 147, 185.

Marcy, William, Secretary of State, USA., 31.
Mackenzie King, William L., Canadian Prime Minister, 207.
Malmö Conference 1914, 94.
Marshall, J. Chief Justice, USA., 22, 69.
McDonald, Ramsey, British Prime Minister, 141.
Mexico, 31.
Michahelles, J., German Minister to Norway, 56.
Millis, Walter, 65.
Moe, Finn, Norwegian politician, 257.
Moore, John, Bassett, 134, 140.
Monroe, James, Secretary of State, USA., 23.
Monroe Doctrine, 213.
Morgenstierne, Wilhelm, Norwegian Minister to USA., 260.
Morriss, Gouverneur, American Minister to France, 20.
Morrissey, A., 65.
Mowinckel government, Norway, 227.
Murray, C. de B., 254.
Mussolini, Benito, 177, 202, 218, 245.

Napoleon, 15, 16.
NATO, 264.
Narvik, 232, 234, 237, 239.
Netherlands, The, see Holland.
New Foundland, 205.
Nicholas II, Czar of Russia, 33.
North Atlantic Pact, 257, 259, 261, 263, 264, 266.
North Sea, 42, 52, 59, 92, 93, 95.
Norway, 9, 28, 29, 51—61, 70, 71, 92, 96, 100—1, 104, 107, 117, 124, 146, 174, 176, 178, 186, 203, 210, 216—244, 259—267, 277—8.
Notter, Harley, 83, 85.

Nuremberg Trials, 144, 276.
Nye Committee, 205.
Nygaardsvold government, 221, 236.

Oppenheim, L., 160.
Oslo Conference 1935, 176.
Oslo States, The, 135, 217, 260.

Page, W. H., American Ambassador to Great Britain, 75, 77, 78, 82, 92, 95, 100, 116.
Palmerston, Lord, 68.
Pan American Union, 109.
Panoy incident, 197.
Paraguay, 134, 161.
Paris Conference 1934, 119.
Paris Peace Conference 1919, 146, 154.
Paris, Declaration of 1856, 30—2, 36, 97, 271.
Paris, Pact of, 136—145, 149—152, 172, 175, 189, 206, 253, 273, 277.
Pearl Harbor, 9, 212.
Perkins, Dexter, 189, 192, 198.
Permanent Court of International Justice, 133.
Peru, 11, 142.
Pittmann bills, The, 164, 166, 199.
Poland, 186.
Polk, James K., President, USA., 100, 101.
Politis, Nicolaus S., 15, 120.
Portugal, 216.
Potts, C. S., 275.
Pradelle, M. de la, French delegate, League of Nations, 145.
Preparatory Commission for Disarmament, 128—9, 131.

Quisling, Vidkun, 233.

Raestad, A. N., Norwegian delegate, League of Nations, 146, 175.
Raeder, E., German admiral, 224, 233.
Reynaud, Paul, French Prime Minister, 202.
Ribbentrop, Joachim von, German Foreign Minister, 218.
Rio Tinto contract, The, 56—7.

Roosevelt, Franklin D., 160, 162, 196, 198, 201—210, 213—215, 218.
Ruhr occupation 1923, 174.
Russia, 14, 26, 30, 46, 50—1, 97, 121, 129, 132, 134, 166, 190, 201, 222—3, 234, 236, 237—8, 257, 262—7, 270, 278.
Russo—Polish War 1920, 133.
Rutgers, M. V. H., Deutch delegate, League of Nations, 131—2, 182.

Saavedra Lamas Treaty, see Argentine Anti-War Pact.
San Francisco Conference 1945, 248, 250, 254, 255, 257.
Sandler, Richard, Swedish Foreign Minister, 187.
Scavenius, E., Danish Foreign Minister, 94.
Scandinavia, 42, 46, 50, 52, 73, 90, 92—4, 104, 106, 115, 117, 142, 172—5, 179, 186, 217—8, 223—4, 226—7, 234, 236, 243, 259—267.
Schanzer, Carlo, 127.
Schempp, Otto, 188.
Schindler, D., 147—8.
Schmedeman, A., American Minister to Norway, 92.
Schwartz-Lindemann government, Sweden, 51.
Seymour, Charles, 74.
Shotwell, James T., 137, 169.
Sino-Japanese War 1937, 167, 197, 273.
Spaak, Paul, Belgian Foreign Minister, 183—5.
Spring-Rice, Sir Cecil, British Ambassador to USA., 115.
Spain, 31, 91, 103, 104, 107, 166, 177, 216.
Spanish—American War, 131.
Spanish Civil War, 165, 229.
State Department, The, 63, 64, 76, 79, 80, 91, 93—5, 97—100, 103, 105, 108—111, 114, 137, 160, 197.
Storting, The Norwegian, 59, 186, 217, 218, 220, 228, 259.
Stimson Doctrine, The, 149, 152.

Stimson, Henry L., Secretary of State, USA., 140, 171.
Stresemann, Gustav, German Foreign Minister, 86.
Supreme War Council, Allied, 237, 239, 243.
Sussex, The, 43, 66, 87, 111.
Sweden, 26, 29, 45, 50—1, 55, 89, 92, 93, 96—98, 100—107, 113, 117, 124, 174—6, 178—180, 186—7, 217—9, 223, 234, 237, 240, 243, 257, 258—263, 265, 266.
Switzerland, 28, 48, 86, 92, 104, 106, 107, 122, 146, 147, 148, 177, 180—3, 185, 188—9, 217, 230, 255.

Tansill, Charles C., 62.
Thirty Years War, 26.
Thommesen, O., 60.
Thomas, E., 15, 76.
Tittoni, M., Italian delegate, League of Nations, 124.
Transito, 50—1.
Tumulty, Joseph R., 85.
Tyler, John, President, USA.,

Undén, Östen, Swedish Foreign Minister, 173, 176, 179, 180, 261.
United Nations, 247—252, 256—7, 260—1, 266, 277.
United States, 9, 15, 18, 19, 20—4, 29, 31, 43—9, 56, 62, 64—118, 121, 132—137, 143, 150, 153, 157—9, 161, 163—170, 172, 190, 195—213, 225, 257, 264, 270, 272—3, 278.
Uruguay, 249.

Vatican, The, 103.
Vayo, Alvarez del, Spanish Foreign Minister, 275.
Venezuela, 110, 111.
Versailles, Peace of, 191—2.
Vigness, Paul, 60.
Vochoc, Vladimir, 254.

Walewski, Count, French Foreign Minister, 30.
Warren, Charles, 168, 170.

Washington Conference 1922, 134.
Washington, George, President, USA., 18, 19, 21, 23, 28.
Washington D.C., 65, 93, 94, 104, 106, 133.
Washington, Treaty of, 32.
Weserübung, 234.
West Indies, 29.
Weygang, Maxime, French general, 240.
Whitlock, Brand, American Minister to Belgium, 87.
Wilkie, Wendell, 203.
Wilhelm II, German Kaiser, 15.

Wilson, Woodrow, 64, 67—70, 73, 76—8, 82—89, 104—108, 113—116, 120, 121, 143, 158, 169, 191, 203, 209, 213—4, 241—5.
Witenberg, J. C., 254.
World War I, 9, 15, 33, 38, 39, 57, 70, 113, 115, 117—20, 135, 144, 145, 152, 154, 158, 161, 170, 189, 216, 222, 225, 227, 241, 255, 272—5.
World War II, 143—4, 195—6, 212, 216, 245, 257, 265, 274.
Wrangel, H., Swedish Minister to Great Britain, 102, 113.
Wright, Quincy, 123, 143, 152, 155, 206, 275.

For Product Safety Concerns and Information please contact our EU
representative GPSR@taylorandfrancis.com
Taylor & Francis Verlag GmbH, Kaufingerstraße 24, 80331 München, Germany

www.ingramcontent.com/pod-product-compliance
Lightning Source LLC
Chambersburg PA
CBHW061428300426
44114CB00014B/1584